Praise for *Good Music, Brighter Children*

"The ear is the first sensory ... ... hows
that sounds and music ha ... ...
development. That's why ... ... your
child's sake!"

> **—Zell Miller,** former governor of Georgia
> and founder of the statewide program,
> Build Your Baby's Brain Through the Power of Music

"Every child instinctively responds—claps, sways, sings, dances,
spins—to music. We are just beginning to recognize music's
power to affect learning. This book reinforces why music, and
all the arts, must be part of plans for educational reform."

> **—Anne T. Dowling,** president, Texaco Foundation

"Sharlene Habermeyer has done an excellent job of compiling
the music brain research in her book *Good Music, Brighter
Children*. We liked it so much, we plan to make this book our
member renewal gift next year."

> **—Pat Page,** executive director, American Music Conference

"I have personally witnessed the way music helps children in
their education and later on in the workplace and society. I
have learned through experience what Ms. Habermeyer's book
expresses clearly on each page: that every child needs and de-
serves to participate in a strong, comprehensive, sequential
music program that teaches musical disciplines integrated with
other academic subjects."

> **—Katherine Damkohler,** executive director,
> Education Through Music, Inc.

"A remarkable testament to the importance of music in our lives
at all ages and in all environments. She not only helps parents
and teachers understand how to develop the musical potential
in children, but explains how music can help all of us develop
more fully in mind, body, and spirit."

> **—Dee Dickinson,** CEO, New Horizons for Learning

"This extraordinary book teaches us how music education, practice in singing, or playing an instrument instills perseverance, determination, self-discipline, and values in children. *Good Music, Brighter Children* must become the focal point for the shift in thinking required to establish music, as well as the visual arts, theatre, dance, and creative writing at the center of public education in America."

—**Eric Oddleifson,** board member, National Arts and Learning Foundation at Walnut Hill

"I have a premonition that one day soon we will wake up, like Woody Allen's character in the film *Sleeper*, to the realization that stripping instrumental music from our elementary schools was a true blunder of twentieth century American education. Sharlene Habermeyer outlines why music is important to learning, and provides parents with excellent suggestions for launching and sustaining a musical influence in the lives of their children."

—**James S. Catterall,** professor of education and co-director of Imagination Project at UCLA

GOOD MUSIC,
BRIGHTER CHILDREN

GOOD MUSIC, BRIGHTER CHILDREN

SIMPLE AND PRACTICAL IDEAS TO HELP
TRANSFORM YOUR CHILD'S LIFE
THROUGH THE POWER OF MUSIC

SHARLENE HABERMEYER

PRIMA PUBLISHING

In order to protect their privacy, the names of some individuals cited in this book have been changed.

All products and organizations mentioned in this book are trademarks of their respective companies.

PRIMA PUBLISHING and colophon are registered trademarks of Prima Communications, Inc.

Photograph on page 1 © John Wood/Index Stock; page 11 © Frank Siteman/Tony Stone Images; pages 29, 100, and 158 © Mark Habermeyer; page 125 © Vcg/FPG Int'l; page 199 © David Waldorf/FPG Int'l; page 215 © Eric Sanford/Index Stock; pages 83 and 241 © Photodisc.

Library of Congress Cataloging-in-Publication Data

Habermeyer, Sharlene.
    Good music, brighter children : simple and practical ideas to help transform your child's life through the power of music / Sharlene Habermeyer.
        p.   cm.
    Includes bibliographic references and index.
    ISBN 0-7615-2150-X
    1. Music—Instruction and study—Juvenile.   2. Music therapy for children.   3. Music—Psychology.
MT1.H115 1999
649'.51—dc21   99-31879
                                                                          CIP

00 01 02 03 HH 10 9 8 7 6 5 4 3
Printed in the United States of America

How to Order

Single copies may be ordered from Prima Publishing, 3000 Lava Ridge Court, Roseville, CA 95661; telephone (800) 632-8676. Quantity discounts are also available. On your letterhead, include information concerning the intended use of the books and the number of books you wish to purchase.

Visit us online at www.primalifestyles.com

TO MY HUSBAND,

MARK,

FOR HIS UNFAILING SUPPORT,

AND

TO MY FIVE SONS,

JASON, RYAN, BRANDON, JAROM, AND TREVOR,

WHO, WHILE OBSERVING WHAT MUSIC HAS DONE FOR THEM,

GAVE ME THE INSPIRATION TO WRITE

THIS BOOK.

CONTENTS

PART

WHY MUSIC

PART

MUSIC IN THE HOME

PART 3

A NEED FOR ADVOCACY: MUSIC EDUCATION IN THE SCHOOLS

PART 4

A CULTURAL HERITAGE

FINALE: BUILDING A LEGACY: A PARENT'S RESPONSIBILITY   243

RESOURCES   259

ACKNOWLEDGMENTS

Every aspect of bringing this book to publication has been a team effort. Even the countless hours writing were not spent in solitude. For those occasions, I received inspiration from Beethoven's Violin Concerto in D, Handel's *Water Music*, Bach's *Brandenburg Concertos*, Mozart's *Requiem* and *Jupiter Symphony*, and Vivaldi's *Four Seasons* . . . to name just a few.

I am grateful to educator Shirley McDonald, who was the first to read my rough manuscript and was encouraging and reassuring from the outset. Her unfailing support, direction, comments, and gentle kindness kept me going despite discouraging moments. I will always value her input on this project.

I appreciate scientist Richard Huber for his constant optimism, for his direct and valid criticisms of the manuscript, for keeping me abreast of vital music information, and for helping me to grasp scientific concepts that were beyond my understanding. This ability to simplify the complex made him invaluable to this project.

Journalist Donna Mackay is a creative wonder! Her quick understanding of the material, her insights, and lively comments were an inspiration to me.

I am indebted to my wonderful, supportive siblings—Alene Villaneda, Jeannette Peck, Geralynn Spencer, Sharon Garn, Talana Kristensen, Diana Mareth, and Howard Peck—who, over the years, have implemented many of these musical ideas as they have raised their children and have given me input on what does and does not work. Their comments on the manuscript were invaluable.

Trusted and treasured friends have read various versions and portions of the text. Their input helped me to further construct and reconstruct my ideas. I appreciate the comments and insights of Joanna Lyons, Jenny Webster, Peggy Stoker, Judy Hribar, Wendy Naylor, Beth Paullin, and Dodi Poulsen.

Many thanks to my agent, Margret McBride, for helping me to find the right publishing house for this book.

Finally, I am deeply grateful for the support from my publishing team: my editor, Jamie Miller, whose vast understanding of music enabled her to help me in diverse, compelling ways. MaryBeth Fontana for all her help and timely assistance. Jennifer Fox, my project editor, for her suggestions, input, and help in creating the polished product. She has been an inspiration to me! I will always be grateful for her attention to every detail. And for Don Zacharias for seeing the project to its conclusion.

INTRODUCTION

I started taking piano lessons when I was five years old. When I was seven, my music teacher told my parents that it was a waste of her time and their money to have me continue studying.

"She hasn't learned the notes in two years, and musically, she'll never amount to anything," she emphatically explained.

Before taking me out of lessons, my mother consulted my father, who asked, "Does she enjoy her music?"

"Yes," my mother said, "very much so."

"Then let her continue with another teacher," my father replied simply.

I will always be grateful for that decision—made by my parents at a time when I was too young to realize the broad implications of severing those music lessons. My parents, while observing the enjoyment I derived from the piano, sensed that my love of music was more important than my ability to play music. As far as my music teacher . . . she was partially correct in her estimation of my musical aptitude. I was obviously not a prodigy, and today my musical talent is certainly not on the virtuoso level (or remotely close!). But, I feel that my connection to music today—and the reason I took lessons through college and into adulthood, acquired a degree in the arts, and still continue to play, enjoy, appreciate, and love all kinds of music—is because of that early and consistent exposure.

Now, many years later, in my own home, the motivation to make music a legacy for our children is a direct result of the musical experiences my husband and I had while growing up. It is a natural desire to pass on to those we love the things we love.

In the early stages of parenthood and like many "first" parents, my husband and I were probably too zealous in trying to be "perfect" parents. We sought and read advice from the experts on how to raise "brilliant" children. Hence our first son, Jason, was exposed to literature and music in utero, and within twenty-four hours after birth, I was reading and singing to him. Playing rhythm instruments, reading, dancing, singing, listening to all kinds of music, group lessons, private lessons, and numerous trips to see music performed "up close and personal" (including a Barry Manilow concert when he was only three) were part of his childhood routine. Our other sons were given similar experiences, but it was Brandon, our third son, who made me seriously look at music not just as an art form—one that added aesthetic experiences to life—but also as a powerful vehicle for achieving academic understanding and success.

Brandon was a cranky baby and was never happy unless he was being held. The only way to get him to sleep was to play not just any music, but choral music. My other sons had loved orchestral music and lullabies as babies, but not Brandon. Choral music was the only sound that soothed his little soul. To keep him asleep at night, we purchased a tape recorder that automatically changed sides, because if the music stopped, Brandon awoke instantly. As a toddler, his language was delayed, and testing in kindergarten revealed sensory, auditory, motor, and visual difficulties. Music would become his lifeline to academic success.

As a young mother, I discovered that if you wanted to learn something and commit it to memory, the key was to set the information to music. For example, we have a long last name—Habermeyer—a challenge for our sons beginning the process of learning to spell their first and last names. When our boys were young, my mother-in-law taught them a little song that helped them to learn how to quickly spell all ten letters. It was the same song that she had taught her children, and most likely our boys will teach it to their children. Seeing how quickly the boys learned anything set to music or with a strong rhythmic cadence later influenced how I helped Brandon in school. Nearly everything he needed to learn and commit to memory, we set to music. His elementary school years were filled with little jingles we routinely made up. When Brandon reached middle school, I started noticing something very interesting. Many other children diagnosed with the same learning challenges as Brandon continued to struggle, despite the fact they had been exposed to the same "one-on-one" programs as Brandon. These were programs that dealt with speech and language, auditory discrimination, sensory integration, and vision therapy. Although these children's learning difficulties lingered, Brandon's improved remarkably. In casual discussions with their parents, I found that the only added benefit Brandon was receiving was music training. Today, because of the research available, I understand more scientifically why music helped him so dramatically.

Scientists have found that music involves both left, right, front, and back portions of the brain, which explains why people can learn and retain information more readily when it is set to music.

First, scientists have found that music involves both left, right, front, and back portions of the brain, which explains why people can learn and *retain* information more readily when it is set to music. This scientific discovery simply confirms what parents have seen when their toddler quickly learns songs, nursery rhymes, and books with rhyming cadences. It is probably why people well into old age can still recite from memory the ABC song they learned as children.

Another possible reason why music may have helped Brandon is how it strengthens the auditory cortex of the brain, which is where most learning difficulties originate. When a child plays the piano, he listens to the pitch of the note being played. In doing so, the neural pathways, called tonotopic maps, found in the auditory cortex are developed. (This topic is covered in Chapter 2.) If music exercises, and thereby strengthens, the auditory cortex of the brain, then it seems logical that learning a musical instrument can help a child with auditory processing difficulties. I do not understand all of the scientific particulars, nor am I certain whether this assumption is correct, but I do know that music played a significant role in helping Brandon overcome his auditory processing problems.

Since 1982, I have lectured on literature and music to parents and educators in the western United States. In the beginning, I presented music as a wonderful art form to expose children to; I explained how music added beauty to their lives, and how music lessons naturally taught many important values (responsibility, perseverance, and so on). After my experiences with Brandon, and after delving more deeply into the available studies on music and the brain (and there are a lot), I changed my focus from the aesthetic to the educational and, in doing so, my lectures on music became more popular. Unfortunately, in our society, we are more motivated by the educational than the aesthetic. Parents, in particular, are more inclined to consistently expose their child to music if they know that Mozart, Bach, Handel, Beethoven, or Vivaldi will make their child smarter as opposed to just knowing that music will enrich their child's life in artistic ways.

During this time, the studies, research, and theories of psychologists, scientists, neuromusicologists, music researchers, medical doctors, and educators influenced and broadened my perception and appreciation of classical music. I read and gathered hundreds of articles from medical journals, periodicals, newspapers, magazines, dissertations, texts from biological music conferences and national music organizations. I consulted and interviewed many experts in these fields. I joined music organizations to learn about their music philosophies, to participate in their conferences and workshops, and to see how their particular approach to music enhanced learning. I then searched for a comprehensive "how-to" book geared to parents on the far-reaching benefits of music to pass on to interested parents at my lectures. Finding nothing under one title, I decided to write this book.

Except for a few examples, you will find that I focus entirely on classical music. This does not mean I do not find other kinds of music wonderful and exciting, but because of the massive amount and variety of music available, the emphasis must be narrowed, and because of classical music's extensive *educational* benefits, the concentration is on classical music.

In Part One, I establish *why* classical music is for you and your child. Part Two gives the nuts and bolts of *how* to accomplish the *why* by turning your home into a powerful musical training center. Part Three focuses on advocacy. It explains the importance of music education in the schools and how an education in music and the arts produces a well-rounded adult who is more valued in his or her work endeavors. Part Four explains the role of and need for music in the nation and how families and individuals can become active supporters of the music community. The Finale, in my opinion, is the most important chapter in the book, as it will give you strong reasons, ideas, and keys for making music a lasting legacy in your home. The Resource section provides lists of music, CDs, books, national music organizations, and Web sites and is a great tool to take to any music store or library.

As you read this book, I hope you will look at and appreciate music in many different ways—a biological human need, an astounding art form that allows us to feel and experience a multitude of sensations, an extraordinary vehicle for enhancing intelligence, and a way to connect and unite people all over the world.

As you read this book, I hope you will look at and appreciate music in many different ways—a biological human need, an astounding art form that allows us to feel and experience a multitude of sensations, an extraordinary vehicle for enhancing intelligence, and a way to connect and unite people all over the world. Over the years, I have looked for a fitting definition of music that would demonstrate the influence it has on all of us. What comes closest is the following quote spoken by Walter Damrosch in 1928, which elegantly portrays the power music has on human life, while concurrently speaking of its divine origin: "Servant and Master am I: Servant of those dead, and Master of those living. Through my spirit immortals speak the message that makes the world weep and laugh and wonder and worship. . . . For I am the instrument of God, I am Music."

PART

WHY MUSIC

$\mathcal{O}$VERTURE:
THE POWER OF MUSIC

[Music] whispers to us dim secrets that startle our wonder as to who we are, and for what, whence, and whereto.

—*Ralph Waldo Emerson*

Music has the power to change us. The advanced civilizations of antiquity—the Greeks, the Romans, the Chinese, and others—viewed music as a powerful force that could change the character of an individual and influence the masses. Confucius believed that music was so far reaching in its significance that it influenced much of what humans did in life and held potential power for both good and evil. He stated, "If you would know if a people are well governed, and if its laws are good or bad, examine the music it practises."[1] These cultures did not consider music a mere art form as we do today . . . they knew and understood its power.

Today, scientists and neuromusicologists—researchers who study how music affects the brain—are beginning to unravel the potential music has on the development of human beings. They know people are born musical; that is, music is a vital part of our biological makeup and is one of the ingredients that make us human. These observers agree that all human beings respond to music on some level, and it has an astounding influence on people's behavior, thinking, and being. Music is one of the first things that babies respond to at birth and one of the last things that people who are dying acknowledge. People who report near-death experiences sometimes tell of the presence of music.[2] We played music during the births of our sons and for my mother-in-law as she lay dying from a malignant brain tumor. In each instance, music created a calm peaceful environment—for one human being entering the world and for another leaving it.

> *Anthropologists believe that music had its beginnings with early man, and since then there has never been a time or a civilization without it.*

Anthropologists believe that music had its beginnings with early man, and since then there has never been a time or a civilization without it. The first evidence of music in cave paintings dates back as much as 70,000 years. Hundreds of cave drawings depict humans engaged in musical activities. Some of these paintings depict bows, which are thought by anthropologists to be used as musical instruments as much as they were used as weapons of war.[3]

Flutes from 30,000 years ago, found in southern France, the Pyrenees, and Russia provide more evidence of music in early man's life. The positions of the tone holes on the flutes indicate that early humans probably created music of artistic significance. More than 40,000 examples of rock carvings illustrating man's involvement in music have been found in caves in northern Italy, Africa, and other parts of Europe.

Universally, evidence shows that songs have been an integral part in the formation of cultures. Records in the form of hymns, chants, and songs have been discovered among the ruins of ancient civilizations. In Asia Minor and Sumeria, clay tablets have been found that contain writings discussing the place and importance of music in those societies.[4] The Greeks linked the creation of music and song to their goddesses, the Muses, who presided over the arts, literature, and the sciences and are told about in their mythology. "Zeus created the world, and the gods viewed in silent admiration all its beauty and magnificence. Then Zeus asked if something was still missing. And the gods answered that one thing was still missing: the world was lacking a Voice, the ultimate voice, which in words and sounds had the gift of expressing and praising all this magnificence. To make such a voice sound, a new kind of divine being was necessary. And thus the Muses were created, as the children of Zeus and Mnemosyne."[5]

Throughout the ages, mankind has produced many forms of music and—whether for religious purposes, rituals, cere-monies, or enjoyment—the human need to create music seems basic to life.

A Musical Universe

We live in a musical universe. In 1772, Johann Bode, a German astronomer, measured the distance between the planets. His mathematical formula was so precise that it later became known as "Bode's Law." He stated that all of the planets possessed mean orbital distances from Mercury, which become progressively greater by the ratio of 2:1 as the planets' distance from the sun increased. The ratio 2:1 means that each planet vibrates twice as fast as its predecessor vibrates and produces a sound with a pitch one octave higher than the previous planet. This ratio is the same as that of the musical tones in an octave, suggesting that the planets themselves form a chain of octaves, with each planet representing one octave. Within this octave, the planets, as they spin on their axes, have an actual tone created by their pitch-frequencies.[6]

To understand this concept, think of the toy tops that children play with. As the top spins around and gains speed, it begins to "hum," and a music-like tone is produced. Scientists measured the tone of the earth in 1960 during an earthquake in Chile. Seismographs showed that the earth "rings" with deep vibrations that are exactly twenty octaves below the lowest sound that the human ear can hear. Approximately every twelve years, the planets become somewhat aligned with one another. If we could hear the combination of these various tones at this time, they would most likely sound like a musical chord. Imagine—the planets are like a gigantic musical instrument resonating in the universe![7]

Stars also produce tones. On August 27, 1998, scientists reported a blast of an unusual star in the earth's upper atmosphere. Kevin Hurley of the University of California at Berkeley said that the star "rang" in x-rays for several minutes, producing an "unheard of" tone in the universe.[8] (X-rays, like a musical note, are measured by frequencies.)

Pythagoras—a philosopher and mathematician of ancient Greece—and his followers, the Pythagoreans, discovered that all music could be understood as numbers and mathematical ratios. More recently, Richard Voss of IBM's Thomas J. Watson Research Center used mathematical formulas to find patterns of music in nature. Music, he says, resembles not the sounds heard in nature, but nature itself. Through a mathematical equation, he linked the underlying musical structure that is found in "flicker" noise (noise found in nature) to a landscape, a range of mountains, or a seascape. "Flicker" noise can be converted to a signature sound and can be compared to how a particular physical system changes over time. Every large mass (a building, a human, a mountain) resonates at a certain "background" frequency that can be measured. If external forces match that frequency, the mass will disintegrate. The Tacoma-Narrows Bridge in Washington broke apart in a "frequency disturbance" as a result of winds. The structure was not engineered properly and was out of tune with its environment, literally. Every structure or mass has this background frequency, and it's referred to mathematically as "flicker noise." This noise is the fingerprint of that mass and all parts of the structure or mass. Although this "noise" is unlike the music of a Mozart, it can still be judged as distinctly music-like. Voss has created realistic-looking artificial landscapes, planets, and clouds using similar equations as a part of a new science known as "fractals."[9]

Animals and Music

Along with music in our universe and musical patterns in nature, it has been found that animals also respond to music—particularly classical music! In February 1985, as many as 3,000 beluga whales were trapped under ice in the waters of the Soviet Union. There were only a few breathing holes in the ice, and the whales had to take turns surfacing for air. Food was running out, the whales were becoming exhausted, and some were even dying. When all seemed hopeless, a Soviet icebreaker, the *Moskva*, came to the rescue. The ship broke through the ice, making an escape path for the whales, but they wouldn't budge. Knowing that whales like music, they tried pop and jazz, but still the whales remained motionless. Finally, the crew tried classical music. It was then that the whales followed the music to the open sea and to freedom.[10]

Birds also respond to classical music. A study by Stewart Hulse of Johns Hopkins University found that European starlings are able to recognize a simple melody in different keys. The researchers concluded that starlings respond to musical features just like humans. In another experiment by Debra Porter and Allen Neuringer at Reed College, pigeons were trained to distinguish the music of J. S. Bach from the music of Igor Stravinsky. They were even able to correctly categorize music from other composers that sounded Bach-like or Stravinsky-like.[11]

Many animals communicate with one another through musical sounds. Baby emperor penguins rely on the *sound* of their parents rather than sight. When their parents go to sea to hunt for food, the baby penguins stay in penguin day-care centers called creches. Upon returning, the parents walk from creche to creche, trumpeting at the top of their lungs. Ann Bowles, an expert on emperor communication states, "Each bird's call is distinctive. When a child recognizes its parent's voice, it comes barreling out to meet it."[12] Dolphins use high whistles and clicks to "see" underwater and communicate with other dolphins. Whales use sounds that resemble songs to communicate with other whales. Frogs sing choruses when they are looking for mates or defending their territory. Elephants communicate with one another using rumbling sounds that are too low for humans to hear, but strong enough for us to feel. They can hear each other from miles away and listen to one another with their huge ears held open.[13]

Music and Learning

Music goes beyond being a powerful force in our universe, a part of nature, and a communication vehicle between the animals of the earth. Proportionately, its greatest impact is on human beings—to our learning processes, brain development, and organization, and the refinement of our entire neurological system. Dr. Gordon Shaw and Dr. Frances Rauscher, scientists at the University of California at Irvine and the University of Wisconsin at Oshkosh—and many others within the brain research community—have shown music to have extensive educational and brain-developing value. Listening to classical music can increase memory and concentration, and studying a musical instrument has been shown to increase spatial reasoning.[14]

When music in all of its forms (singing, playing a musical instrument, listening to classical music, and so on) is a part of the home environment, it creates a positive atmosphere, one which is conducive to learning and aids in the acquisition of early language. When music is taught comprehensively and sequentially in the schools, it increases math, science, reading, history, and SAT scores. It also reaches at-risk students by increasing their confidence and those with learning disabilities by making the learning process easier. Additionally, studying a musical instrument helps develop imagination, invention, creative thinking, communication, and teamwork skills—precisely those attributes needed for a twenty-first century global work force.[15]

Listening to classical music can increase memory and concentration, and studying a musical instrument has been shown to increase spatial reasoning.

An education in music and the arts has been shown to be an essential ingredient for our children's future success. With the passing of the Goals 2000: Educate America Act in 1994 and the National Standards for Arts Education, the importance of the arts has been nationally recognized, and with a collaborative effort between schools, arts organizations, and corporations, music and arts education can become a reality for children in schools across our nation.

Communicating Emotions

But no matter what potential music has in developing the intellect, how it describes us as human beings and how it affects us emotionally are by no means insignificant. Donald Hodges, editor of *Handbook of Music Psychology*, relates the following story: In 1978, when NASA was preparing to launch *Voyagers* 1 and 2 into space, they called Carl Sagan to head up a special team. The team's job was to devise a means of communicating with extraterrestrials, should the spacecrafts be captured or discovered. The scientists agreed that because of the universal appeal of music, it would be the most effective way of communicating to aliens what humans are all about. The spacecrafts would show our scientific technological side, but music would show our emotional nature. Music from all over the world was recorded and sent aboard the *Voyagers* to explain to others what we are like as human beings.[16]

The 1990s have been dubbed the "decade of the brain," because of the explosion in brain research. Scientists have found that the cortex represents 85 percent of brain mass and handles our intellectual functions. The remaining 15 percent—the limbic system—handles our emotional functions, which scientists feel may be vital to our survival. Dr. Marian Diamond, professor of anatomy at the University of California at Berkeley, found that giving tender loving care to aging rats increased their life spans.[17] These results implied that the emotional area of our brain is as necessary for the well-being of the individual as the intellectual side—if not more so. Dr. Paul MacLean at the National Institute of Mental Health believes that our brains are composed of three separate units: the reptilian brain, which controls basic movements and survival instincts; the mammalian brain, which is made up of the limbic system that is responsible for our feelings and emotions; and the neo-mammalian brain, or neo-cortex, which is the intellectual core of the human mind. Dr. MacLean believes that the emotional, or limbic system of the brain is so powerful that it can either facilitate or inhibit learning and higher-order thinking skills.[18]

Because recent studies demonstrate that music seems to involve the brain at almost every level, music may be the key to providing, in part, this emotional balance. Anne Blood, who conducted studies at McGill University in Montreal, found that the "neural mechanisms of music may have originally developed as a way of communicating emotion as a precursor to speech, offering

insights into how the mind integrates sensory information with emotion and meaning."[19] The research indicates that music and the arts utilize both the cortex and limbic systems. Both are essential for learning that lasts and—as Diamond found—for our very survival. You simply cannot study music and the arts without *feeling* joy, happiness, love, tenderness, sorrow, humor, and so on, and when we allow these emotions to be a part of the learning process, our education becomes richer, more meaningful, longer lasting, and has greater impact in our lives. As Diamond suggests, "One without the other is only half an experience."

> *You simply cannot study music and the arts without feeling joy, happiness, love, tenderness, sorrow, humor, and so on, and when we allow these emotions to be a part of the learning process, our education becomes richer, more meaningful, longer lasting, and has greater impact in our lives.*

Mark Jude Tramo, a neurobiologist with the Harvard University Medical School, concurs, "Music is biologically part of human life, just as music is aesthetically part of human life."[21] In short, music is essential to human life. Music has power.

CHAPTER 2

$\mathscr{M}$USIC AND THE BRAIN: NOTHING IS MINOR ABOUT MUSIC

Science will . . . produce the data . . . but never the full meaning. For perceiving real significance, we shall need . . . most of all the brains of poets, [and] also those of artists, musicians, philosophers, historians, writers in general.

—Lewis Thomas, Scientist

Centuries ago, Plato said, "Music is a more potent instrument than any other for education." Today, because of the advancement of technology, we can see more clearly why this statement is true. A growing field known as neuromusicology (the study of how music affects the brain) has advanced significantly in the last ten years. Scientists have found that music has the ability to train the brain for higher levels of thinking—the kind of thinking involving problem solving, inference, arriving at conclusions, comparing and contrasting the similarities and differences between two or more objects, analyzing, synthesizing, and evaluating information. A recent study found music to be a powerful tool for increasing spatial-temporal reasoning, which is the ability to perceive the visual world accurately and form mental images of objects. In other words, it is the mind's ability to see in very detailed pictures and to recognize, compare, and find relationships among the patterns and details of an object.[1] The temporal element involves a child's ability to think ahead. In learning music, one must be able to play a note, then a series of notes, then a series of chords, and be able to look ahead at the music and determine where and what will be played next. In 1994, Drs. Gordon Shaw and Frances Rauscher, scientists at the University of California at Irvine, conducted an experiment showing a causal link between spatial reasoning and music. They divided seventy-nine college students into three groups. Each group was given a cutting and folding task. One group heard ten minutes of Mozart's Sonata in D for Two Pianos, K. 488, another group heard ten minutes of minimalist (Philip Glass's *Music with Changing Parts*) and rhythmically repetitive music (Ian Rich's C-Level Productions mix of *Mortal Stomp* and *Carry Me Through*), and the control group was in silence. Nothing of significance occurred with the latter two groups, but the students who listened to the music of Mozart experienced an increase in their spatial IQ of eight to nine points in just ten minutes! Although the effect was temporary, the scientists believed that a particular organization of the elements in the music caused the improvement in spatial-temporal reasoning. This phenomenon has since been dubbed the "Mozart effect."[2]

The scientists wondered if merely listening to music could cause an increase in spatial-temporal reasoning could the effect be prolonged by studying a musical instrument? To find out, the researchers tested thirty-three three-year-olds in a Los Angeles preschool—three-year-olds were chosen because the cortexes of their brains are still maturing.[3] They divided the children into two groups and provided eight months of keyboard and singing lessons to nineteen of the children. Fourteen of the children made up the control group and did not receive any music training. The training consisted of a weekly ten- to fifteen-minute private keyboard lesson, daily practice periods, and a daily thirty-minute singing time. After eight months, they tested the children. Five tasks were used to test the children's spatial reasoning: arranging pieces of a puzzle into a meaningful whole; matching depicted patterns using flat, two-colored blocks; placing correct color pegs into holes below a series of pictured animals; performing a geometric design task; and describing what was "wrong" or "silly" about a picture. The spatial-temporal reasoning of those in the control group increased by only 6 percent, but those who had received the music training increased their spatial-temporal reasoning by an impressive 46 percent![4]

Next, the researchers took another group of seventy-eight preschool children and divided them into four groups. One group consisted of thirty-four students who were given private daily piano lessons. A second group of twenty students had ten minutes of private computer training each day, and twenty-four children were divided among a singing-only group and a no-lesson group. After six months of training, the four groups were tested. Those in the piano group had the most dramatic improvement in spatial-temporal reasoning—their scores increased by 34 percent.[5]

In 1998, the scientists explored how a computer math game called "Spatial-Temporal Animation Reasoning (STAR)" coupled with either piano lessons or English-language training affected students performance in math. The four-month study focused on 170 second-graders from an elementary school in Los Angeles. One group of children studied the piano keyboard and the math video game, another group received English language training and studied the math video game, and a third group, the control group, had no exposure to these lessons. After four months, both groups of students who had received training in the computer game showed a 100 percent increase in their math skills as compared to the control group. Additionally, the students who had piano keyboarding along with the computer game did a striking 27 percent better on questions devoted to fractions

and proportional math than those students who received training in English language and the math video game. Teachers
of the group who studied the keyboard also reported that
these students demonstrated better attention and concentration abilities.[6]

The Importance of Patterns

This research brings up questions: How did the scientists determine there *could* be a link between spatial-temporal reasoning
and music? And why is spatial-temporal reasoning important? To
understand this link, it is important to realize the significance of
patterns. There are patterns found throughout the universe and
in the functions of our bodies. We see them in the frequency of
lunar eclipses, in the changing of the seasons, in sunspots, and
tree rings, in our heartbeat, hormonal cycles, and brain waves.
Simply put, just about everything in life has connecting patterns. Music has been defined as an ordered *pattern* of sounds.[7]
The structural patterns found in music and math are similar; in
fact, so similar that the Pythagoreans considered music one of
the four branches of mathematics.[8] In the sixth century B.C.,
Pythagoras said, "There is geometry in the humming of the
strings. There is music in the spacing of the spheres." Eric
Wright, of the Irvine Conservatory of Music, who worked with
Shaw and Rauscher, said, "When you look at music, it truly is a
mathematical production."[9]

   Many of the great composers enjoyed math and understood
its pattern relationship to music. Bach loved mathematical structure, patterns, and order, which can be observed most readily in his
music. It comes as no surprise that the first music to be put on the
computer (an orderly, structured device) was the mathematical
music of Bach. Mozart also loved math. Just before his sixth birth-
day, he discovered math and ". . . suddenly the house erupted with
figures scribbled on every bit of space—walls, floors, tables, and

chairs. This passion for mathematics is plainly in close alliance with his great contrapuntal facility."[10] Interestingly, musicologists refer to Mozart's music as a "science" and describe his music as "architectural" because it is built around the same mathematical proportion and elemental structure laws as are found in many famous cathedrals.[11] Confirming the relationship between music and math, Martha B. Denckla of the National Institute of Health in Bethesda, Maryland, said, "Music and mathematics are very similar in that both are *par excellence*—when performed well—duets between the two sides of the brain."[12]

Likewise, the patterns found in the brain and those found in music are similar. Recently, researchers using data from SQUID—superconducting quantum interference device, which measures the brain's electrical activity—determined that the arrangement of the tonotopic map in the auditory cortex of the brain is much like that of a piano keyboard, with equal distance between octaves.[13] Tonotopic maps are pathways in the brain and are involved in determining the pitch of a note played on a piano. Studies show that these "maps" are about 25 percent larger in musicians than non-musicians, demonstrating that musical experiences during childhood influence the development of the auditory cortex.[14]

Dr. Shaw also has found similar patterns in music and the brain. Over the last twenty-five years, he has created computer models that map the mathematical patterns that neurons make when they fire in the brain. He found that the neurons are organized into patterned columns that "talk" to one another by

> *Confirming the relationship between music and math, Martha B. Denckla of the National Institute of Health in Bethesda, Maryland, said, "Music and mathematics are very similar in that both are par excellence—when performed well—duets between the two sides of the brain."*

sending out electrical impulses. Shaw and researcher Xiaodan Leng assigned musical tones to each of the columns and found that the brain was organized into what appeared to be musical themes. They then picked a piece of music that most closely resembled the musical themes on the computer model, which in this case was Mozart's Piano Sonata in D for Two Pianos, K. 448. It was determined that if the music exercised the same brain circuits responsible for spatial reasoning, then spatial reasoning would naturally increase. When they tested the students, that is exactly what happened. The music—with the patterns and themes similar to those found in the brain, increased spatial-temporal reasoning. The results were even more dramatic when the students were given ongoing keyboard lessons. The research showed that when children study music, patterns in the brain are affected, which has an impact on the way brain circuitry is developed in the first few years of life.[15]

"Music involves structured sequences of patterns," Shaw says.[16] The conclusion—music could enhance brain function. The music lessons led to a sustained improvement in certain spatial skills in young children, suggesting that both functions exercise the same brain circuits. So, as a child learns a musical instrument, he is exercising two functions at once—learning to play a musical instrument and increasing spatial-temporal reasoning skills.

Spatial-temporal reasoning is the kind of reasoning used in higher levels of math and science. Children with strong spatial-temporal reasoning enjoy chess, more abstract advanced mathematics, and have a greater understanding of science. For instance, they understand ratio and proportions better and consequently do better on proportional reasoning tasks. These elements are important in understanding many difficult math and science concepts that are taught in school.[17] Because musical training increases the ability to comprehend higher-level math, science, engineering, and physics concepts, it is considered essential for optimal thinking capabilities.[18]

The skills associated with spatial-temporal reasoning are found in many different professions. They are crucial elements in the worlds of the surgeon, the pilot, the artist, the scientist, and the engineer. Many of these peoples because of their ability to visualize, can "see" three-dimensionally or see the intricate details of an object in their mind. Dr. Ben Carson is one of the top pediatric neurosurgeons in the world. In 1987, he separated the Binder twins, who were joined at the skull. He talks about his ability to see three-dimensionally and how this acute inner vision has increased his capability to understand physical relationships between objects. People say he has "gifted hands" because of his visual abilities. Dr. Carson is also a gifted musician and mathematician.[19]

While flying, many pilots have an innate visual sense of direction, a mental map of where they are, even if they are surrounded by clouds. Artists and architects see and observe in their minds how the elements of space, line, shape, color, patterns, and balance come together to form a completed building or picture. Some people with strong spatial reasoning skills are daydreamers as they think, imagine, create, and invent pictures and ideas in their minds. Some don't necessarily do well in school, either. An example of one such person is found in the following description of a very spatially intelligent and scientific child:

> Once there was a boy who consistently made a poor adjustment to school. In fact, in his senior year of secondary school he got a certificate from his doctor stating that he should leave school for six months. He was not a good all-around student, hated tests and exams, and did not make high grades. He had no school friends and his speech was delayed. Some teachers found him a problem and described him as dull. His father was ashamed of his lack of athletic ability. Who was he? The theoretical physicist and Nobel prize–winner Albert Einstein, whose curiosity and perpetual sense of wonder lasted his whole life.[20]

Einstein was daydreaming—taking a ride through the universe on a beam of light—when he came up with his theory of relativity. It was his acute visual imagination, and not his formal training in physics that led to his discovery of one of the most significant theories of all time.[21] He was also a gifted violinist and felt that music helped him to organize his thoughts. Historian Eugene Ferguson said, "Pyramids, cathedrals, and rockets exist not because of geometry, theories of structures, or thermodynamics, but because they were first a picture—literally a vision—in the minds of those who built them."[22]

Thomas Armstrong, educator and author of *7 Kinds of Smart*, believes spatially intelligent people need to be more valued in society, and that their skills and abilities of being able to see things so accurately in the mind's eye will be greatly needed for the challenges of the next century. He illustrates his point with the story of the space shuttle disaster, demonstrating the impact spatially intelligent people can have in the world . . . if listened to. "Apparently, the *Challenger's* poorly designed O-rings failed to remain flexible in cold weather and thus allowed a leakage of fuel that led to the explosion that destroyed the spacecraft. This flaw was spotted by spatially intelligent technicians, but overruled by analytically oriented and politically motivated supervisors who were perhaps less able to visualize the consequences of the problem."[23]

Music for a Brighter Future

The discovery of the correlation between math, music, and spatial-temporal reasoning will have significant ramifications for the next century. The American Mathematical Society warns that the United States is heading for a shortage of math capability that could undercut its economic and military strength as it enters the 21st century.[24] In 1990, the National Science Foundation estimated that the United States would face an annual shortage of 9,600 doctoral-level scientists, and by the year 2000 this country would need nearly half a million more scientists and engineers than it will be able to produce. By the year 2010, the shortfall of professional scientists and engineers will approach 1 million, if current trends persist.[25] If music enhances brain functioning for higher-level math and science skills and, as a result, keeps us competitive in a global economy, it is something we as parents and educators need to provide for our children—now!

Frances Rauscher advises, "It's important to involve children in music, the more the better. If you can't afford music lessons, get them a simple keyboard. If you can't afford a keyboard, sing to them."[26]

If music enhances brain functioning for higher-level math and science skills and, as a result, keeps us competitive in a global economy, it is something we as parents and educators need to provide for our children—now!

An increase in spatial-temporal reasoning is just one of the positive effects that music training has on brain development. Donald Hodges reports that magnetic resonance imaging (MRI) shows that certain areas of the brain—the *planum temporale* and *corpus callosum*—are larger in musicians than in non-musicians and even more exaggerated for those musicians who started training before age seven. (The *planum temporale* plays an important role in language and in early auditory processing. The *corpus callosum* transfers information from one hemisphere of the brain to the other.) From this, the researchers concluded that music training can affect brain organization.[27] Neurologist Dr. Gottfried Schlaug of Beth Israel Deaconess Medical Center in Boston found that male musicians have significantly larger brains than men who have not had extensive musical training. He found that the cerebellum, which contains about 70 percent of the brain's neurons, is about 5 percent larger in expert male musicians. Dr. Schlaug believes that the cerebellum grows larger as a result of constant practicing by the musician as he develops those motor skills needed to play an instrument.[28] Dr. Frank Wilson, assistant clinical professor of neurology at the University of California School of Medicine, San Francisco, reports that learning to play an instrument refines the development of the brain and the entire neurological system. It also connects and develops the motor systems of the brain in a way that cannot be done by any other activity. Dr. Wilson believes that learning a musical instrument is vital for the total development of the brain and individual.[29] Another researcher, Dr. Jean Houston of the Foundation for Mind Research concurs, and believes that the brains of children not exposed to music arts education are actually being damaged because these nonverbal modalities help them with skills such as reading, writing, and math.[30]

One of the most remarkable aspects of learning a musical instrument is that both sides of the brain are utilized. Psychologist Dr. Howard Gardner of Harvard University states, "Most musical capacities seem to be represented chiefly in the right hemisphere . . . but it is far too simple to conclude that music is principally a right-hemisphere function . . . as an individual becomes more skilled in music, capacities that were initially housed in the right hemisphere are found increasingly in the left hemisphere. It seems as if with musical training, a significant proportion of skills migrate across the *corpus callosum* into the linguistically dominant hemisphere."[31]

Dee Dickinson, CEO of New Horizons for Learning in Seattle, Washington, cites research showing that when a child listens to classical music the right hemisphere of the brain is activated, but when a child studies a musical instrument both left and right hemispheres of the brain "light up." Significantly, the areas of the brain that become activated are the same areas that are involved in analytical and mathematical thinking.[32] Dr. Wilson has cited data from brain-scan research studies performed at the University of California at Los Angeles. These data show that studying music involves more left and right brain functions than any other activities studied.[33] Dr. Lawrence Parsons at the University of Texas in San Antonio also found that music involves the entire brain. "We find that harmony, melody, and rhythm had distinct patterns of brain activity. They involved both the right and left sides of the brain," he said.[34] He found that melody affects both sides of the brain equally and that harmony and rhythm predominantly activate the left side. The conclusion—music seems to involve the brain at almost every level, and when the entire brain is being utilized, learning is significantly enhanced. Additionally, because learning to play a musical instrument involves daily practice, studies show that coordination, concentration, and memory are heightened, which leads to greater visual and hearing acuity.[35]

In 1982, at North Texas University, researchers Dr. Barbara Stein, C.A. Hardy, and Herman L. Totten conducted an experiment to see what effect, if any, certain music had on the memorization and retention skills of students. Using the *Water Music*—music that Handel created as a court composer at the request of King George I for his trips down the Thames River—they tested graduate students' ability to learn twenty-five vocabulary words either in silence or while listening to the *Water Music* being played in the background. The results of the test showed that the students who listened to the music while learning the words did remarkably better than those who learned the words in silence. The researchers believed that utilizing both sides of the brain dramatically increased learning.[36] They also examined elements in the music that could have caused the students to memorize the words more easily. They turned to the work of Georgi Lozanov, a Bulgarian doctor and psychiatrist who extensively studied music and memory. Lozanov found that listening to very specific music with a very specific rhythm, particularly music from the Baroque period, caused the rhythms of the

body—the heartbeat, the brain waves, and so on—to synchro-
nize themselves to the beat of the music. When the heartbeat
slowed down, the mind was able to work more effectively and ef-
ficiently. For years, psychologists have claimed that if we relax
our body, we will be able to remember better what we study.[37]
Lozanov also found that although the music caused the body to
relax, the mind remained alert and able to concentrate on very
strenuous mental work. With a slower heartbeat and an alert
mind, the electromagnetic frequency of the brain changed to approximately 7.5 cycles per second.[38] This frequency is also referred to as the Schumann Resonance, alpha mode, or the range
of meditative thought in the brain. Dr. Norio Owaki, a Tokyo researcher, did a ten-year study on specific kinds of sound patterns
that can induce alpha brain waves. He found that music and
sound could, indeed, change brain wave activity.[39]

As far back as Bach, the effects of certain sound patterns
and their ability to cause relaxation and concentration were understood. History relates an interesting story about a series of
musical pieces written by Bach that were later used for Count
Kayserling, who had constant problems with insomnia. After
hearing this music played for a short time, the count was able to
relax and felt less tense. These pieces have since been called the
Goldberg Variations, in honor of the count's friend and musician,
Johann Goldberg, who came and played the Bach music each
time the count had difficulty relaxing or sleeping.

Try playing classical music as background music while your
child is studying or doing other homework. (See the Resource
section for specific examples.) According to the studies, he or
she should be able to concentrate, focus, and memorize facts easier. However, don't expect your child to tell you how much easier it is to study with Bach playing in the background. More than
likely, your child will not notice—but you will. Many people
have reported remarkable experiences using music from the

Baroque, Classical, and Romantic periods while studying. (The musical periods will be discussed in more detail in Chapter 10.)

Deborah Cave was teaching part time, tutoring, and attending law school. To help herself focus, concentrate, and block out the daily stresses while studying for her law classes, she played in the background music from the Baroque period. She felt it made a significant difference in her effectiveness for memorizing and retaining the material. During law school, Deborah took two very difficult take-home exams. Both times she played Handel's *Water Music* in the background. She states, "When the music stopped, I hit the repeat button. I found that the music was a critical factor in helping me to organize my thoughts." She ended up with the highest grade in the class on the first exam and a 97 percent on the second one, which was the second-highest grade in the class and her highest grade in law school. When she sat down to take the California Bar Examination, Handel's *Water Music* immediately began playing in her mind. She relaxed instantly and went on to successfully pass the exam on her first try. Deborah firmly believes the music made a significant difference in her ability to absorb, retain, and retrieve information during law school and was an important element in her ability to focus during the bar examination.

Joan Erzer Behrens, who is very organized and focused, was skeptical about whether music could help her. Usually when she listened to music in the background, she would analyze the music instead of concentrating on the task at hand, so she started out by playing the music very softly in the background. In a few days, she noticed that the music did indeed become "background" music, and she was able to focus and concentrate more effectively than ever before.

Lauren Smith was recently divorced, in her fifties, and had gone back to school to complete a master's degree. Overwhelmed by stresses, she was unable to focus on her studies and considered dropping out of school to wait until her life calmed down. As a last effort, she began playing Handel's *Water Music* in the background while she studied. Within days, she noticed a remarkable improvement in her ability to absorb, retain, and retrieve the information from her classes. Music can and does make a difference!

Through the use of sophisticated equipment in this "decade of the brain," scientists are now able to see how the brain functions as never before. A baby's brain at birth contains 100 billion neurons, which is as many nerve cells as there are stars in the Milky Way. At birth, the brain contains nearly all the nerve cells it will ever have, but the pattern of wiring between them has not yet stabilized.[40] This wiring depends on the rich sensory experiences the child is exposed to during the early years of life. If a child is deprived of a stimulating environment, the brain will suffer.

Hands-on parenting cannot be underestimated in its effect on young children and their brain development. As parents, we must provide numerous, ongoing, and enriching experiences that will nourish our children's brains. Music is such an experience.

Researchers at Baylor College of Medicine have found that children who are not given opportunities to play or who are rarely touched develop brains that are 20 to 30 percent smaller than normal for their age.[41] The opposite also can occur. Researchers at the University of Illinois found that lab animals in an environment of stimulating activities developed 25 percent more synapses per nerve cell and 80 percent more blood vessels to nourish each cell. The conclusion—"rich experiences really do produce rich brains."[42] Scientists now realize that a baby comes into the world primed for stimulating environmental experiences that will shape her intellect and future. These facts have profound implications for parents. Hands-on parenting cannot be underestimated in its effect on young children and their brain development. As parents, we must provide numerous, ongoing, and enriching experiences that will nourish our children's brains. Music is such an experience.

As we have learned, all human beings are born musical and will respond to music. Because classical music, with its complex repetitive patterns, has far-reaching effects on the child and his brain development, it is the *perfect* experience. As you read this book, you will learn specific ways to increase children's brain functioning, enlarge their capacity for learning, and profoundly enrich their lives—through classical music!

PART

MUSIC IN THE HOME

CHAPTER 3

HOME: SET THE TONE WITH MUSIC

If the child is not filled at least once by the life-giving stream of music during the most susceptible period, between his sixth and sixteenth years, it will hardly be of any use to him later on. Often a single experience will open the young soul to music for a whole lifetime.

—Zoltán Kodály

Beth Perry grew up in the West, the third of eight children. Her life was somewhat void of material possessions, but rich in educational and cultural experiences. Whatever she and her siblings lacked in worldly belongings, their parents made up for by exposing them to the arts. Music was an integral part of their home and lives. Her parents took the family to the opera, ballet, symphonies, and art museums, many of which were free. Libraries were also a frequent destination. Somehow they afforded piano, flute, clarinet, violin, and saxophone lessons for all eight children. Beth learned to play the familiar childhood tunes of John Thompson on a wonderful old black upright piano that had belonged to her grandparents.

Music was important to her parents because they had grown up with musical experiences that their parents had offered them. Their extended families abounded in musical talent and among them were mandolin players, violinists, pianists, and opera singers. It was a natural course of events for them to pass on to their children their love for the arts.

One of the musical experiences Beth remembers was the free concerts offered by the Utah Symphony Orchestra. Conductor Maurice Abravanel, a Russian Jew, was responsible for teaching thousands of children to appreciate music and follow proper concert etiquette. She remembers how he would peer out over the audience with searching eyes before beginning the program, looking for anyone who was whispering or walking down the aisles. When he found an offender, he would emphatically point his baton at the person and yell, "Freeze!" The children in the audience learned very quickly to respect the musicians and their music!

Beth's husband was fortunate to have had a similar early exposure to music while growing up in San Francisco. Today, they both continue to love and enjoy music and the arts. Like the homes they grew up in, their home is filled with music, and they now take their children to concerts, ballets, and operas, thus passing on an important family legacy.

Whenever someone starts a new business, analysts say the three most important things to consider are "location, location, location." Likewise, the keys to having your children love and appreciate classical music are "exposure, exposure, exposure." The first exposure to music usually comes from the home—and the good news is that parents do not have to be musicians, or schooled in music, to introduce their children to classical music. Any home can become a musical training center. In this chapter, we explore many ways to accomplish this with ease and pleasure. With parental help, children can reap many important benefits that come from early musical exposure and training such as early language, reading, and math development, as well as listening, memorization, and thinking skills.

As you begin to expose your children to music, you will find that they have an innate or natural capability for music. Dr. Frank Wilson confirms this and believes there are natural musical qualities that are a part of every human being. He said, "I am convinced that all of us have a biologic guarantee of musicianship. This is true regardless of our age, formal experience with music, or the size and shape of our fingers, lips or ears. . . . We all have music inside us and can learn how to get it out, one way or another."[1]

The first exposure to music usually comes from the home— and the good news is that parents do not have to be musicians, or schooled in music, to introduce their children to classical music.

The ideas given in this chapter are not difficult to follow. They do take a little time and effort, but the time you spend exposing your children to music and giving them opportunities to learn a musical instrument becomes a powerful investment in their future. Plus, as you progress in this labor of love, you will witness music's capability to positively affect your children socially, intellectually, physically, and emotionally. Let's begin by exploring different ideas you can use to accomplish this from pre-birth through high school.

Pre-Birth (In Utero)

Glen Gould, the famous concert pianist, reports that his mother played the piano for him constantly while he was developing in utero. Sergei Prokofiev, the famous Russian composer who wrote *Peter and the Wolf*, also was exposed to music before he was born. His pregnant mother played the piano every day for him, exposing him to the music of Chopin and Beethoven. Today, scientists agree that a child's music development may start before he is born. Approximately twenty-two days after conception, a little heart begins to beat. This distinct rhythmic beat is similar to the mother's heartbeat and to the rhythmic patterns found in the symphonies of Mozart, Beethoven, and Brahms.[2] As the development of the baby continues, so does the rhythmic fashion in which the baby moves his arms, his legs, and his torso. Already the baby is producing music!

Studies have been done to determine whether the unborn fetus is able to hear sounds coming from outside the uterus. As early as 1925, researcher S. Peiper found that a five-week old fetus responds with sudden movements to loud sounds coming from outside the body of the mother and, by the twenty-fourth week, the fetus listens to sounds all the time.[3] Many pregnant singers report that their babies seem much quieter when they sing. Perhaps the fetus is responding much like the newborn does to his mother when she sings a soothing lullaby. Other mothers report that when they practice a musical instrument, their babies become more active.[4] When Donna Adams was pregnant with her second and third sons, she was taking piano lessons and practicing daily. The pace of the song she was practicing determined whether or not the baby was calm or active. As newborns, they both responded to music. When the stereo was playing, they would turn their heads in the direction of the music, and it would calm them when they were upset. Orchestral lullabies and soothing vocal music would help them fall sleep.

During the last twenty years, expectant parents have been encouraged to not only talk and read to their unborn children, but to play classical music and sing to them, as well. When a mother sings and talks to her unborn baby, she is exposing her to the sound and nuances of her voice. Because of this daily exposure to singing, the baby will immediately recognize her mother's voice at birth. To support this, scientists have found that just moments after birth a baby will turn in the direction of the mother's voice, and by the end of the first week she can identify her mother's voice from a group of female voices (much like the baby emperor penguins talked about in Chapter 1).[5]

Today, many fathers are becoming involved in prenatal activities, too. Researcher Sarah Lopez from the University of California, San Diego, found that when fathers use a pregaphone to talk to their unborn child, they reap big rewards. A pregaphone is an instrument that has a mouthpiece to talk into, with a trumpet-shaped part that fits on the mother's stomach and can amplify the father's voice. With it, fathers are able to sing and talk to their child in utero. From this simple exercise, newborns recognize the father's voice as quickly as they do the mother's. Lopez calls this phenomenon "father presence."[6] It is not absolutely necessary to use a pregaphone when communicating with an unborn infant; it is thought that just by singing and talking close to the mother's stomach the baby will still hear.

In 1985, Rene Van deCarr said that prenatal infants are in a "prenatal university." He instructs parents to expose their prenatal child to music, poetry, and children's literature. He has found dramatic developmental differences between those children exposed to music and literature in utero and their siblings who were not.[7]

Donald Shetler, professor emeritus of music education at the Eastman School of Music in New York, found dramatic increases in language development and memory skills in children exposed to music in utero. In the Eastman Pilot Study (1980 to 1987), headphones were placed directly on the stomachs of the expectant mothers, exposing the fetus to five to ten minutes of both sedating and stimulating music each day. Within four to six weeks after birth, he met with the mother and child to watch and observe the baby. Shetler noted that the most remarkable development was observed in children between the ages of two and five. Their memory skills were stronger, and their speech patterns were developed earlier with greater articulation, sophistication, and organization than their siblings who were not exposed to music in utero. For example, a two-year-old girl in the study was able to sing a thirty-two-measure song with chromatic intervals and key changes. She sang with excellent speech clarity and used expressive dynamics and gestures. Another little girl, not quite two, sang twelve songs from memory and was able to play the piano with independent fingering. She used excellent verbal articulation and expressed herself in complete sentences. A four-year-old boy in the study identified the sounds made by a wide variety of musical instruments that he was hearing for the first time. He played and improvised his own songs on various rhythm instruments. When his mother played different beats on a drum, he was able to imitate them.[8]

Although musical studies on babies in utero are continuing, these earlier studies suggest that by singing, talking, and reading to the unborn child, parents can give them a significant advantage in early language, memory, and music development.

The experience Sheryl and Mike Hatter of Chicago had with their first-born child supports the finding of this research. During this pregnancy, both were going to school and living in an apartment. Not having a piano to play, they constantly sang, talked, and read to Jason as he was developing in utero. When he was only five months old, he said his first word; at nine months he was talking and singing in short sentences, and by the age of two he had taught himself to read. He memorized poetry and books with a strong rhythm very quickly. He also loved to sing, dance, and was able to correctly beat out different rhythms on his little drum.

Although musical studies on babies in utero are continuing, these earlier studies suggest that by singing, talking, and reading to the unborn child, parents can give them a significant advantage in early language, memory, and music development.

MUSICAL EXPERIENCES FOR YOUR UNBORN CHILD

- If you play a musical instrument, play it each day for your unborn baby.

- Place headphones on your stomach during pregnancy and play ten minutes or more of classical music that is both calming and stimulating (see Resource section for suggestions). Shetler found when mothers played stimulating music, their babies responded with sharp, rapid, or agitated movements. When the mothers played sedative music, the babies responded with rolling or soft motor movements.

- In the car, at work, and at home, play the music of Mozart and other composers for your unborn children. Studies indicate it may increase their spatial-temporal reasoning, even in utero! In 1998, Dr. Frances H. Rauscher found that rats exposed to Mozart's Sonata (K. 448) in utero plus 60 days postpartum performed better in a maze learning environment than rats exposed to white noise, minimalist music (Philip Glass), or silence. The rats were tested for five days in a T-maze and by day three, the rats exposed to Mozart in utero completed the maze quicker and with fewer errors than the other rats. By day five the rats that listened to Mozart continued to outshine the other rats. The researchers believe that the patterns within music can influence or re-wire an animal's internal neural network.[9]

- Sing to your unborn child. You may not have an operatic voice, but your child doesn't care . . . to him you have the most beautiful voice in the world!

- Take classical music to the hospital to play while your baby is being born. It makes for a very relaxing, peaceful atmosphere for both mother and baby. Former governor Zell Miller of Georgia has made it possible through private donations for the parents of every newborn in Georgia to be given a classical music recording to play for their baby. He hopes the parents will play the music often in the baby's presence because of the findings showing that music increases intelligence. Atlanta Symphony conductor Yoel Levi helped select the music for the recordings. And following the timely actions of Governor Miller, other organizations are now supporting the concept of exposing newborns to classical music. The NARAS Foundation—the nonprofit music education and preservation arm of the National Academy of Recording Arts and Sciences—and Mead Johnson Nutritionals recently launched a national program titled "Smart Symphonies." Its purpose is to raise awareness of the benefits of exposing infants to classical music. Beginning in May 1999, a compact disc, which features Grammy-winning classical music, will be included in Enfamil Diaper Bags that will be given to more than a million new mothers as they leave the hospital. Recording Academy president and CEO Michael Greene states, "There are few things more important than giving our children every scientific and cultural advantage possible. The Recording Academy had dedicated itself to aggressively supporting research into the educational and developmental benefits of music and helping to put those findings to practical use."

Infants (Birth to Age Two)

In the late nineteenth and early twentieth centuries, orphanages for babies were called foundling homes. The death rate in these homes was nearly 100 percent. Although the children received enough food, and the shelter and clothing was adequate, they still continued to die. When a baby came into the home, the caretakers would enter "condition hopeless" into the records, knowing all too well that eventually the baby would die. This condition became so prevalent that it was even given a name: "marasmus," a Greek word meaning, "wasting away." No one could find the cure because they were unable to trace the cause of the malady. Then, quite by accident, both cause and cure was discovered. An elderly woman was hired in a German foundling home. Each day this loving woman went from child to child, holding them, talking to them, singing lullabies, and caressing them. Miraculously, the babies began to thrive. It was then that the authorities realized that these infants had been dying from a lack of love. Researchers now know that a baby less than one year old will die without enough love.[10]

Mothers throughout the ages have communicated love and warmth to their infant child through the singing of lullabies and songs, and through talking, and touching. These simple activities also give the baby a feeling of security and protection. Peter Ostwald, professor of psychiatry at the University of California, San Francisco, has found music to be a strong conveyer of love and security between mother and baby. In his research, he noticed that infants respond positively to the musical qualities of their mothers' voices. When the mothers sang lullabies to their babies, it signaled to the baby that it was safe to go to sleep. Ostwald also found that infants who are sung to by their parents will have a much stronger emotional bond to them.[11] More than forty years have passed since Mark Schutz's German grandmother sang lullabies to him as he slumbered. He was just a toddler, yet he clearly remembers the sound of her voice, the German language she spoke, and her hands gently rubbing his back as he drifted safely off to sleep.

Although mothers all over the world sing lullabies to their babies, the lullaby format can be very different from culture to culture. They do not necessarily need to be soft and soothing for a child to go to sleep or to feel secure. John Baily and Veronica Doubleday, professors at the Department of Music at Columbia University, found when studying the music systems in Afghanistan that even though lullabies are the first musical experience that Herati children are exposed to, the form is much different than lullabies sung in the United States. Women swaddle their babies as they *vigorously* rock them to sleep in their cradles. Instead of the lullaby being soft and lilting, these songs consist of highly rhythmic sounds and repeat the phrase, "*Allā Huwa*" or "He is God."[12]

Whether the lullaby is soft and soothing, or vigorous and highly rhythmic, singing regularly to your baby has significance in terms of early language development. Language occurs as a gradual process. First, the baby in utero moves in a rhythmic motion, much like the rhythms and cadences found in speech. After birth, a baby hears and responds to the musical tones of the mother's voice as she communicates with her tiny infant. "Motherese" is a term that some psychologists use to describe the speech patterns a mother uses when she talks to her baby. It is a highly rhythmic musical jargon between parent and baby and not only strengthens the child emotionally, but helps with his budding language development.[13] As a mother pats and sings to her infant, he will wave his arms and kick his legs in rhythm to the mother's voice. As a mother coos and talks to her baby, the infant will respond with noises and coos similar to the mother. Researchers have found that babies less than six months old are actually able to "sing" back pitches and simple melodies sung to them.[14] Patricia Kuhl, a neuroscientist at the University of Washington in Seattle, discovered this to be true in a study that she and her colleagues recently completed. They found that the mother's singsong melodious cadence with fluctuating pitches is nature's way of teaching the beginning of language to the receptive infant.[15] Remarkably, studies have also found that babies as young as four months can recognize out-of-tune notes and changes in

> *Whether the lullaby is soft and soothing, or vigorous and highly rhythmic, singing regularly to your baby has significance in terms of early language development. Language occurs as a gradual process.*

melodies, all of which add to early language development.[16] Dr. Robert Garfias, professor of anthropology at the University of California at Irvine, believes music can have a tremendous impact on language development in children. Through research, he has found that music and language are inseparably linked as a single system in the brain. This system is acquired in the earliest stages of infancy and continues as the child processes the sounds of human voices around him.[17] Additionally, singing songs to infants may influence how quickly the child later learns math and languages. Eric Oddleifson, chairman for the Center for the Arts in the Basic Curriculum in New York, talks about a Japanese master mathematics teacher whose almost two million students have demonstrated math abilities beyond their years. The teacher was asked, "What would you say is the most effective way of heightening children's mental ability at the earliest possible stages?" He answered, "The finest start for infants is to sing songs. This helps to elevate their powers of understanding, and they register astounding speed in learning math and languages."[18]

MUSICAL EXPERIENCES FOR YOUR INFANT (BIRTH TO AGE TWO)

- Sing or play songs to your newborn as often as possible throughout the day, especially while you are bathing, dressing, and feeding him.

- At night, play soothing classical music or vocal lullabies as he falls asleep. There are many wonderful lullabies in the record stores. Choose a variety to play to your child and watch to see which are his favorites. (See Resources section.)

- Play musical games and fingerplays. Clap the beat as you sing, and take his hands and clap the beats along with him. He will be able to pick up the rhythm very quickly. There are many wonderful fingerplays–*Where Is Thumbkin; The Farmer in the Dell; The Brave Old Duke of York; The Wheels on the Bus; Trot, Trot to Boston; Where Is the Beehive,* and so on.

- Purchase age-appropriate musical toys and rhythm instruments. Xylophones, bells, and rattles are wonderful beginning instruments.

- As you sing to your child, vary the tempo, the softness, and the loudness. Make your voice go up and down from low sounds to high sounds.

- Encourage him to mimic the musical sounds and songs you sing to him. The Papouseks, developmental researchers from West Germany, found that infants as young as two months old were able to imitate the pitch and intensity of the songs their parents sang to them.[19]

- Expose him to age-appropriate musical experiences and classes offered in the community.

- Videotape your musical experiences together, no matter how insignificant they may seem. Later, your children will love watching themselves creating music as infants.

- Two wonderful videos to play for your child (ages one month to thirty-six months) are *Baby Mozart* and *Baby Bach.* The video series was developed by Julie Clark, a former teacher in Colorado, and combines color, shape, texture, and the music of Mozart and Bach to create a dazzling visual and audio experience for your young child. These tapes are a *must* for babies! (See Resources section to order.)

Preschoolers (Ages Two to Five)

Research indicates that music continues to have a powerful influence on a preschooler's language development, as well as his

motor, listening, and memory skills. Sally Rogers, assistant professor of psychiatry at the University of Colorado Health Sciences Center, believes that giving your preschool child a chance
to experience a wide variety of musical activities can enhance
his learning of language—which develops rapidly between the
ages of fifteen months and three years—and at the same time
teach him valuable motor skills.[20] As a child learns to clap to the
beat of the music, or as he uses triangles, blocks, and sticks to
beat out the rhythms, or as he marches to different cadences, his
physical coordination, his timing, and his thinking develops, according to Dr. Carla Hannaford, author of *Smart Moves*. She
states, "Movement is an indispensable part of learning and
thinking."[21] He will also gain memory skills as he learns to sing a
variety of songs with different rhythms. Aural, or listening skills
will be developed as he listens to the varying pitch, rhythm, and
harmony of a multitude of songs, and various pieces of music.
Dancing to the music, marching, singing, whistling melodies,
humming tunes, and playing musical games with other children
all boost the child's growing language, listening, and motor
skills. "These early musical experiences can help children develop physical coordination, timing, memory, visual, [listening],
and language skills," confirms Dr. Frank Wilson. "When they
work to increase their command of music and exercise musical
skills in the company of others, they gain important experience
with self-paced learning, mental concentration, and a heightened personal and social awareness."[22]

Preschoolers also can develop early math abilities when
learning a keyboard instrument. Drs. Frances Rauscher and Gordon Shaw found that preschoolers who had eight months of keyboard lessons had a greater ability to work mazes, draw geometric
figures, and copy patterns of two-color blocks—all important
spatial skills that later help with higher forms of math. "If you're
working with little kids," says Shaw, "you're not going to teach
them higher mathematics or chess. But they are interested in

and can process music."[23] Clearly, early music education offers a pleasurable and effective way to prepare a child for the learning tasks of school.

MUSICAL EXPERIENCES FOR YOUR PRESCHOOLER (AGES TWO TO FIVE)

- Continue with all the musical activities previously mentioned.

- Provide all kinds of rhythm instruments for your child to experiment with. Making rhythm instruments with your child can be a fun and creative experience, but keep in mind that rhythm instruments that are purchased will have a much better tone quality to them. These pure sounds are important for your child to hear and experience.

- Purchase age-appropriate tape recorders and CD players, and teach your child how to use them. Let your child start her own classical music collection of CDs and tapes. While you are building your collection, borrow CDs and tapes from the library, as it will give you a chance to preview the music before making an investment.

- Give children scarves, feathers, or ribbons, and turn on classical music and let them dance, sing, and improvise to the music.

- Play clapping games to see if they can match a variety of simple and complex rhythms.

- Read to and help your child memorize all kinds of poems and Mother Goose rhymes that have a strong musical rhythm.

- Read stories about great composers, instruments of the orchestra, and general music books—*The Nutcracker, Mozart*

Tonight, and so on. (See Resources section for more suggestions.)

- Play marches in the morning as your child is getting ready for the day. She will enjoy marching to the bath, to dress, or to eat. The strong rhythmic beat will help her accomplish these tasks with ease, as well as keep her focused on the task at hand.

- Play music for your child throughout the day. "Absolute musts" include:

  Saint-Saëns: *Carnival of the Animals*

  Prokofiev: *Peter and the Wolf*

  Britten: *The Young Person's Guide to the Orchestra.*

  Tchaikovsky: *The Nutcracker*

  Dukas: *The Sorcerer's Apprentice*

- Play classical music while your child is going to sleep at night and when she's getting up in the morning. A favorite is the "Classical Kids" series. (See Resources section for list.)

- Another excellent series to play at night and in the morning is called, *The Musical Lives of the Great Composers*, with A. A. Hannes as the narrator and the Vienna Symphony Orchestra. This series gives interesting facts about the composer, as well as playing a variety of music written by the composer. (See Resources section.)

- Enroll your child in group music classes, appropriate for her age and development.

Elementary (Ages Five to Twelve)

By the time children enter kindergarten, they start the momentous task of learning to read. Prior to entering kindergarten and while in kindergarten, exposure to music can help with this task and make it significantly easier. An explanation of how this happens will make the connection clear. As children memorize the lilting tunes of Mother Goose rhymes, use rhythm instruments, and play musical games and fingerplays, they are learning about the patterns that formulate the sounds, rhythm, and blending of syllables that make up words. This is a one-skill learning pattern necessary for beginning readers. In her book *Endangered Minds*, Jane Healy confirms the importance of early rhymes and music when she says,

As children memorize the lilting tunes of Mother Goose rhymes, use rhythm instruments, and play musical games and fingerplays, they are learning about the patterns that formulate the sounds, rhythm, and blending of syllables that make up words.

"Reading specialists tell us children's ability to discriminate and create rhyming words, as well as their sense of rhythm, are closely related to early reading ability. A child who has absorbed over and over—through the *ears*, not the eyes—such common word parts as 'fun, sun, run,' or 'fiddle, diddle, middle' as well as the *melody* of their language is statistically destined to have an easier time learning to read."[24]

Before your child enters kindergarten, exposing him daily to a variety of songs and Mother Goose rhymes will make the evolution of reading easier for him. Once he is in kindergarten, continue teaching him songs with a strong rhythm. The *Alphabet Operetta* by M. Manley Little is wonderful and uses alliteration (combinations of words that sound alike); is fun for the child to sing along with; and is a great way to learn the sounds of letters, syllables, and words. Frequently reading poetry that has a clear musical rhyme is also helpful to children's language and reading skills. Hearing the combination of sounds, syllables, and rhyme further enhances reading ability. The poetry of Jack Prelutsky is an excellent example. It is not only filled with humor, but has wonderful rhyming words and phrases, too. Try "singing" his poetry and you will be amazed at how quickly your child is able to memorize twenty or thirty lines of poetry as music, rhyme, and language come together. "Bleezer's Ice Cream" from *The New Kid on the Block* is a great Prelutsky poem, and children immediately hear and *feel* its strong rhythm—"Cocoa Mocha Macaroni, Tapioca Smoked Baloney, Checkerberry Cheddar Chew. . ." are some of the delightful rhyming word combinations.

While your child is in elementary school, have her memorize a fun poem and song each week. Choose poems and songs that have a well-defined rhyme, such as *I Point to Myself, Itisket, Itasket,* and *Little Rabbit Foo Foo.* You will start an educational (and fun-filled) tradition in your home, as well as increase your child's reading, language, vocabulary, and memorization skills. These exercises will also confirm to you the power that music has in developing those skills necessary for language and reading. Dr. Hannaford believes that the most natural way for children to learn when they are starting school is through "image, emotion, and spontaneous movement," all of which are found in these simple and fun musical activities.[25]

Elementary age children are great imitators. If they see their parents listening to classical music, they will want to listen to it. Parents can also lead the way by reading books to their children about classical composers and musicians, taking them to local concerts, or playing musical games with them. These activities will have a significant influence on their attitude toward music, particularly classical music. They will grow up knowing that good music should be a part of their life and that it makes life more rewarding and interesting. In homes all over the world where music has a significant, long-lasting impact on the child, the parents are active participants. In Afghanistan, for example, children born into musical homes are exposed to the sounds of music and encouraged to engage in musical activities at a very early age. The parents set the example by taking the children to musical celebrations where the parents themselves are involved playing musical instruments. In these settings, the child is given access to musical instruments and opportunities to observe his parents' and older siblings musical skills. It is through imitation and experimentation that young Afghan boys and girls learn to play instruments. These children grow up believing that music is what life is all about.[26] Parents in every part of the globe can have the same influence on their child. Example and parent participation speak volumes to the child. Musical involvement by the parents starts a cycle that can repeat itself for generations, bringing enjoyment and pleasure into the lives of countless family members.

It is usually sometime in the elementary years that children begin private music lessons. (In the next chapter, we will discuss how to choose an instrument and teacher.) This is a big step as far as the commitment required from both child and parent. Realizing that learning a musical instrument is valuable to the child in multiple ways will make this commitment easier. When a child learns a musical instrument, most of his senses are being utilized. For example, a child learning the piano is using his eyes to read the music, his ears to hear the correct notes, his hands to play the notes, and his feet to coordinate and play the pedals. All of this requires a level of concentration, memory skills, motor coordination, and symbol recognition. Both sides of the brain, as well as the front and back portions of the brain are being used to accomplish this incredible feat. Not only is the child experiencing the enjoyment that comes from learning a musical instrument, he is also learning skills that will help him succeed in school and beyond. (See later chapters for more detailed discussion of this topic.)

MUSICAL EXPERIENCES FOR YOUR ELEMENTARY AGE CHILD (AGES FIVE TO TWELVE)

- Continue with all of the musical ideas previously suggested, making them age appropriate.

- To help your child with his reading skills in the early elementary years, continue to sing and memorize songs and poetry with a strong rhythm and rhyme. Besides the poetry of Jack Prelutsky, check Tom Glazer's songbooks, *Eye Winker, Tom Tinker, Chin Chopper,* and *Do Your Ears Hang Low?*

- Play musical games with your child involving math, spelling, and reading. Young children learn their ABCs faster when singing the ABC song. As you drill your child in his math facts, sing the facts to a rhythm. He will learn them much faster and with greater ease. Fifth-graders can learn all fifty of the United States quicker and easier when they learn the song, "Fifty Nifty United States." Kathy Carroll, a science teacher in Washington, D.C., developed a cassette tape called *Sing a Song of Science,* which helps students learn science material. She developed the tape after watching her students respond to a little jingle she had made up about matter. She noticed the children writing down the jingle in their notebooks (a first!) and then coming back to school the next day singing it. Kathy knew she was on to a very positive learning experience for her students and, as a result, developed this tape. By using this tape at home, your child will learn many interesting things about science that they can then share at school. (See Resources section.)

- While driving in the car, play musical guessing games. Call it "Name that Tune" (after the popular TV show). Use either the classical music station on the radio or a classical tape that you can play in your car. Try to identify the piece of music, the composer, and the period in which the music was written (Baroque, Classical, Romantic, Twentieth Century). Some wonderful CDs to help your child recognize musical periods and the composers of those periods are *Mozart TV*, *Bibbidi Bobbidi Bach*, or *Heigh Ho! Mozart*.

- Play guessing games that require recognizing the different instruments of the orchestra. Once your child knows them by their individual sound, have them try to categorize them into their correct "family," such as the strings, woodwinds, percussion, and brass. Listen many times to *The Young Person's Guide to the Orchestra* to become familiar with each instrument's distinct sound. You will be amazed how your child's listening skills will improve by playing this simple game.

- Play "Twenty Questions." Possible categories include musicians, composers, or instruments of the orchestra.

- Continue with your child's group music lessons until you decide to enroll him in private lessons. Although every child is different, a good time to begin private lessons is between the ages of three and eight.

- Invite someone from your neighborhood who is taking music lessons to come to your home and share a piece of music or a song with your child.

- Take your child to age-appropriate symphonies, musicals, ballets, or chamber orchestras. (See Chapter 10 for more information.)

- Rent videos about music and musicians and watch them together as a family. Examples: *Beethoven Lives Upstairs*, *Amadeus*, *Shine*, *Mr. Holland's Opus*.

- Organize a yearly talent show in the neighborhood. It should be a low-key, non-competitive get-together where the kids on the block can have fun just sharing their talents. Who knows, this may encourage others in the neighborhood to work at developing their talents. Don't forget to videotape these events for future memories.

- As children are doing their homework, play music from the Baroque or Classical periods in the background. It helps with concentration, absorption, and organization of information. We call this our "study music," and some favorites include Handel's *Water Music*, the *Mozart for Your Mind* CD, and any of Bach's *Brandenburg Concertos*. (See Resources section.)

- Compliment your child on all her musical efforts.

Junior and Senior High School (Ages Twelve to Eighteen)

Academic Preparation for College: What Students Need To Know and Be Able To Do is a handbook published by the College Board to help high school students prepare for college. It states, "Preparation in the arts will be valuable to college entrants whatever their intended field of study. The actual practice of the arts can engage the imagination, foster flexible ways of thinking, develop disciplined effort, and build self-confidence."

By the time your child is entering junior and senior high school, competition for her time becomes more intense, but don't let her give up her music! Remember, keeping your child involved in music is an investment in her future. You may rationalize, "Okay, Jenny has had a few years of piano lessons. It's been good for her, but now life is going to get very busy with school, sports, and other activities. She won't have time to practice, and I'm not going to waste money on unprepared lessons. Besides, she's not going to be a concert pianist. I guess it's

> *By the time your child is entering junior and senior high school, competition for her time becomes more intense, but don't let her give up her music! Remember, keeping your child involved in music is an investment in her future.*

time to quit." Wrong! Children don't have to become concert pianists to gain the lasting benefits that come from continuous study of a musical instrument. Today, as well as in years past, parents understand the importance of their children furthering their education by going to college, but the competition is getting more and more difficult. It is a well-documented fact that students involved in music do better in school. They are more responsible, dependable, and have a greater degree of self-discipline. They tend to be far more creative and innovative, and their critical- thinking skills are considerably more advanced. Additionally, the College Entrance Examination Board has found that students involved in the arts perform better on SATs (Scholastic Achievement Tests). The Board states, "Students of the arts continue to outperform their non-arts peers on the SAT. In 1995, SAT-takers with coursework/experience in music performance scored fifty-one points higher on the verbal portion of the test and thirty-nine points higher on the math portion than students with no coursework or experience in the arts. Scores for those with coursework in music appreciation were sixty-one points higher on the verbal and forty-six points higher on the math portion. And longer arts study still means higher SAT scores: In 1996, those who had studied the arts four or more years scored fifty-nine points higher and forty-four points higher on the verbal and math portions, respectively, than students with no coursework or experience in the arts."[27]

All of these reasons, plus others that will be discussed later, should be sufficient motivation for parents to keep their children actively involved in music throughout their high school years. Their chances for making a lifelong commitment to music will be stronger if they continue with it during the high school years. Recall that Dr. Wilson believes *all* children are born with an innate musical nature and, with nurturing, it can blossom, giving enjoyment and satisfaction their entire life.

Diana Vaupel of Corpus Christi, Texas, repeatedly told her children, "When you're eighty years old, you're not going to be out kicking a soccer ball, but when you are eighty you can still enjoy music and play an instrument." Her father is proof of that. At eighty, he still plays the piano and finds tremendous enjoyment from his music.

MUSICAL EXPERIENCES FOR YOUR JUNIOR AND SENIOR HIGH SCHOOL STUDENT (AGES TWELVE TO EIGHTEEN)

- Encourage older children to be an example to younger siblings in regard to practicing their instruments. After seeing the movie *Shine*, one seventeen-year-old boy became very enthusiastic about his music. He wanted to play more difficult pieces and, as a result, began to practice more. His enthusiasm was electrifying to his younger brothers. They followed his example and began practicing more and asking their piano teacher for more difficult pieces. Pretty soon, the three of them were fighting over practicing time on the piano. Remember: example is powerful!

- Take your child to more sophisticated concerts. Check the local newspaper, community, and local colleges for a variety of choices. If possible, arrange for a backstage tour. If it is an opera or a musical, they will gain much more from the experience if they understand some of the details that make the actual performance seem flawless. (More on this in Chapter 10.)

- Let them join a record company that produces classical music and allow them to choose CDs for the family, as well as starting their own collection.

- If possible, arrange for your child to meet with a real composer. Network with other parents to find out about the composers in your area. See if they are child-friendly and would welcome the opportunity to meet and encourage another budding musician. (Contact "Meet the Composer;" see the Resources section for details.)

- For holidays and other special occasions give musical gifts—subscriptions to concerts, plays, or symphonies. Encourage grandparents to give tickets to a symphony or musicals.

- Hold family music recitals and invite the grandparents and any other extended family. It will give your child a chance to "show off" in front of family and friends in a non-threatening environment.

No matter what the ages of your children, you can start now to build musical traditions in your family.

• Start a "Hall of Fame" in your home with either statues or pictures of famous composers. Talk regularly about the greatness and strength of these men and women and their dedication to the arts. As a family, choose a composer each week and enjoy an evening together listening to their music and discussing interesting facts about their life. Thomas Carlyle said in his book *Heroes and Hero Worship,* "Great men taken up in any way are profitable company, for we cannot so much as look upon a great man without gaining something from him."

The ideas presented here can be your guide to making your home a musical training center, and your consistency in implementing them will ensure its success. No matter what the ages of your children, you can start now to build musical traditions in your family. You will find that these traditions will become valuable treasures that can be passed down from generation to generation.

$\mathcal{M}$AKING SOUND CHOICES: CHOOSING AN INSTRUMENT AND TEACHER

Musical training is a more potent instrument than any other for education.

—Plato

A recent poll found that there are approximately 62 million people in the United States who play a musical instrument, and 97 percent of parents polled believe that children benefit from a music and arts education by becoming more creative and imaginative.[1] Thousands of statistics like these are available to illustrate how far-reaching music is in our lives. Music provides a meaningful, lifelong learning experience. It gives our children a critically important outlet for their emotions and feelings, it helps to develop their sense of creativity and wonderment, and gives them a sensitivity to the world and people around them. Because music develops the whole child, it will have a profound influence on whatever he decides to do in life. In addition to music helping our children learn in school, it can bring joy, beauty, and happiness into their personal lives. These three elements alone will contribute to our children having richly rewarding lives.

Getting Started

When children are young, parents can provide them with the many wonderful musical experiences previously discussed, but eventually parents will need the help of professionals to further their children's music education and enjoyment. Music lessons, both group and private, are readily available in most communities. Early involvement in a group music class enlarges a child's musical experiences and prepares him for the concentration and commitment required for private lessons, when the time comes.

Early involvement in a group music class enlarges a child's musical experiences and prepares him for the concentration and commitment required for private lessons, when the time comes.

MUSIC PHILOSOPHIES

In the music community, you will find a variety of methods and philosophies regarding how to best introduce a young child to music. The five most well known music philosophies are: Dalcroze, Kodály, Orff-Schulwerk, Yamaha, and Suzuki. The following sections offer a brief description of each.

Dalcroze

Dalcroze was started in Switzerland by Emile-Jaques Dalcroze. In a Dalcroze class, children move their bodies to the beat of the music in a very systematic, rhythmic way called eurhythmics. The body is trained like an instrument. Attention, concentra-

tion, and memory are required. Dalcroze teaches a child to understand complex rhythms.

When a child hears the music, she moves her body in sync
with the rhythms. By merging the senses of seeing, hearing, feeling, and moving to the music, the child enjoys a complete musical experience. The training to become a Dalcroze instructor is
both extensive and intensive and, as a result, there are only a
few licensed teachers in the United States. The principles of
Dalcroze also form the foundation for both the Kodály and the
Orff philosophies.

Kodály

Zoltán Kodály developed the Kodály method in Hungary, utilizing singing, reading, writing, and creating music. Singing is the
core of the Kodály method. Kodály himself said, "I sang before I
could speak, and I sang more than I spoke." He taught that
through singing a child learns relationships between sounds.
Children learn to sing on pitch and eventually are able to look
at a piece of music and sing it with perfect pitch without the aid
of any instrument. The Kodály method calls this type of singing
solfege, and it takes a great deal of practice. While singing, the
children use certain hand signals called *curwen* that reinforce
their learning. Seeking to preserve the cultural and national
heritage of Hungary, Zoltán Kodály, along with his colleague
Bela Bartók, gathered together thousands of folksongs from vil-
lages and towns all over their country. Part of the Kodály philosophy includes teaching children these folksongs, as well as those
from other parts of the world.

In 1996, I attended a conference for the Organization of
American Kodály Educators (OAKE), at Brigham Young University in Provo, Utah. At the conference, I heard a Kodály children's choir perform. It was some of the most beautiful singing
I've heard from a young chorale group. These children clearly

understood music and how to make perfect musical sounds. They lived in different parts of the United States and had come to the conference to perform for the educators. Although they had rehearsed together only briefly, their voices blended in perfect pitch and harmony, and they sang as if they had been singing and performing together for years. It was both impressive and inspiring.

Orff-Schulwerk

Orff-Schulwerk was started by German composer Carl Orff and his associate Hunild Keetman. Orff's philosophy is, "Out of movement, music; out of music, movement."[2] Clapping, stamping, patting the hands on the lap, and finger-snapping are the four body movements that make up the Orff experience. Through play activities and the use of rhythm instruments such as drums, sticks, blocks, and bells, children learn music patterns and how to keep a beat. Orff's melody instruments include wooden xylophones and metal glockenspiels (glockenspiel means "bell-play" in German). This method is a group experience, and the children learn to be team participants through songs, games, rhymes, and dances. The Orff-Schulwerk program has been translated into eighteen languages and is taught all over the world using the traditional music and folklore of the country in which it is taught. There are more than 10,000 Orff teachers in the United States.

Yamaha

Genichi Kawakami of Japan founded the Yamaha method. He said, "If the education method is correct, the same results will be obtained anywhere in the world." His method requires parents to be actively involved in their children's music experience. Young children are taught musical pitches, rhythm patterns, and harmonies. Using an electronic keyboard, students learn keyboarding and sight playing. They are also involved in such activities as

singing, ear training, group performance, music arranging, sight
singing, and theory. Later, the children are encouraged to compose and perform their own music. The program usually starts at
age three. The Yamaha method has been established for more
than thirty years and is in forty-two countries worldwide.

Suzuki

Suzuki was founded by Shinichi Suzuki in Japan. He believed
that, given the proper musical learning environment, all children could learn and reach their potential. His approach to
teaching music is based on how a child learns language. First,
they listen to the sounds, and then they try to imitate those
sounds. Eventually, they mimic words, then phrases, and finally,
whole sentences. Using this same method in music, Suzuki students first listen to a note, then they imitate that, then the
process is repeated with a musical phrase and, finally, an entire
piece. With patience, love, and encouragement, parents and
teachers teach the child to play the violin, cello, viola, flute, or
piano. Each step is mastered with constant repetition. Suzuki believed talent is no accident of birth, but is developed through
hard work, effort, and education.[3]

CHOOSING THE RIGHT PROGRAM FOR YOUR CHILD

In choosing a music program for your child, consider her personality and interests and the philosophy that would make the best
fit. If one particular program or philosophy doesn't work for your
child, try another. There are many music programs in communities all over the world that embrace several philosophies successfully. Perhaps a combination, rather than just one method, may
work best for your child. A group class is a good way to start a
one- to five-year-old. Here are some things to consider.

- Check around your community to see what music classes are available. Try local universities, community arts and music facilities, recreation centers, and child education programs.

- Network with other parents to see what music classes their children have enjoyed and why. Seek opinions from parents whose children are similar to yours in personality and temperament, but remember that what works for one child does not necessarily work for another child.

- Prior to enrolling your child, attend a class and observe the teacher, the program, and the other students. First, does the teacher seem happy to be there? Does she seem to enjoy teaching? Is she responsive and positive to the children? Does she relate equally well to both girls and boys? Does she have control over the class? Keep in mind that a class is only as good as the teacher who teaches it.

- Observe the program after educating yourself on its philosophy and goals. Ask yourself, does it meet my expectations? Does the program provide varied and interesting experiences for my child? Does the program accomplish its goals?

- Observe the other children in the class. Do they seem happy? Do they seem to enjoy what they are doing? Are they having fun or do they seem bored?

- If the program is for children ages one to three, select a class that includes movement, rhythm, singing, dancing, listening, and the use of rhythm instruments. By age four, enroll them in classes that include an introduction to the instruments of the orchestra, notation, keyboarding, and learning about the lives of the great composers.

After exposing your children to group lessons for a few years, they will be prepared to take the next step: *private lessons*.

PRIVATE MUSIC LESSONS

Deciding when to begin private music lessons, selecting an instrument to study, and choosing the right teacher can be challenging and fun! Scientists talk about "windows of opportunity," meaning the optimum periods of time that children learn. Although humans are learning constantly throughout their lives, there are times when scientists believe learning is much easier. For music, that window is between the ages of three and ten. The brain is primed in such a way that it is able to process new information quickly and effectively. By introducing music lessons to the child during this time, brain circuits become permanently wired, and the child never forgets how to play that musical instrument.

Pediatric neurobiologist Harry Chugani of Wayne State University's Children's Hospital of Michigan has had personal experience with this theory. He started taking piano lessons with his young daughter. Although she learned easily, he did not. However, as a child, he had taken guitar lessons, and when he went back to the guitar he was excited to find that he was able to recall what he had learned many years prior and in his own words, "the songs [were] still there."[4]

Does this mean that if you have a child over ten, she won't learn a musical instrument easily and that you should forget the idea of giving her music lessons? Definitely not! In his book *Never Too Late: My Musical Life Story*, John Holt, an educator and musician, advocates that learning is a lifelong process. At the age of fifty, he took up the cello and, by practicing intensely, was able to join a chamber orchestra and string quartet. Says Holt, "Teachers say that if we don't learn to play musical instruments as children we will never be able to learn as adults . . . not so. Of course, it is nice, if we come freely to music, to come to it young, but if we don't come to it then, we can later. It is never too late."[5]

Joseph Sparling, who co-authored *Learningames*, agrees, "You want to say that it is never too late, but there seems to be something very special about the early years. And yet, there is new evidence that certain kinds of intervention can reach even the older brain and, like a microscopic screwdriver, rewire broken circuits."[6]

Although scientific research shows that a young child can learn to play a musical instrument easier when she is young, don't panic if you missed the "window of opportunity." Just start lessons as soon as possible. The challenge now becomes choosing a musical instrument and the right teacher to teach that instrument.

Choosing an Instrument

According to a Gallup poll on instrument popularity among the 62 million amateur musicians in the United States, the piano is the instrument of choice of 34 percent. Twenty-two percent chose the guitar; 6 percent, drums; 5 percent, flute; 4 percent each, clarinet, organ, saxophone, and keyboard; and 3 percent, trumpet and violin.[7]

Before your child chooses an instrument to learn, it is worthwhile (and fun!) to listen to some of the music that "features" that instrument. This will enable both you and your child to hear what the instrument sounds like, its range of versatility, and how it is combined with other instruments of the orchestra to produce its varied and unique sound. Below are some of the things to consider when selecting an instrument to study and a repertoire sampling of music that "shows off" the particular group of instruments, along

Before your child chooses an instrument to learn, it is worthwhile (and fun!) to listen to some of the music that "features" that instrument.

with interesting stories and anecdotes about people, instruments, and compositions of music.

Vocal

The human voice is considered an instrument and is actually the first instrument we learn. It is regarded as the most beautiful and perfect of all instruments. Long ago, instrument makers tried to make instruments where the sound most resembled the human singing voice. The term "voice" is still used by instrument makers and tuners today, as they make adjustments in improving the sound of an instrument.[8] Likewise, it is possible for our voices to sound like instruments of the orchestra, as illustrated by the following story.

In the early 1940s, three young Dutch sisters, Antoinette, Helen, and Alette Colijn, living in the Netherlands East Indies, were sent to a women's Japanese prison camp on the island of Sumatra. The world was experiencing war, and people everywhere were affected. At the camp, conditions were horrible— the food scant, the guards brutal, and disease rampant. Desperately wanting to lift the morale of the women prisoners, an Englishwoman, Norah Chambers, who had studied at London's Royal Academy of Music, decided to form an orchestra made up of human voices. Among the participants were Antoinette and Alette. On the day of their performance, excitement filled the air as thirty women, wearing ragged prison attire, stood before the other women prisoners prepared to sing. Another Englishwoman, Margaret Dryburgh, stepped forward and said, "This evening we are asking you to listen to something new: a choir of women's voices producing music usually performed by an orchestra. The idea of making ourselves into a vocal orchestra came to us when we longed to hear again some of the wonderful melodies that uplifted our souls in days gone by.

So close your eyes and imagine you are in a concert hall hearing a world famous orchestra."[9]

They began to sing the largo from Antonin Dvořák's *New World Symphony*. No words were used by the singers, only the musical syllables "ah," and "loo" to imitate the various sounds of the orchestra. They continued to sing such pieces as Chopin's "Raindrop Prelude," Handel's "Pastoral Symphony" from the *Messiah*, and Debussy's "Reverie." The prisoners were spellbound, overtaken by memories of better times and places.

That night in the barracks, the women talked of the seeming miracle that had taken place. It was learned that Margaret Dryburgh had written down all the music and Norah Chambers had arranged the music to be performed by voices instead of instruments—and all from memory. The choir performed four more concerts that year, each time uplifting the prisoners from their brutal conditions.

After the liberation in 1945, the three Colijn sisters moved to America. Thirty-five years later in 1980, Antoinette Colijn found her precious sixty-eight-page booklet of the vocal orchestra scores sung in the prison camp. Having sung in a church choir at Stanford University in Palo Alto, California, she decided to donate the music to the university for preservation. Because of the moving story behind the music, the Peninsula Women's Chorus of Palo Alto began practicing the music for a special "Song of Survival" concert. In 1983, nine of the original prison-camp singers flew to California to witness the performance, among them Norah Chambers.[10] It was a riveting emotional experience for the survivors.

Today, in all parts of the world, women's choirs have performed "Song of Survival" music and, in 1997, the movie *Paradise Road* brought the story to millions. This story illustrates not only the power of music to lift our spirits in the most desperate of circumstances, but the tremendous versatility of the human voice.

Considerations for Selecting Vocal Training

- If your child enjoys singing, get her involved in group singing classes, school choirs, church choirs, or children's chorale groups. Serious vocal training does not come until later.

- Intense vocal training is started between the ages of twelve to fourteen for girls and fifteen to sixteen for boys. Starting lessons too soon can damage a child's voice. (This does not include the kind of singing mentioned above.)

- The American Chorale Directors Association in Laughton, Oklahoma, reports that children's choirs are forming across the nation as more music programs are cut in the schools. Presently, there are about seven thousand children's choirs nationwide, and the number is growing. Look into opportunities in your community for choirs that your child can join. They may be affiliated with churches, schools, community education programs, or the local university. At El Camino College in Torrance, California, longtime music instructor and choir director Jane Hardester started a choir for children ages seven to thirteen. They are enrolled in the college and receive credit for their participation. Hardester and her partner, Diane Simons, have big plans for their choir. They want to create both advanced and beginning music ensembles that will give performances in the community. "Everyone loves children's choirs, and we want to make this one great!" says Hardester, who sees this as an answer to the diminishing music programs in the schools.[11]

Vocal Repertoire Suggestions

Mozart: "Pa-Pa-Pa-Pa" (*The Magic Flute*)

Humperdinck: "Brother, Come Dance with Me" (*Hansel and Gretel*)

Offenbach: "The Doll Song" (*The Tales of Hoffmann*)

Mozart: Queen of the Night's aria—"Der Holle Rache" (*The Magic Flute*)

PIANO

The piano, the heaviest of all musical instruments, is considered a percussion instrument because the strings are struck by hammers. The early pianos came in many shapes and sizes, with the makers always striving for elegance and beautiful tone quality.

One of the most popular pieces of children's music ever written for two pianos (and a few strings) is Camille Saint-Saëns' *Carnival of the Animals*. Not only was Saint-Saëns a composer, he was also a writer of poems, plays, and books. He composed *Carnival of the Animals* in 1886, under the title *Grand Zoological Fantasy*. It was actually composed as a private joke and performed at a Mardi Gras concert for a few of the composer's friends. The original music was scored for two pianos and a small instrumental ensemble, but it was later changed and orchestrated by the composer for a larger instrumental group. Interestingly, Saint-Saëns refused to let the score be performed in public or published during his lifetime. Two months after his death in 1922, the Colonne Orchestra in Paris, with Gabriel Pierne conducting, performed *Carnival of the Animals* to the delight of hundreds. Some conductors felt that the reason Saint-Saëns did not want the music published while he was alive was that serious audiences would not understand the humor he was trying to portray in the music. There are fourteen sections describing lions, hens, roosters, wild asses, tortoises, elephants, kangaroos, fish, cuckoos, birds, fossils, pianists (early pianists are dangerous beasts!), and swans. In the late 1940s, Columbia Records commissioned Ogden Nash to write a series of humorous verses for *Carnival of the Animals*, which are still included in recordings today. Children love this piece of music and have a great time mentally visualizing the animals Saint-Saëns musically describes. It also gives piano students an opportunity to appreciate the versatility of the piano.

Considerations for Selecting the Piano

- The piano is a wonderful first instrument for many children to learn. It is one of the easiest instruments to play and sounds good immediately for two reasons. First, when you push down a middle C, that's what you hear. With string instruments, you have to have a good ear to "find" the correct note. Second, in a short time your child can "sound" good because they play many sounds at once, unlike the woodwinds and brass that play one tone at a time.

- In learning the piano, children can see a direct linear relationship between the keyboard and the musical scale, which is not true for learning stringed instruments.[12]

- As a pianist, you never need an accompanist. It is pretty much a solo instrument and one that sounds wonderful by itself.

- A disadvantage in playing the piano is that pianists usually do not play with other musicians. A child learning the piano will not have the group experience that she would get from playing instruments used in a band or orchestra. For some children, the group experience is very important, so take into consideration your child's personality when choosing the piano to study. (Note that in today's business world, teamwork skills are very important, and a child learns teamwork skills when playing in a band or orchestra.)

- Another disadvantage is that, in a performance setting—such as playing at a rest home, for a funeral, or even for a church program—your child is at the mercy of the piano that is available. A piano can be out of tune, have keys that stick, or other problems that make it difficult to play. I've personally experienced all these problems in the past. Many times, people who arrange a musical program don't understand the importance of performing on a quality instrument. A rather humorous story is told of Count Basie, the famous bandleader, who told a club owner whose piano was always out of tune, "I'm not returning until you fix it." A month later, the owner called Basie and told him everything was fine. However, when he returned to the club, the piano was still out of tune. "You said you fixed it!" an angry Basie exclaimed. "I did," the club owner replied. "I had it painted."[13]

Piano Repertoire Suggestions

Saint-Saëns: *Carnival of the Animals*

Chopin: Waltz, Op. 64, No. 1 "Minute Waltz"

Mozart: "Rondo alla Turca"

Beethoven: "Fur Elise"

Rimsky-Korsakov: "Flight of the Bumblebee" (from *The Tale of Tsar Sultan*)

STRINGS: VIOLIN, VIOLA, CELLO, DOUBLE BASS

The stringed instruments had a rather shady beginning in the early seventeenth century, with the fiddlers of the time referred to as "scurvy thrashing scraping mongrels."[14] But time has changed that perception, and today the stringed instruments serve as the front position in a symphony orchestra, and the violin is considered the king of instruments.

The exquisite violins created by Nicola Amati and Antonio Stradivari in the seventeenth and eighteenth centuries still continue to be in demand today because of their beautiful tone quality, which amazingly gets better with age. Today, a Stradivari can cost $3 million! The secret of how these violins were made died with the creators themselves and, although scientists have studied the varnishes, the thickness and shape of the wood, and the molecular composition of the wood under powerful microscopes, no one can explain what makes these violins so unique.

Fascinating stories abound of priceless Amati and Stradivari violins stolen from their owners, only to turn up decades later at the deathbeds of the thieves. One remarkable story is that of Vahan Bedelian, who in 1915 was to be sent to his death in what is now the Syrian desert. It is there that 1.5 million Armenians died at the hands of the Turks. Bedelian defended himself with neither gun nor sword. On the eve of his appointed journey to death, Bedelian picked up his violin and performed mournfully and passionately before a Turkish general. The general listened and then, with champagne in hand, said, "A talent like you we need. You should not be sent to the desert." Bedelian's life was spared, and he lived to teach the violin to many, including his son, Haroutune, who attended London's Royal Academy of Music at age fifteen and became an accomplished violinist.[15]

Considerations for Selecting a String Instrument

- The strings are a high-demand instrument. An orchestra usually needs a combination of at least sixty violins, violas, cellos, and basses.

- There is a wonderful, large repertoire written for the string instruments.

- The first few years of learning a string instrument can be difficult and will require patience and encouragement from parents.

- Playing a stringed instrument requires a good ear. Because there are no frets to mark where the fingers are placed, the violinist must learn exactly where to put his fingers to play "in tune."

Stringed Instrument Repertoire Suggestions

Beethoven: Violin Concerto in D Major, last movement

Brahms: Concerto for Violin and Cello, last movement

Dittersdorf: Concerto for Double Bass in E-flat Major

Debussy: String Quartet, second movement

WOODWIND INSTRUMENTS: FLUTE, PICCOLO, BASSOON, CLARINET, OBOE, SAXOPHONE

The wind instruments are varied in their sound and appearance. Some are made of wood, while others are made of silver, gold, or other metals. In an orchestra, there are usually three flutes, one piccolo, three oboes, three clarinets, and three bassoons. There are also an English horn, a bass clarinet, and a double bassoon. They are considered non-resonating instruments because once the musician has stopped blowing, the sound stops. Good breath control is very important when playing all of the wind instruments.

A delightful example of a piece of music that is beloved by children everywhere and that uses several wind instruments for solo passages is Sergei Prokofiev's *Peter and the Wolf*. Prokofiev, the Russian composer, is probably best known for this children's work which he called, "a present not only to the children of Moscow, but also to my own." Although a very controversial figure, Prokofiev had the innate ability to look at the world through a child's eyes. He loved fairy tales and imaginary play. Realizing that children love and intently listen to music, he wrote a number of pieces for them, his most popular and engaging one being *Peter and the Wolf*. Being rather childlike himself, Prokofiev understood how children think and was able to bring exciting characters and events into this work. Each character and its personality is memorably represented by an instrument of the orchestra, with most of them being from the wind section. The excitable bird is represented by the flute; the waddling duck by the melancholy sound of the oboe; the cat's graceful gliding steps by the clarinet; Peter's grandfather by the rich sound of the bassoon. The wolf is portrayed by the growling sound of the brass, the hunters by the bass drums, and Peter is played with loving warmth by all the strings of the orchestra. *Peter and the Wolf*, in typical fairy-tale fashion, addresses itself to a child's sense of courage, adventure, and risk taking (and a little bit of disobedience) with, of course, a happy ending as Peter saves the day and marches triumphantly with the other characters at the end.[16]

Considerations for Selecting a Woodwind Instrument

- The child has a group experience when learning to play a wind instrument.

- Winds get to play many solo passages in an orchestra, as they often carry the melody. Their tone both blends and contrasts with the strings.

- Woodwind players are often called upon to play their "sister" instruments, as well. For instance, a flutist can be asked to play the piccolo; the oboist, the English horn; and the bassoonist, the larger contrabassoon. The saxophone and clarinet players also are able to easily switch from an alto sax or bass clarinet. And in rare instances, musicians are able to play more than one woodwind at a time. Saxophonist Chang-Kyun Chong, a Korean immigrant, plays tenor, alto, and soprano saxophones simultaneously. He has always liked the big band sound and, not having his own orchestra, he decided to improvise. He started out playing two saxophones, which he found to be fairly easy, but it still lacked the sound he was looking for. By adding a third saxophone, he achieved his goal, but it was quite difficult blending three instruments with different tones and in different keys. Practicing two hours a day at a local park for three years helped him hone his skill.

Audiences are skeptical when he wraps his lips around three mouthpieces, spreads his arms around three horns and his fingers over six sets of keys, but the sound he produces impresses everyone.[17] So, if your child decides to play more than one woodwind simultaneously, remember the success of Chang-Kyun Chong and rest assured that anything is possible!

- A child can learn to play the winds in a short amount of time with positive results.

- Wind instruments are not as expensive as the string instruments.

Wind Instrument Repertoire Suggestions

Prokofiev: *Peter and the Wolf*

Debussy: "Syrinx," for unaccompanied flute

Weber: Bassoon Concerto in F Major

Creston: Concerto for Trombone

Mozart: Clarinet Concerto in A Major, last movement

BRASS INSTRUMENTS: TRUMPET, TROMBONE, FRENCH HORN, TUBA

The brass instruments were originally made from the horns of beasts, elephants, bulls, and boars. Consequently, these instruments have been associated with great strength and power. A famous biblical story is told of how Joshua, leader of the Israelites, and his army blew on their horns as they marched around the city of Jericho. So great was the sound that the walls tumbled to the ground and the Israelites took possession of the city.

Today, brass instruments have gained wide popularity and are used in jazz, dance, and brass bands. A piece of music that is both brilliant and jubilant and is scored for nine trumpets, nine horns, twenty-four oboes, twelve bassoons, a contrabassoon, three pairs of timpani, and assorted drums is Handel's *Music for the Royal Fireworks*. King George I of England commissioned Handel to write the music to commemorate the signing of the Treaty of Aix-la-Chapelle. A huge victory pavilion was built to serve as the place for this event and the spectacular fireworks display. The king, of course, wanted equally spectacular music for the occasion, so he requested that Handel use only military-type instruments and no strings. At first, Handel was concerned, but in the end he was able to give the king the electrifying sound he wanted. The disappointing fireworks display took place on April 27, 1749, with Handel's monumental music the only redeeming part of the entire event. The overture is magnificent, with a marvelous interplay between the wind and brass instruments.[18]

Considerations for Selecting a Brass Instrument

- The child has a group experience when learning to play the brass instruments.

- Brass instruments are very versatile—they can play both loud and soft melodies of music.

- Children wearing braces will have a hard time playing these instruments.

- Children with an overbite do very well with this instrument, but those children with an underbite have difficulty.

- Children learning a brass instrument will develop a "stiff upper lip," and will learn about the concept of embouchure, which is how you hold your lips around an instrument. The mouthpiece is held against the upper lip, and the muscles of the lip control the pitch. If the lip becomes tired and limp, the notes will split or crack.

Brass Instrument Repertoire Suggestions

Handel: *Music for the Royal Fireworks*

Handel: *Water Music*, alla hornpipe

Mozart: Horn Concerto No. 4, last movement

Mussorgsky: *Pictures at an Exhibition*

Rossini: Overture, *William Tell*

PERCUSSION INSTRUMENTS: CYMBALS, DRUMS (TIMPANI), MARIMBA, XYLOPHONE, BELLS, CHIMES, TRIANGLE, AND OTHERS

The percussion section is made up of many different and exciting instruments that are either banged together or banged on with a stick or sticks, but they do not necessarily have to have a loud sound. The drums can be used to emphasize the music's rhythm and how it changes. Cymbals, castanets, chimes, and triangles can be used to add an interesting and added dimension to the music, such as what you would hear in Tchaikovsky's *Nutcracker Suite*. Although the history behind each of the percussion instruments is fascinating, the cymbals have the longest history and date back to the second millennium B.C. Today, the best cymbals come from either Turkey or China and are made by a secretly guarded formula of copper and tin. After the percussionist of the orchestra clashes the cymbals, he holds them high in the air so everyone can see them and to allow the sound to resonate throughout the hall.

An excellent way to hear all the individual percussion instruments (and other instruments, as well) is by listening to Benjamin Britten's *The Young Person's Guide to the Orchestra*. This marvelous recording is considered the most popular symphonic work of the twentieth century. According to Ted Libbey of National Public Radio, "This 1946 score by Britten has made more friends than any other work of English music, with the exception of Handel's *Messiah*."[19] Using Henry Purcell's *Abdelazer* as the main theme, Britten demonstrates how each instrument of the orchestra plays an important part in a musical score. The theme is first heard with all the instruments of the orchestra playing, and then each section of winds, strings, brass, and percussion instruments is played. Individual instruments in each section have an opportunity to have the "spotlight." The percussion section includes such instruments as the kettle drums, bass drums, cymbals, tambourine, triangles, side drum, Chinese block, xylophone, castanets, gong, and whip. The percussion instruments play separately and then together to show how the individual sounds complement one another. In the end, Britten, using his fugue and Purcell's theme, brings all the instruments together for a dramatic climax. (A fugue is a composition with three or more musical lines that enter at different times in the piece, creating a counterpoint with one another.)

Considerations for Selecting Percussion Instruments

- A percussionist can learn to play all the percussion instruments, but it is important for the player to have a steady sense of rhythm and a very good ear. Most percussionists start by playing the bells. Playing the mallet instruments requires the ability to read music.

- These instruments can play melodies, solos, and accompaniments.

- The most popular percussion instrument is the drum. The technique involved in playing drums takes time to learn well, and a percussionist must have a strong sense of rhythm and be able to read music rhythm patterns. In an orchestra setting, the person playing timpani, or kettle drums, is usually an individual who has had a great deal of experience playing with an orchestra and understands how the drums contribute to the music. It is definitely not as simple as one would think.

Percussion Instrument Repertoire Suggestions

Tchaikovsky: *Nutcracker Suite*

Tchaikovsky: *1812 Overture*

Britten: *The Young Person's Guide to the Orchestra*

Grieg: *Peer Gynt* Suite No. 1

Gounod: *Funeral March of a Marionette*

GUITAR

Although the guitar is considered a string instrument, it is discussed separately from the other string instruments because of its versatility and association with both classical and rock music. The first known guitar existed as early as 1,000 B.C. among the ancient Hittites. The Moors introduced it into Spain in the twelfth or thirteenth century, and the early form of the guitar as we know it today was made in Spain during the sixteenth century. The guitar is often used to accompany singing. In 1860, the guitar began a decline and was not accepted in musical circles as a serious instrument. There were several reasons for this. First, despite the fact that there was a great deal of music for the guitar, it had not been written by any of the great composers. Both Franz Schubert and Hector Berlioz were guitarists, but they wrote very little music for the guitar. Second, the music that was written for the guitar could not compare to the quality of music written for other instruments. As a result, serious classical musicians did not play the guitar.

It was Andrés Segovia, a self-taught guitarist, who brought the classical guitar up to the same standing as the other serious classical instruments, and he dedicated eighty years to doing so. He accomplished this by exposing people to the music of the guitar in concerts and by extending its repertoire. As he traveled around the world performing in concert, people everywhere were astounded not only by his talent as a musician, but also by the brilliance of the guitar in the hands of someone who knew how to play it skillfully. Next, he focused his energies on convincing prominent composers to write music for the guitar. One of the first great composers to do this was Manuel de Falla. Many others followed including, Villa-Lobos, Paganini, and Weber. Segovia also worked tirelessly with guitar makers to improve the quality of sound and volume of the instrument. In 1947, because of Segovia's influence, Albert Augustine developed the nylon guitar string. Finally, Segovia went to colleges, universities, and music conservatories, convincing them of the importance of establishing a seat for the classical guitar. Because of his efforts, music departments today have included the guitar in the curricula and have professors of guitar. Today, classical guitarists the world over owe a debt to Andrés Segovia for establishing the guitar as a serious and respected instrument.[20]

The guitar is a very popular instrument with teens. They especially like the electric guitar (introduced in 1936) because of its association with rock-and-roll bands. They also like the fact that they can increase the volume on an electric guitar because it can be used with an electric amplifier.

Considerations for Selecting the Classical Guitar

- Invest in a good guitar teacher, so your child does not pick up any bad habits. Don't just allow them to "teach themselves" the guitar. (Many teens just want to learn the guitar from a friend.)

- Once a child learns the guitar, he can transfer these skills to other fretted instruments, such as the banjo or ukulele.

- When she is first starting lessons, encourage your child to learn on a nylon-string or classical guitar as opposed to an acoustic guitar. By starting on a classical guitar, your child will develop a good technique foundation, which will give her greater versatility to play with either a band or an orchestra.

- If you have a child who is getting tired or bored with the instrument he is now playing, and if you are concerned about your child wanting to quit music lessons, try the guitar. It is a very social and popular instrument.

Guitar Repertoire Suggestions

Vivaldi: Guitar Concerto in D

Andrés Segovia: *Macarena*

Villa-Lobos: *Bachianas Brasileiras No. 5*

Schubert: *15 Original Dances* (for flute, violin, and guitar)

After carefully weighing the advantages and disadvantages of each instrument, make a decision with your child on which instrument would be best suited for them. Once this decision is reached, the next step is finding a good teacher.

Choosing a Teacher for Private Lessons

A good teacher is worth his or her weight in gold. He or she can make all the difference between a child having a positive feeling about music or not wanting to have anything to do with learning a musical instrument. Barbara Spencer will never forget her sons' first piano teacher. Wendy Waring was a dedicated and inspiring teacher with the rare gift of relating to all children. She literally made every lesson fun and exciting, but she was also a tough taskmaster and insisted on pieces being played musically. Wendy helped them to understand the music by telling them stories about the composers, their music, and the circumstances of when and why they

A good teacher is worth his or her weight in gold. He or she can make all the difference between a child having a positive feeling about music or not wanting to have anything to do with learning a musical instrument.

wrote these pieces. Timing and correct rhythm was of utmost importance. Clapping, singing, and tapping were all forms of helping them to "feel" and play the correct beat.

Each week while waiting for their lessons, her boys were given crayons, paints, and markers for creative expression. The teacher's weekly exuberance was electrifying, and Barbara's sons loved piano lessons because of Wendy's unique style. Wendy also became involved in her students' lives and was interested in their hobbies, school, and friends. She planned outings at the tide pools, the beach, and at parks along with her other students. She was sensitive to their moods when they came for lessons and listened to their opinions regarding pieces they were interested in playing or not playing. Unfortunately, after three years of an ideal situation, she stopped teaching to have more time to spend with her son, a very gifted vocalist. But for Barbara's sons, it was a phenomenal experience. After Wendy, they went through a period of "trial and error" before finding another teacher who related well to them and had high musical standards. Although John Reith's style is much different, they have found him to be the perfect personality for teens. He knows when to be fun, when to be serious, when to be tough, and when to lighten up. Barbara feels that because of John's influence and personality, her boys continued with their music during the tumultuous teen years.

The importance of a good teacher cannot be overstated, but finding an outstanding teacher is difficult. Rich Christensen teaches band and symphonic orchestra at Dobson High School in Mesa, Arizona. He insists on high musical standards by inspiring his students to work hard, pursue excellence, and respect each other. His symphonic orchestra was selected to play in the "World's Largest Concert," aired by PBS in March 1997. It was the first time a public school musical group had been invited to perform in this annual event. They also received an invitation to perform in Chicago for approximately ten thousand music teachers from all over the world, and their achievements have been touted in *Music Educators Journal,* a national magazine. Mr. "C" (as his students affectionately call him) recently received a teacher fellowship through the National Symphony Orchestra at the Kennedy Center for Performing Arts in Washington, D.C. His formula for success was summed up by one of his students, who wrote an essay for English about a person who most influenced her life goals. The student wrote, "When I have felt unable to perform, he has expressed his faith in my ability. He tells us how much he cares about us, and he lets us know that he is there for us if we need him. . . . I am indebted to him for . . . showing me the satisfaction of a life dedicated to serving and sharing with others."[21]

American-born Dorothy DeLay, a violin teacher at the Juilliard School of music in New York is considered to be the best violin teacher in the world. Some of her students have included Midori, Itzhak Perlman, Cho-Liang Lin, and Nadja Salerno-Sonnenberg. What makes her so special? She shares some of the very same qualities that made Wendy Waring an extraordinary piano teacher and Mr. Christensen an outstanding music teacher. She loves her students and shows it, is very patient and understanding of their feelings and moods, is involved with other aspects of their life, and knows how to get the very best musicianship from her students.

Of her, Itzhak Perlman said, "When you get right down to the nitty gritty, it's that she believed in me. There was a time when my parents and Miss DeLay were the only people in the world who believed I could have a career. The fact that I was disabled—a lot of people looked at me with distorted vision. And she never did. She was able to see."[22]

Showing that Miss DeLay respected her students' independence, Midori said, "Unless it's really strange (the music), Miss DeLay lets me do what I want."[23]

Miss DeLay has high expectations of her students and, although she's very patient, she expects them to work hard. Nadja

Salerno-Sonnenberg came to lessons for seven months without her violin because she just wanted to spend the time talking. Miss DeLay was very patient and then finally said to her, "If you don't come in next week with your violin and a piece prepared, you're out of my class and I'm kicking you out of Juilliard. I'm not kidding."[24] This scared Nadja enough that for her next lesson she had learned the entire Prokofiev Violin Concerto. After that, she started practicing thirteen hours a day and reached her goal of winning the 1981 Naumburg Competition.

Isaac Stern, who has known Miss DeLay for many years, summed it up when he said, "What Miss DeLay does is to give an enormously solid physical base to her students, but also allows them to keep a measure of their individuality instead of stamping them. She has a sense of responsibility to young psyches and an ability to arouse in them a devotion, which she returns tenfold. The result is that she's the most effective violin teacher in the world."[25]

It is rare to find a Wendy, a Mr. Christensen, or a Miss DeLay, but as you are beginning this process of choosing a teacher look for the following qualities:

- Find a teacher who has a degree in music. Consider teachers belonging to such organizations as the Music Teachers National Association, but do not rule out teachers who do not belong to such organizations. It is possible to find excellent teachers who do not affiliate with music organizations.

- Interview several possible music teachers. Ask questions regarding their length of time teaching, their expectations, and methods of teaching.

- Keep in mind that a concert musician does not necessarily make a good teacher.

- Ask to attend a recital, so that you can observe the musical abilities of the students. If the teacher doesn't have recitals, find another teacher. Recitals motivate the child to complete and polish their music. They also help to keep student enthusiasm at a high level.

- Ask the teacher if she involves the students in music competitions. Skilled teachers know when, how, and if, they should involve a student in a competitive musical atmosphere.

- Choose a teacher who will complement your child's personality. A teacher with lists of credentials and glowing recommendations may not be right for your child. One teacher may relate to one of your children, but not another. Consider finding another teacher for the other child. It may mean the difference of that child sticking with her music or quitting.

- Trust your instincts with teachers. If it doesn't "feel" right, it probably isn't right. A rather interesting incident occurred while I was interviewing a teacher for my son. As she was telling me about her own two daughters, she suddenly exclaimed (obviously without thinking), "I have two little girls, and I'm so glad because I hate boys." Because I am a mother of five sons, the last person I want involved with my child is someone who hates boys.

- As a child gets older, he may want to help select the pieces he plays. Make certain the teacher is flexible and will listen to the student when making these decisions.

- Question the teacher on what emphasis she places on counting and rhythm. If a child doesn't play the correct rhythm, they're just playing notes on a page. Students who struggle with the music are usually having difficulty with the timing. Many teachers have the student tap or clap out the rhythm before they start playing the piece. Counting out loud should be part of the process. Rhythm and timing are probably the

most important aspects of the music and should be empha-
sized by the teacher.

- Discuss with the teacher the length of the lesson time, as well
  as how much time your child should be practicing each day.

- Get in writing the policy and procedures of the teacher regarding absences, vacations, sicknesses, tardiness, make-ups,
  and payment schedule. It is important that you understand
  the rules and are willing to abide by them.

- Once you have carefully decided on a music teacher, give him
  or her every consideration. Teachers are professionals trying
  to make a living by bringing music into the lives of your children. They need parental support and help. Show the teacher
  every courtesy that you would any professional. Take the time
  to express your appreciation. It is one of the greatest needs of
  human beings.

  With the right teacher and instrument, your child is ready
to embark on an exciting musical journey.

CHAPTER 5

$\mathscr{P}$RACTICING: KEEPING THE TEMPO

If I don't practice for one day, I know it; if I don't practice for two days, the critics know it; if I don't practice for three days, the audience knows it.

—Jan Paderewski

Mom," wailed Jason from the piano bench, "how long do I have to practice?"

"Until you're eighteen," she replied, "so keep practicing!"

This scenario is a familiar one in many homes. Getting a child to practice consistently can be a challenge. Few children enjoy practicing day after day, except perhaps Mozart who hated to *stop* practicing. Midori, one of the great violinists of our day, loved to practice the violin for hours each day when she was barely four years old. Then, of course there was Handel, whose mother hid a clavichord in the attic so that at night he could secretly practice without his father knowing. (Handel's father wanted him to become a lawyer and *not* a musician) But, unlike

Mozart, Midori, and Handel, most children need encouragement and gentle prodding to practice their musical instruments.

Additionally, there may be reasons why children do not want to practice. When Jennifer Peck was growing up, the piano was down in the basement, where it was dark and creepy. She was only seven, and hated to practice by herself in a place that was frightening to her. When she was in junior high school, she started taking organ lessons, and because her family didn't have an organ, she practiced on the one at their church. The building was huge, and she had to lock herself in. It didn't help that she was in a church, she was still frightened, couldn't concentrate on the music, and spent most of the time paralyzed with fear.

Finding out why your child does not like to practice does not necessarily solve the problem, but knowing why can be helpful as you seek to find ways to motivate and encourage her. In this chapter, we discuss some ideas on motivating children to practice that have worked for different families across the nation.

Getting Your Child to Practice

In the Spencer home in Fort Collins, Colorado, they have only three laws that are non-negotiable. They feel that a few well-placed rules can be very powerful, and that too many rules lose their effectiveness. One of these non-negotiable laws is that each child must choose a musical instrument, or instruments, and learn to play it, through consistent practice, until the child enters college. Their goal is not to produce musical virtuosos but rather to instill within their children certain values and skills that learning an instrument can teach, as well as help them gain a deep appreciation and love for music. If the child wants to continue lessons in college, their parents will continue to support her.

Right from the beginning, the Spencers set down the rules for practicing while their children were excited about this new adventure of learning a musical instrument. Before the first lesson, they drew up a contract explaining the terms of practicing, commitment, and expectations. Once everyone agreed to the rules, both parents and the child signed the paper. A copy of the contract was given to the child, so she would have something she could see, hold, and look at whenever she wants to. For young children, this is important because "seeing is believing." The contract is now binding and cannot be broken until they leave for college. (Although I am sure an attorney could find a loophole!)

> *Losing enthusiasm about practicing is a very common occurrence with children because they are experiencing the discipline of doing something each day, which is not easy.*

Usually about three or four months into the lessons, the fun and excitement begin to wane. "This is hard work," "I don't like this anymore," and "I think I want to quit" are typical comments heard when this happens.

When this happens, Mrs. Spencer whips out the contract and says, "Sorry. Talk to me when you're eighteen, when the contract becomes null and void."

Losing enthusiasm about practicing is a very common occurrence with children because they are experiencing the discipline of doing something each day, which is not easy. When your child sends you this message, it is time to seriously look at ways to motivate and convince her that learning a musical instrument can bring big dividends and is worth the sacrifice, even though the benefits seem intangible and distant.

It is important to remember that in life there are many things we do that start out fun and exciting, but that eventually become difficult and frustrating. Developing a talent, doing homework, working at a job, learning a difficult subject, or practicing an instrument are all things that have their challenging moments. For instance, in the early years, learning math and science involves many fun hands-on activities and the use of manipulatives (such as pattern blocks, algebra tiles, and fraction bars), but sooner or later the student must learn the complexities and abstractions of the subjects that take *real* studying and commitment. Oftentimes when this happens, students lose interest, become overwhelmed, or their grades drop, particularly if there is no one to give the help and support they need. Many educators understand this dilemma. George Tressel of the National Science Foundation, addressing teachers of the nation said, "At an early age, you try to develop the enthusiasm, but then in high school there does come a time when science is not easy. Science is hard." And according to John Tyrell, senior science advisor for the Boston City schools, "Theories abound as to why kids lose interest [in science]. Basically, the high schools blame the elementary schools, and the elementary schools blame the parents."[1]

In many ways, learning a musical instrument can be compared to learning science or math. It starts out rather simply when learning the basics, but eventually gets more challenging, and then the interest wanes. When this happens, absolutely do not throw up your hands and let your child quit, no matter how much he complains, nags, or whines. Stick to your original commitment, keeping in mind that in the long run, you will be happy you did and so will he. By not allowing your child to give up, you are teaching him a valuable lesson of life. It is called perseverance. How many adults do you know who, when looking back at their childhood, wish their parents had not allowed them to quit their music? When I speak to audiences about this subject, invariably, many people share stories of unfulfilled dreams of learning a musical instrument. They quit because it got difficult, and their parents allowed it.

You wouldn't allow your child to stop going to school if he got discouraged or didn't like the homework, would you? So, what do you do when discouragement is at a high and enthusiasm is at a low? In two words . . . motivational bribery! Be a firm believer in finding out what motivates your child and then pursue it. Ask yourself, "What motivates me? Would I go to work each day for free just because I love to be there with my peers, or because I enjoy the discipline of hard work?" Of course not! You are there because you are paid to be there. You may love your job, but you still need that reward called a paycheck. Our children are the same. They need some kind of a carrot in front of them acting as an incentive when things get difficult. That "carrot" may be money, extra privileges, a special toy, or whatever. When using rewards, give your child something that *they* ask for and want, and not something that you, the parent, feel they should have or would be an exciting reward for them. If the parent decides on the particular reward or motivation, it usually doesn't work. Let them decide what they want and are willing to work for. Some children want a trip to the ice cream store, to see a movie with a friend, or some money. Keep in mind, too, that there will always be children who will consistently practice their musical instrument because they love to, but they tend to be the exception and not the rule. All of the Spencer children started out loving to practice, but they *all* went through a period when they hated it and wanted to quit. Because of the connection between consistent musical training and development of the intellect, it is important to do whatever is necessary to keep your child interested and enthusiastic.

Surprisingly, the Spencer children's desire for a reward did not last long. It was usually in the first three years that they needed the little boosts of encouragement. After that, they no longer seemed interested in rewards. What changed? "By this time," their mother states, "they were reading the music well and were practicing successfully on their own. Their confidence had increased through achieving a substantial level of musical proficiency—the music had become its own reward!"

Many parents have shared similar experiences about both their struggles and successes in getting their children to practice.

It seems that children who are the most successful at consistent practicing have parents who consistently help and encourage them. For example, the Jacob family from Provo, Utah, is a remarkable musical family of eleven children. Among them, they play violin, viola, cello, harp, and piano. When their parents play with them, they are a complete chamber orchestra! Not only are they accomplished musicians with the talent and expertise to perform beautifully, but they immensely enjoy what they do. It is amazing how their mother is able to inspire eleven children to consistently practice day after day. She confides that music has been an integral part of their lives since they were babies. She and her husband started the children in music lessons when they were very young, making practicing a daily routine and encouraging them with charts, stickers, money, and other rewards. They felt that each one of their children had a special musical talent and, as parents, their job was to provide the necessary encouragement, support, and to help make those talents become a reality. Mrs. Jacob said, "I had a vision for my children in regard to music; I wanted them to come to love and appreciate music, to have it a natural part of their lives, and in turn, be able to share their musical talents with others." They have had this opportunity by being participants in ensembles, orchestras, and string quartets, and in doing so, have generously shared their musical gifts, expertise, and knowledge with their community, school, and church.

The Braun family in Los Angeles is another example. They have three very musically gifted children and each one plays the violin. Although the parents do not play instruments, they have always loved and appreciated classical music and wanted to give their children an opportunity to develop their musical talents. Today, their two older sons have played with several symphony orchestras, including the Disney Young Musicians Symphony Orchestra at the Hollywood Bowl in Los Angeles. How do their parents get them to practice each day? "Although I don't read music," their mother said, "in the beginning, I sat with them each day, encouraging them, praising them for their efforts, showing an avid interest in what they were doing, and explaining to them that developing a talent takes hard work.

"Not only do they work hard with their music," she continues, "they have transferred that perseverance to their studies at school, as well. They understand, first hand, that to accomplish anything worthwhile in life takes hard work and effort."

Nineteen-year-old Mikel Poulsen of Bremerton, Washington, has been playing percussion since the fourth grade. Although he started out playing the piano, he switched to percussion to play in the school band with his friends. His parents bought him a sixty dollar used snare, and Mikel was on his way. Practicing each day was not always an easy task. His mother, a non-musician, found that Mikel liked her to sit with him, even if it was for only ten minutes. Through the interest she showed and her generous praise of what he was accomplishing, Mikel felt validated. She states, "It was not really a big sacrifice. I enjoyed sitting with him and listening to him play. I didn't play a musical instrument when I was young, and I wanted this for my children. It gave me great pleasure seeing how much he enjoyed it." Mikel's mother also suggests attending all their music concerts in elementary, junior, and senior high school. She says, "When you show continued support for and interest in your child's music, the child will motivate himself, even when you think you can't stand to hear, 'Hot Cross Buns' played one more time." In high school, Mikel played in percussion ensemble, jazz band, jazz combo, wind ensemble, and marching band. He won the regional contest for snare drum and marimba solo and went on to compete in the state competition, and placing in the top ten for snare. Mikel's interest in and dedication to music also won him tuition scholarships to college, and he continues to study and play music in the college arena.

Jacqueline Paullin of Palos Verdes, California, was in utero when her parents began singing to her. As a toddler, she loved to sing, and Raffi became a religion in their home. Her father sang to her and exposed her to classical, blues, and rock-and-roll. At six, Jacqueline began taking piano lessons. At fourteen, she started voice lessons. Practicing has never been an issue. Her mother explains, "Music has been a part of Jacqueline's soul since birth. From the beginning, she has shown a passion and love for music. We believe that her music is one of those special God-given gifts, and her desire has always been to develop it. Because of that, she has willingly and with consistent discipline, practiced on her own. Knowing how other parents struggle getting their children to practice, we feel fortunate." Jacqueline has performed at church, funerals, high school, and at community events.

In all of the examples, the parents took an active role in their children's music development by being involved and interested and by being there when their children needed encouragement and support.

When a child is learning a musical instrument, he is learning long-term perseverance. It is a different kind of perseverance than completing a homework assignment for school or finishing a project for work; most of these tasks are done within a few days or weeks. The kind of perseverance learned from practicing a musical instrument day after day, year after year, communicates to the child that some talents take years to develop and can only be realized through daily practice and patience, but that the results are definitely worth the effort. When a child learns a difficult piece, the inner satisfaction he feels will boost his confidence and help him to have the desire to continue with his instrument. Once again, the music is its own reward. Consider the following ideas as your child begins to play an instrument.

- Draw up a Contract of Expectation. Establish rules of practicing and a statement of commitment regarding the study of the instrument. By putting it in writing, you will avoid any misunderstanding later on. Be sure to give a copy to your child to keep. The importance of consistent practice is illustrated in Shinichi Suzuki's comment, "You don't have to practice every day . . . only on the days that you eat."

- Establish a time each day for practicing. For consistency, try to make it the same time every day.

- Sit with your child during practice sessions. Even if you cannot read music, be there for support and encouragement. The key to a child's early musical success requires the parent and child to become a unit. Think back when your child was first learning to read. Didn't you listen to him each day to encourage and praise him for his successes and efforts? Learning a musical instrument can be similar to learning to read. To a beginner reader, words and letters can look foreign. The same is true with music. Those black notes on the page look like a foreign language to a beginning music student. The only time it is not a good idea to sit with your child when he practices is if you tend to get frustrated or angry while working with him. In this case, do not sit with him and do not feel guilty about it. It would be counterproductive if you were to sit there and criticize him for every mistake he makes. A possible alternative could be to have your spouse or an older sibling sit with him, or you can listen to your child practice . . . from another room.

- Successful learning is a group effort. Children need support, encouragement, and help from parents, teachers, grandparents, and other family members in the learning process. It is particularly important for fathers to support their children's efforts. The Department of Education found that children whose fathers were actively involved in their school activities did significantly better in their schoolwork and were less likely to repeat a grade or get expelled. And this is regardless of parents' income, race, ethnicity, or education.[2] The same can be said about learning to play a musical instrument.

When the father becomes part of the supportive team, the child will work even harder to learn a musical instrument and will be less likely to give up. A child senses when parents are united in helping him to accomplish a task. Those children who develop their talents to a high level almost always have a support group that is deeply committed and involved in what they do.

- Have your child regularly put on performances for the family. It is a way for her to experience the enjoyment and fun that comes from sharing her hard-earned new skills with an audience with whom she's comfortable.

- As always, be generous with praise. Cognitive theorist Kurt Fischer says that a child's innate problem-solving ability is enhanced 400 percent by practice combined with praise from an adult. When children receive praise for their efforts, their learning and musical skills are tremendously accelerated.[3]

- Be patient. Learning to play a musical instrument involves learning many complex skills at once, and your child will need to receive a great deal of patience and love.

Each day as your child practices her instrument, the discipline required for consistent practicing becomes easier as habits are formed and valuable lessons are learned. One of these lessons is that hard work and discipline pay off, especially when a performance goes well at a recital, school talent show, or family gathering where people applaud her obvious talents. Quickly forgotten are the tedious hours of practice, and the motivation to continue to work hard is revitalized. Trombonist James Kraft of the National Symphony describes practicing like this: "Practicing is like putting money into the bank. Performing is like taking money out of your bank account."[4] This statement becomes a truism for any endeavor that the child pursues in life, and the best part is that he learns these lessons from the most influential of teachers . . . experience.

The Virtuoso

When Jay Webster was eighteen months old, he would climb on a chair, reach up to the stereo, and put music on to sing and dance to. By the time he was three, he was studying the violin and taking group music lessons, which he immensely enjoyed. At seven, Jay started taking private piano lessons. Eight months later, with positive comments from the judges, he won second place in the duo division at the Southwest Music Festival at California State University, Dominguez Hills. At eleven, he performed from memory an hourlong recital on piano and organ. At twelve, he lost this intense interest in the piano. He continued taking piano lessons until he went to college, but not with the same focus. Today, at twenty-one, he still loves music, particularly classical music, but is happily pursuing a degree in journalism.

Each day as your child practices her instrument, the discipline required for consistent practicing becomes easier as habits are formed and valuable lessons are learned. One of these lessons is that hard work and discipline pay off, especially when a performance goes well at a recital, school talent show, or family gathering where people applaud her obvious talents.

There were many reasons why Jay lost interest in seriously studying the piano, but regardless of the reasons, his parents did not feel he would have ever become a concert pianist, nor were they grooming him for such. The ongoing interest and the willingness to work hard at the piano simply was not there. The goals for children studying music should not be to transform them into a virtuoso, but rather to help them realize their full potential in all aspects of life and to instill in them a love of music.

Henry David Thoreau said, "The woods would be very silent if no birds sang except those that sang best." What Jay's parents wanted, and what they saw happen, was that he learned many valuable lessons such as responsibility, perseverance, and dependability that carried him through life's challenges. Additionally, Jay acquired increased inner confidence in his abilities and a love for the arts, which forever will enhance the quality of his life—and he didn't need to become a virtuoso to do so.

Many parents who see signs of genius in their young child feel compelled to relentlessly develop those talents immediately, fearing if they do not that the child's potential, however dramatic it may be, will be lost . . . forever. This potential could be in music, sports, math, or any other subject in which the child shows exceptional talent at an early age. Actually, nothing could be further from the truth.

Lauren A. Sosniak, an associate professor of education at the University of Illinois at Chicago, conducted a study that gives a very clear outline on how exceptional talent is developed. Twenty-one concert pianists were interviewed to find out what was involved in developing outstanding achievement in music and how this relates to the overall development of talent. The data that formed the basis of her study were drawn from a much larger project entitled *Development of Talent Research Project* by B. S. Bloom and involved thousands of gifted individuals with many different talents. Ms. Sosniak found the following:[5]

- Development of a talent takes a long time—an average of seventeen years of hard work from the time the child begins training until she receives international recognition.

- All of the pianists interviewed started out playing a musical instrument with no intention of becoming concert-level performers.

- Surprisingly, they did not show any unusual talent at an early age. Their parents gave them lessons because, like many parents, they felt that learning a musical instrument was a positive thing.

- It wasn't until they were thirteen or fourteen, after spending several years taking lessons and practicing daily, that the teacher or parent realized they could accomplish more with their music. At this point, the focus of their music changed.

- From that point, the pianists started spending a lot more time practicing, giving serious attention to the details and technicality of the music.

- They got involved in musical competitions, summer camps, auditions, and public musical activities.

- Eventually, after working with some of the finest piano teachers and developing a music style uniquely their own, they reached their goal of concert status.

The musicians in the Sosniak study did not start piano lessons with the intent of becoming concert pianists—it was a natural evolution. If their parents saw talent, they did not push it. Some of the parents were not even musical themselves. By the time the students realized they wanted to seriously pursue music, they also were willing to work hard. Violinist Isaac Stern confirms this gradual process of music development and says, "Somewhere along the line, the child must become possessed by music, by the sudden desire to play, to excel. It can happen at any time between the ages of ten and fourteen. Suddenly the child begins to sense something happening and he really begins to work, and in retrospect the first five years seem like kinderspiel, [or] fooling around."[6]

Yo-Yo Ma is an excellent example of the evolution of a virtuoso. Ma began playing the cello at age four, and six months later he was playing Bach suites. His father taught him, but was careful not to put too much pressure on his young son. In fact, he insisted that young Ma practice only thirty minutes a day, learning only two measures of music, but playing them technically perfect. By following this system, he had memorized three Bach suites at the young age of seven. When Ma was fourteen, it was obvious to people in the music business in New York that he was virtuoso material, but his father wanted his son to be "normal." Therefore, Ma did not enter competitions, and he rarely gave concerts. He said, "My father wanted us to be educated, good people first and musicians second." It was while he was at Harvard pursuing a liberal arts degree that he began to realize how very important music was in his life. It became clear to him that his first desire and priority was music. Today, he is internationally recognized as one of the greatest cellists in the world.[7]

Another example of emerging musical talent is Wynton Marsalis, the famous jazz/classical musician. He was raised in a musical home, and his father was an accomplished musician. His mother, understanding the importance of music, took the time to expose her children to music programs offered in the community. Marsalis was six years old when he started to play the trumpet. His father did not force him to practice, but rather encouraged his young son and made lessons available to him. When Marsalis turned twelve, he realized that music was something he was very interested in, and he began practicing every day. He learned about "shedding," which is what jazz musicians call burning the midnight oil and practicing hard. He began "shedding" up to six hours a day. With serious dedication to his music, along with parental encouragement and help, Marsalis has become a nationally renowned musician.[8]

Extraordinary musical talent, such as demonstrated by Wynton Marsalis and Yo-Yo Ma, is not forced, but evolves gradually with the support, patience, and encouragement of family, friends, and teachers. Howard Gardner said, "The challenge of musical education is to respect and build upon the young child's own skills and understanding of music, rather than simply to impose a curriculum that was designed principally to ensure competent adult musical performances. The ready exploration of bits and the intuitive sense of the form and contour of a piece are precious experiences, which should not be scuttled if a full flowering of musical talent is to occur in later life."[9]

Whatever musical road your child chooses, the evolution and process involved takes the time and patience of parents and child.

Additionally, it takes serious dedication and hard work from the child. All great composers through the ages have known and practiced this simple formula of perseverance and eventual success. As Johann Sebastian Bach put it, "I was obliged to work hard. Whoever is equally industrious will succeed just as well." Thomas Edison believed the same. He said, "Talent is 99 percent perspiration and 1 percent inspiration." Children everywhere who are developing their musical talents will agree that it takes their own personal commitment of working hard to achieve any amount of success.

The musical journey will be different for each of our children. Some will achieve concert status, some will enjoy playing a musical instrument with the school band, while others will enjoy listening to music with a deep love and appreciation. Whatever musical road your child chooses, the evolution and process involved takes the time and patience of parents and child. This concept is illustrated in nature by the indra swallowtail butterfly. Laboratory scientists have carefully chronicled its life cycle. An egg is laid at just the right spot on the food plant, and within five days it hatches and grows into a black caterpillar with yellow-orange dots. When it reaches maturity, the caterpillar creates its own chrysalis. Most emerge after two years, but some take up to seven years to come forth out of the chrysalis. Unexpectedly, it

begins to emerge, no longer the spotted caterpillar, but a gorgeous black butterfly. Scientists and observers, understanding the indra swallowtail growth, patiently wait and give time a chance.[10] As you watch your child emerge musically, encourage him to work hard, enjoy the journey, and finally . . . appreciate the destination.

$\mathscr{N}$OTEWORTHY: LEARNING VALUES THROUGH MUSIC

Learning is experience. Everything else is just information.

—*Albert Einstein*

Many articles have been written on the importance of and necessity for young people to develop marketable skills for their future endeavors. In 1991, the U.S. Department of Labor issued a report urging schools to teach for the future workplace. Some of the areas the report recommended to be incorporated within the curriculum instruction were working in teams, self-esteem, communication, creative thinking, imagination, and invention. Interestingly, these qualities all grow out of the acquisition of the basic values of hard work, diligence, perseverance, self-discipline, and so on. In the past, these traits and values were formed as children worked, lived, and developed their talents within the family unit and community. In turn, these became qualities that sustained and enriched families, neighborhoods, communities, and the nation. But change comes and not always to our benefit. The traditional home of a two-parent family, extended grandparents, and other family members is no longer the "norm." The nucleus of the family is changing because many families find it necessary for both parents to work. Parents today are balancing hectic schedules, trying to provide for the basic needs of the family, leaving little time for teaching values to their children. Many feel there are simply not enough hours in the day, or they are too tired to put forth the additional effort after working all day then facing a myriad of household duties to keep the family running. There are also parents who worry *how* best to teach basic values that will enable their child to lead a balanced, productive life. Because values are being taught "hit and miss" in the home, the schools have tried to pick up the slack by adopting programs for the classroom that teach values. But reading, discussing, or hearing stories about values does not teach them effectively. It takes experiences with the discipline of daily routines, disappointments, challenges, problem solving, and difficulties to teach children values and traits that they can utilize in a future job, as a future parent, and as a contributing member of society.

Confucius said, "Hear . . . and forget. See . . . and remember. Do . . . and understand." It is through this simple "do" where the learning sticks and the values take hold. Thomas Stanley, Ph.D., who co-authored *The Millionaire Next Door: The Surprising Secrets of America's Wealthy,* says that wealth is built on hard work, perseverance, planning, and, most of all, self-discipline.[1] Remarkably, when children learn to play a musical instrument, they acquire these values and traits, as well as others that will benefit them in their future work and will help them to be successful, be it financial or otherwise.

This chapter discusses how one learns to work hard, to persevere, to be self-disciplined, as well as how one acquires many other skills and values needed to achieve success in life, all through the process of music education.

The Value of Hard Work

The amount of energy we put into developing a talent—such as learning a musical instrument—determines its strength, force, and impact in our lives. Will it become a talent that we enjoy throughout our lives, or merely something we will say we briefly experienced? To accomplish the former requires diligent effort.

When children expend the consistent effort required to learn a musical instrument, they discover that the discipline of this day-to-day task will affect how they approach their other responsibilities in life, such as the effort they put into their school studies or the degree of diligence they give to the development of other talents. Through this hands-on experience, they come to realize that success in anything is the result of consistent hard work. The great composers learned that hard work was the key to creating beautiful music that would last through the ages. Bach credited hard work to the prodigious amount of music he composed in his lifetime. Haydn, a deeply religious man, worked hard composing music, not only mentally but also spiritually. If he began to have difficulties organizing his musical ideas, he would stop and pray to God, asking if he had sinned or erred in any way and, if so, would God forgive him. In the words of a well-known saying, "he worked as though everything depended on him and prayed as though everything depended on God." George Frideric Handel, who wrote *Messiah*, the most famous oratorio of all time, did not write this monumental work easily. Even though it took

> *When children expend the consistent effort required to learn a musical instrument, they discover that the discipline of this day-to-day task will affect how they approach their other responsibilities in life, such as the effort they put into their school studies or the degree of diligence they give to the development of other talents.*

him only twenty-four days to compose 260 pages, Handel never left his house during that time, and rarely left his room or stopped to eat. He was completely absorbed and obsessed with the task at hand, feeling driven and inspired to complete the work. Sir Newman Flower, one of Handel's biographers said, "Considering the immensity of the work and the short time involved, it will remain, perhaps forever, the greatest feat in the whole history of music composition." After his first performance of *Messiah*, Handel was congratulated by Lord Kinnoul on the excellent "entertainment." Handel very simply replied, "My lord, I should be sorry if I only entertain them. I wish to make them better."[2]

Although most of us will never reach the level of talent of these great men of music, we can all benefit in many areas of our lives from the consistent hard work we put into developing our own potential. For example, young Dat Nguyen, a blind Amerasian orphan from Saigon, learned at an early age the importance of hard work as he developed his musical talents. As a beggar on the streets of Saigon, he met a man named Mr. Truong, one of Saigon's finest music teachers and who, like Dat, was also blind. Mr. Truong, feeling sorry for the young boy, took Dat and his sister into his home and cared for them. Mr. Truong taught Dat the piano, several string instruments, and how to read in Braille. When Dat was eighteen, he heard a radio performance of Andrés Segovia playing the classical guitar. Dat knew instantly that he wanted to learn to play the guitar like Segovia, so Mr. Truong began teaching him. In 1991, Dat and his sister were given the opportunity to come to the United States under a program that brought Amerasian children to the country. He was sent to live in Orange County, California, under the sponsorship of Thanh Vu, who had fled Vietnam in 1975. Dat attended California State University at Fullerton, and while there met David Grimes, who headed the university's classical guitar program. Grimes encouraged Dat to enter the Southern California American String Teachers Association contest. In preparation, Dat practiced eight hours a day. On the day of the competition, Dat nervously wondered why he had ever decided to compete against so many talented people, but after playing the first few notes of *Nocturno* by Federico Moreno Torroba, he became so absorbed in the music that he forgot everything and everyone around him. Dat won the competition and went on to win the statewide American String Teachers Association competition. Hard work paid off! He continues to work hard and is currently writing songs to raise money for Vietnamese refugees in the Philippines to come to the United States.[3]

Although developing a talent can seem like a lifelong commitment to a painstaking process, the rewards for the individual, as well as the people they impact, is immeasurable. Thanks to Handel's hard work, we have today for our enjoyment *and* inspiration, *Messiah*. Because of Dat Nguyen's hard work in developing his musical talents, he has been able to earn money to help many Vietnamese come and enjoy a better life in the United States.

Gaining Perseverance and Determination

We live in an age of instants: instant photocopies, instant food, instant photos, instant communications, and more. Although many of these instants make our lives easier, they also can give our children a distorted view of life and how goals are achieved. Many children grow up expecting instant results in life, never learning to work for or wait for a reward. When things don't come easily or immediately, they give up. For this reason, studying a musical instrument becomes a priceless lesson. As a child begins to learn to play the flute, for example, she soon realizes that this is not going to be done in an "instant." It will take time, patience, perseverance, determination, and the ability to stick to the task, day after day, year after year, to play the flute with any degree of proficiency. Learning to read notes, to develop hand-eye coordination, to listen, and to count rhythms is a process involving perseverance. As she works through the difficulties and challenges of learning an instrument, she soon learns that determination and perseverance equal success. Likewise, the perseverance a child learns by practicing her instrument can be, as the experiences of many demonstrate, transferred to other areas of her life. For instance, when subjects in school are difficult, she will continue to try her best until the assignment is completed, confident that eventually she will be successful. When life throws her a curve, she will not give up, but will work harder with even greater diligence and perseverance until she reaches her goal.

Although most of the great composers suffered personal adversity, they persevered and went on to write beautiful sonatas, symphonies, and operas. Beethoven, despite his progressive deafness at an early age, wrote perhaps his greatest music after going completely deaf. Bach suffered blindness and diabetes, yet continued to compose music. George Frideric Handel suffered a debilitating stroke that put him in a rest home. The world felt that a great life had come to a close. With dogged persistence, he shuffled his way to the organ each night after everyone had gone to bed, forcing his fingers to slowly play each key on the organ. The nuns who heard him were amazed at his unfailing courage and determination. Eventually, he made a complete recovery and went on to write many great pieces of music.

Although the composers of past eras experienced and rose above adversities through determination and perseverance, so have many of the great musical people of our day, such as opera singer Denyce Graves. Graves grew up in poverty in Washington, D.C., in the 1970s with her mother and two siblings. Although they lacked material possessions, their home was filled with singing and music. At an early age, Graves had a strong, clear voice that impressed her teacher, Judith Grove, who encouraged the young girl to audition for acceptance into the Duke Ellington

School of the Arts. Grove was impressed with Graves's voice, but even more so with her perseverance and determination, which Grove felt would be her key to success. Graves was accepted to Ellington, and there she decided to become an opera singer. By working hard, she was able to graduate early from Ellington. She went to study voice at Oberlin Conservatory of Music in Ohio, and from there she went to the New England Conservatory to study voice. As Graves was preparing to compete for the National Council Auditions of the Metropolitan Opera, she began noticing phlegm in her throat and a pain in her vocal cords, which forced her to withdraw from the competition. After visiting dozens of specialists, she was finally diagnosed with a thyroid condition and was given medication that cleared up the problem. Free to pursue her goal, she went to the Houston Grand Opera, playing the part of Emilia in *Otello*. But in the back of her mind was her lifelong dream to perform at the Metropolitan Opera House in New York. Finally, that day arrived, and on October 7, 1995, she played the lead role in Bizet's *Carmen*. Years of determination and perseverance had paid off as she received a standing ovation from a spellbound audience. The *New York Times* said of Graves, "Few Carmens bring such beauty and sensuality to the role."[4]

An old saying illustrates the tenacity, perseverance, and determination of those like Graves, Handel, Bach, and Beethoven: "Man is like a postage stamp. He may get licked, depressed, stuck in a corner, and sent from post to post, but he will always succeed and arrive in the right place if only he will stick to it."[5]

Learning Self-Discipline

While perseverance is learned over time, self-discipline is exercised as the day-to-day task of practicing an instrument is accomplished. For many children, this is not easy. As we already discussed, parents can help by establishing a time each day for practicing and then by monitoring the sessions. During practice time, it takes self-discipline to work on the difficult measures of a piece. Instead of viewing those measures as something to avoid, a child over time learns that they are a challenge that can be solved by breaking the piece into workable parts, and that troublesome situations in life can be solved in the same way. As he masters these difficult areas in the music, he learns that difficulties in life cannot be ignored, but must be confronted and addressed to be successfully resolved. Facing problems and working on them eventually leads a child to conquer them.

The difference between the person who daydreams about goals and the person who accomplishes his goals is self-discipline.

Self-discipline is a quality that helps children not only start a task, but also finish it. Later in life, the lessons they have learned from facing challenges head-on and solving them will be a vital asset in whatever they choose to do. In life, we often admire the person who has the self-discipline to never lose sight of his goal. Likewise, we have little respect for those individuals who have no control over their actions, appetites, passions, and whims, and who never get past dreaming about their "good intentions." The difference between the person who daydreams about goals and the person who accomplishes his goals is self-discipline.

Eleven-year-old Sally Kikuchi is not one who daydreams about her music goals. In fact, she demonstrates self-discipline beyond her years. She practices between four and six hours a day, depending on whether or not she is preparing for a competition. Sally knows that, to fulfill her dream of studying at Juilliard and eventually becoming a concert pianist, she must sacrifice other things to accomplish her goal. Her self-discipline toward her music has paid off. She has won numerous awards and honors for her playing, including the Maurice K. Parness Concerto Competition for Young Artists in 1997 and 1998, and first place in the open solo, open Chopin, and open Baroque categories for 1997 and 1998 at the Southwestern Youth Music Festivals.[6]

In a speech given at the National Symposium for Music Education (March 1992) in Washington, D.C., the importance of self-discipline and its relationship to learning a musical instrument was noted. "As a child begins to understand the connection between hours of practice and the quality of a performance, *self-discipline* becomes self-reinforcing. It is only a short jump from that realization to making the connection between self-discipline and performance skill in life [emphasis added]."[7]

The Benefits of Responsibility

"I'm the one that writes my own story—
I decide the person I'll be.
What goes in the plot, and what does not,
Is pretty much up to me."[8]

—*Carol Lynn Pearson*

We are "pretty much" responsible for what we accomplish in our life—the decisions we make, as well as the talents we develop. Music teaches responsibility effectively over time. It is a gradual process that develops as a child grows in maturity and inner motivation. Responsibility comes in music training when the child realizes that ultimately he alone is accountable for any successes he will have with his instrument. Accepting this responsibility is shown in his willingness to practice consistently each day, even when no one is checking up on him. When he practices and finally masters various musical skills, he demonstrates that he has taken responsibility for solving difficult musical passages. If he plays in a band or orchestra, he is confronted with the important responsibility of not only learning his part of the music, but also performing it well with the other musicians.

As a child matures, so does his understanding of responsibility. Eventually, a child will enjoy being responsible because it will add structure and organization to his life, which in turn will help him to do what needs to be done to successfully reach his goals. He will enjoy taking charge of his life and actions. He will learn not to blame others or find scapegoats when things go wrong with his musical performances. He will face his challenges, explore them, and take responsibility for the outcome. As a result, his confidence and self-worth will soar.

These same dynamics make responsible people valuable figures in the workplace. Unfortunately, in today's society there are many people who choose *not* to take responsibility for their actions and blame others when their lives don't turn out how they imagined. Michael Levine, a Beverly Hills publicist, has seen many people in his line of work not take responsibility for their actions. He feels that personal responsibility is so important that he is advocating the building of a "Statue of Responsibility," to serve as a reminder that we are each responsible for our actions and that, "with liberty comes responsibility." He says, "Many believe that our society has arrived at or near a state of chaos. It is my belief that is because we have placed our emphasis almost entirely on the concept of liberty, to the exclusion of personal responsibility."[9] He hopes that this statue will serve as a powerful symbol of the importance of responsibility.

Years ago, William Ernest Henley commented on personal responsibility in his poem *Invictus*. He wrote, "I am the master of my Fate/I am the captain of my soul." We *are* the masters of our fate and the captains of our souls. It really is up to us to do, to become, and to be. Therefore, even if personal responsibility were the only benefit derived from music training, it would be worth any amount of effort and sacrifice to provide this valuable learning experience for your child.

The Value of Teamwork

In the United States, we tend to be an "I" culture. We prize the individual over the group. Most cultures outside of the United

States are "we" cultures. Cooperation and collaboration are the rule where people move together or not at all. There is a saying in Japan that goes, "The nail that stands up gets hammered down." In many "we" cultures, to be singled out is an embarrassment and praise for the group is the standard.

Actually, there is strength in both philosophies, but the balance of the two is the most powerful of all. Playing a musical instrument encompasses both philosophies. In a band or orchestra, each musician is responsible for how he or she plays individually, but the group must work together as a team to create a beautiful blended sound. By doing so, they learn cooperation, team spirit, and the power that comes from working together for the greater whole. As we think about it, nearly every aspect of our life requires a certain amount of team effort: activities at school, home, church, and work. Certainly one of the top qualities that employers look for in potential employees is their ability to work as part of a team.

More and more colleges and universities are looking at prospective applicants who have been involved in activities where they learned and demonstrated team skills. These are young people who set themselves apart from the rest by being organized, working well with others, and accomplishing more with their time. Studies have shown that successful college students are those who show a high level of achievement and teamwork in their high school activities and not necessarily from their SAT scores, class rank, and grades in school.[10]

Fred Hargadon, dean of admissions for Stanford University, in a 1983 interview said, "We look for students who have taken part in orchestra, symphonic band, chorus, and drama. It shows a level of energy and an ability to organize time that we are after here. It shows that they can carry a full academic load and learn something else. It means that these particular students already know how to get involved and that's the kind of campus we want to have."[11] Additionally, social scientists believe that social intelligence is more valuable than academic intelligence. You could be a genius, but if you can't cooperate and work with others, your intelligence will not be your greatest asset.

Over the past thirty years, Rebecca Marsh has had numerous opportunities to accompany vocalists, choral groups, and general audiences in a number of musical settings. She has learned that it takes a team effort to be successful as an accompanist. On one occasion, which she will never forget, "team effort" took on a very significant meaning. She was called at the last minute to accompany a young vocalist for a funeral. Arriving at the funeral home, she found that the organ was situated behind a thin wall with the sound projected to the audience by speakers suspended from the ceiling. The problem was (and it was a big problem) that she would not be able to see the vocalist, nor could she hear the speaker announce the musical numbers. It required someone to run back to where she was sitting and tell her to start playing. It was unnerving, to say the least, particularly because she had not even practiced with the young woman who was singing. This was a classic case of the blind leading the blind. Fortunately, the three worked closely together as a team—the vocalist, the runner, and Marsh—and because of this (and only because of this) it turned out successfully.

In a like manner, it is essential that members of an orchestra work together as a team to perform flawlessly and successfully. The Odessa Philharmonic Orchestra in the Ukraine was, at one time, a very successful orchestra that played to packed audiences but, under stifling Soviet rules, it had languished. Some members had become discouraged and had even thought of leaving and going to other orchestras. Then in 1991, a young American, seeing great potential in Odessa and needing a new challenge in his life, accepted the post as conductor for fifty dollars a month. His first task was to raise money for desperately needed musical supplies for the musicians. With three thousand dollars collected from family and friends, he purchased bow hair to refit the entire string section and mutes for the brass and string sections. His next goal was to help each of the musicians earn the necessary money to live, which they could do by touring abroad. To do this, they needed to perfect their skills up to a world-class level of performance. An enormous team effort was expended as each musician worked with a fervor and purpose they had never before experienced. Individual rehearsals with each section, plus four-hour practice sessions with the complete orchestra was a daily routine and reinforced their one desire and goal: to perform abroad in the West. In late 1991, their first opportunity to perform outside the Ukraine presented itself. They went to Austria and performed the marches of John Philip Sousa, Gershwin, and others for the Bregenz Spring Festival. It was an enormous success, and people loved the unique experience of hearing a Ukrainian orchestra performing American music. This moment also became a turning point for each member of the orchestra. By working together with greater intensity, they eventually reached their goal and performed throughout the United States, with their dream performance in New York at Carnegie Hall.[12] Music teaches teamwork!

Developing Creative Thinking, Imagination, and Invention

Nothing can match the human mind when it comes to thinking, creating, imagining, dreaming, and inventing. When we are young, we dream about castles in the air and what our future may hold. As we get older, our dreams just get better planned. It was imagination that showed young Albert Einstein how to measure the distance an object travels through space at the speed of light. The world of light, power, and communication were the inventive thoughts of Thomas Edison. Thomas Jefferson followed his own creative and innovative thoughts when he wrote the United States Constitution. (Coincidentally, all three were musicians.) It was Michelangelo's imagination that saw a statue in every block of marble he chipped away at, and Leonardo da Vinci, one of the most creative men who ever lived, dreamed dreams never known before in science, music, art, math, and engineering. He was the embodiment of the Renaissance spirit of intellectual curiosity and creativity.

Every great achievement is at first and for a time, only a dream and a part of someone's creative imagination. The story of sculptor Gutzon Borglum, who was working on a head of Abraham Lincoln, is an excellent example. As he chipped away at the marble, a cleaning woman swept up the pieces and threw them away. She was amazed as she watched the head of Lincoln emerge from the stone under the sculptor's hand, until at last the work was finished. She could no longer hold her wonder and said, "Mr. Borglum, how did you know that Mr. Lincoln was in that stone?"[13]

When we think of someone who is creative, we usually think of a person who is talented in the arts. But Pablo Picasso said, "Every child is an artist. The challenge is to remain an artist." Young children, uninhibited and easygoing, freely express creativity in their play with others. As children grow older, their natural creativity will wane unless it is nurtured. That nurturing can be accomplished through music education. Studying a musical instrument teaches and reinforces creativity in young children. As we have learned, the brain, like a muscle, can be developed through exposure to a rich environment of learning experiences. The mental process of learning music utilizes the whole brain. Music students are developing those areas of the brain that expand human creativity. They broaden their thoughts of originality, independence, curiosity, and flexibility, as they interpret, analyze, and break apart the music in new and interesting ways. Creativity then becomes the natural process behind approaching situations in life in innovative ways.

Music through the ages has been a way for young musicians to creatively express and communicate their feelings, thoughts, and concerns to others. In 1792, Joseph Haydn used an innovative way to convince his boss, Prince Nicolaus, that he and the other court musicians were in need of a vacation. Haydn composed a piece of music that conveyed their feelings. He called it the "Farewell Symphony." During the music, the musicians, one by one stopped playing and walked quietly out of the room with the music under their arms. The prince got the hint and gave them a vacation.

Music students are developing those areas of the brain that expand human creativity. They broaden their thoughts of originality, independence, curiosity, and flexibility, as they interpret, analyze, and break apart the music in new and interesting ways.

Creativity will become one of the most important skills for people entering the twenty-first century. As information rapidly expands and changes, people will need to be flexible and able to apply their knowledge, skills, and experiences in many different directions. Those individuals who have honed their creative skills through participation in the arts will have no trouble adapting and being successful.

Building Confidence

The Norwegian Research Council for Science and the Humanities found that students who study a musical instrument, or who are involved in the arts, are more likely to succeed in school because their confidence in themselves is higher.[14] Confidence stems from an inner belief in oneself and one's abilities. A child with confidence in his abilities demonstrates optimism and is not devastated by challenges or setbacks. He feels secure about who he is and his ability to reach goals. When a child masters the complex task of learning a musical instrument or singing with a chorale group, his confidence begins to soar. Confidence also can come from something as simple as playing well in a recital. A successful performance at a recital gives a child an inner sense of accomplishment and satisfaction. Through the self-expression afforded in musical participation, he sees himself as unique and talented. A child cannot be gifted in every area, but he needs a chance to discover his uniqueness on which confidence is built.

Have you ever observed a child after a recital? If so, you might have seen a child who was bursting with confidence and excitement and could hardly wait to pick out a new piece to learn. Dan Rather talks about the confidence he felt as a young boy performing on woodblocks in a recital: "It is thrilling to be sitting in a group of musicians playing (more or less) the same piece of music. You are part of a great, powerful, vibrant entity. And nothing beats the feeling you get when you've practiced a difficult section over and over and finally get it right. (Yes, even on the woodblock.) And you think *you're* excited when you get that song right: imagine how your *mother* feels. You can see it in her face: relief and pride. Big pride."[15] And this confidence continues to build upon itself with each new piece mastered.

Children who study a musical instrument oftentimes demonstrate their confidence by doing better in school and also in their future jobs. In the work force, confident, self-assured individuals are often the leaders and strength of an organization. Instead of trying to "keep up with the Joneses," they *are* the Joneses! They set the standards that others try to emulate.

Confidence in oneself helps a person to get through the challenges and difficulties of life. Despite critics' condemnation, Igor Stravinsky was a confident composer, willing to defy the traditions of musical composition by introducing an entirely new direction in music. He attained instant fame with two ballets, *Firebird*, a ballet based on a Russian legend, and *The Rite of Spring*, which premiered in Paris on May 29, 1913. During the performance of *The Rite of Spring*, a riot broke out in the theater.

Some people cheered, while most screamed and threw things. Despite this initial reaction, *The Rite of Spring* became an enormous success and was credited with changing the whole course of music. His fame spread worldwide. Stravinsky's actions demonstrate that confident people have the courage to "slay the sacred cow" of tradition by using their talents in innovative ways and thereby raising the level of creative expression to new heights.

Developing Critical-Thinking Skills

Critical thinking has been on the lips of educators now for at least fifteen years. During this time, teachers have flocked to seminars, classes, workshops, and educational conferences to learn how to teach the rising generation to think, to analyze, and to solve problems. Not surprisingly, they are finding that students who play musical instruments are better thinkers than those who do not. This is because the very process of learning a musical instrument requires, if not demands, critical-thinking skills. A child may start out learning notes on a page, but eventually rhythm, syncopation, phrasing, the use of different "voices," or parts of the music, all have a critical part in making the music musical. Music students need to carefully analyze how the composer may have wanted the piece to be played. Decisions are made regarding interpretation of phrases and passages. They analyze, take apart, and evaluate each piece. Music is not just developing hand-eye coordination or symbol recognition, but interpretation, thinking, and problem solving, as well. Developing these skills while they are young gives them the tools they need for the future.

Alan Gooden, a seasoned science teacher, laments the fact that children today simply cannot think. This situation is not unique, but is fast becoming a common thread, weaving itself throughout our nation's schools. The future for young people who cannot think is a dismal one because employers are looking for people who have the abilities to think and solve problems to meet the challenges of a progressive twenty-first century. At the Nashville Music Forum, Susan Driggers of Bell South Corporation said, "At perhaps no other time have music and arts education been more important. Apart from their obvious benefits, music and the other arts produce critical thinkers, people who are decision makers. In the information age, our company needs people with the critical thinking skills to analyze data and make judgments."[16]

Lifelong Learning

At School Sisters of Notre Dame in Mankato, Minnesota, is a rather unique group of elderly nuns who are exceptionally active and alert. Their average age is eighty-five, with many of them in their nineties and some 100 and older. Their secret to productive longevity: disciplined, lifelong learning! Interested in their remarkable vigor, scientists have studied this order of nuns and have found that their activities, which include earning college degrees, teaching, reading, doing puzzles, playing musical instruments, studying politics and current events, working math problems, and writing in journals, are constantly challenging their minds. In short, exercising the brain is a way of life at the nunnery.

The nuns' way of life was summed up by Dee Dickinson, who said, "In order to prepare human beings to be lifelong learners in a world of escalating change and uncertainty, it is essential that they become not just knowledgeable, but as fully intelligent as possible."[17] The sisters' accomplishments clearly show us that through the process of lifelong learning, we can remain active and alert well into old age. Arnold Scheibel, head of the Brain Research Institute at the University of California at Los Angeles, says, "Anything that's intellectually challenging can probably serve as a kind of stimulus for dendritic growth, which means it adds to the computational reserves in your brain."[18]

Scientists at the Salk Institute for Biological Studies in La Jolla, California, and at Princeton University recently discovered that intense mental exercise could spur the growth of new brain cells throughout our lives. Mental challenges that required spatial relationships and timing (which are required in learning a musical instrument) had the greatest effect in developing new brain cells.[19]

Studying a musical instrument—which works the sides, front, and back portions of the brain—can act as a high-powered stimulus for dendritic growth. Many musicians and composers have kept their brains alert by actively playing and composing music throughout their lives. Stephane Grappelli is one such musician who, throughout his eighty-nine years as a French jazz violinist, performed for audiences all over the world. He once said, "I will play until the final curtain."[20] And he did just that! Until he died in December 1997, he was performing with precision and classic beauty—"an advertisement for the sheer joy of playing jazz."[21]

Studying a musical instrument—which works the sides, front, and back portions of the brain—can act as a high-powered stimulus for dendritic growth. Many musicians and composers have kept their brains alert by actively playing and composing music throughout their lives.

George Stevens, ninety-one, of Highland Park, California, is another. He has enjoyed singing with the oldest non-university men's singing club in the nation, which began in 1888. Stevens joined in 1928, when he was twenty-two years old and, except for a hiatus during World War II, has sung with this group his entire life.[22]

Even younger musicians, realizing the importance of music to their mental well-being, are making lifelong commitments to the study of music. Case in point: The Caduceus Jazz Ensemble, in Springfield, Missouri, was formed by fifteen physicians and two medical administrators who created the group out of a need for entertainment at an employee Christmas party. Their first performance was such a success that they now give performances throughout the community, despite their hectic schedules and pagers that go off during rehearsals. Their common bond is their love for music, and they have every intention of keeping their group together well into old age!

NAMM, The National Association of Music Merchants, in Carlsbad, California, is hooking up inactive musicians with other musicians in their locale in the Weekend Warrior program, giving them an opportunity to enjoy, utilize, and share their musical talents with others. After just four short rehearsals, these musicians are ready for a performance at a local venue! (See Resources section.)

You may conclude that if you want to remain mentally active and alert throughout your life, one sure way to do it is through an ongoing, lifelong study of a musical instrument. As the nuns of Mankato have proven, learning can continue throughout life and, as Arnold Scheibel's research has shown, it *should*. Scheibel notes that, "All of life should be a learning experience, not just for the trivial reasons, but because by continuing the learning process, we are challenging our brain and therefore building circuitry. Literally. This is the way the brain operates."[23]

Lifelong learning is not just a catch-phrase of the nineties, but can be an actual physical reality. Scientists now know that humans experience another growth spurt at about age thirty, particularly in regard to the refinement of muscle movement in the hands and face. Fine motor coordination increases, and pianists and violinists are able to move their fingers with greater agility. Vocalists are able to command a greater range with their vocal cords, and actors are better able to subtly control their facial muscles and express any emotion just with their face.[24]

Twenty-seven-year-old Leif Ove Andsnes, winner of the 1998 Gilmore Artist Award, said this regarding this later refinement of growth, "I was fed the myth that basic technique must be mastered before twenty, but to my surprise, I've developed as much in the last couple of years. My capacity for learning is greater now because of a larger frame of reference."[25] So, we can expect patterns of growth throughout our life. We are a work in progress as long as we keep developing, striving, and learning. On a higher level, there is a deep satisfaction and knowledge that comes from continuous involvement with the arts that cannot be calculated. The quest for knowledge and self-improvement is endless. It seems that the more we know, the more we want to learn, and the more we realize there is so much yet to know.

Appreciation, Sensitivity, and Love of the Arts

Historian Arthur M. Schlesinger said, "If history tells us anything, it tells us that the United States, like all other nations, will be measured in the eyes of posterity not by its economic power nor by its military might . . . but by its character and achievement as a civilization." The arts give beauty and meaning to our lives, and they are the means by which the character and achievement of a civilization are measured. Monuments fall, civilizations perish, but artistic creations survive. One cannot study a nation without studying the music, art, and literature of that nation. It is through the arts that we understand and appreciate both the individual and the culture. For this reason, it is always interesting to visit a history, art, or science museum. The artifacts behind glass speak of the artistic talent of civilizations of bygone years and give us a picture of its daily life. It does not matter if we are looking at examples of an early musical instrument, pottery of the Incas, or Viking weapons of war—they all possess elements of creativity and artistic design and tell us much about the people who made them.

Music speaks to the inner reaches of the soul, giving solace to the mind as well as the body. It has the power to uplift us when life is collapsing around us. The poignant true stories that follow are moving examples of music's power.

Vedran Smailovic, a cellist with the Sarajevo Opera, watched as a bomb fell and killed twenty-two starving people while they waited in line to get bread. Using music to fight back his emotions, he dressed in full concert attire and played the cello each day for twenty-two days in the crater that the shell had made. With bombs exploding around him, he courageously played Albinoni's mournful Adagio in G minor for those who died so senselessly. Miraculously, he was never hurt. People in the village responded with love and brotherhood, as did the rest of the world. "The Cellist of Sarajevo" and his music became a universal symbol of hope and peace. His act illustrates the power of music to communicate love and sorrow for the victims in a war-torn country filled with hatred and its power to help heal the wounds.[26]

Herbert Zipper's life was changed in an instant when the Nazis marched into Austria in March 1938. He was a talented Viennese musician and conductor who enjoyed the life of the cultural elite. Rounded up and sent to Dachau along with many of his musician friends from the Munich Philharmonic, his life became a brutal existence. Determined to make things better, he and others began to make roughly hewn violins and other instruments from spare wood. They formed a secret orchestra and, on Sunday afternoons, performed for the other men in camp. Astonishingly, they were never caught.

Zipper said, "I realized in Dachau that the arts in general have the power to keep you not just alive, but to make your life meaningful even under the most dreadful circumstances."[27]

Zipper and his friend Jura Soyfer wrote a song entitled *Dachau Song,* and in a few short months all one thousand inhabitants of Dachau knew the song. It spread from camp to camp and became "one of the powerful and tightly embraced resistance songs during the Holocaust."[28]

United States Air Force pilot Clair Cline was a prisoner at Stalag Luft I in Germany during World War II. As a child, he had learned to play the violin, but he had also loved fixing the broken violins and other stringed instruments of neighbors. As he languished in prison, desperately trying to combat boredom, he decided to make a violin made from wooden bed slats. Using a small pocketknife, a table knife, and a piece of broken glass for fine scraping, he began his project.

From spring until late November, he worked feverishly until, finally, the violin was complete. Because it was close to Christmas, he began learning some carols. On Christmas Eve, he pulled the violin from under his bunk and began playing some of the carols. A few of the men hummed along. When the guards ordered silence in the prison, the room grew quiet, but then Cline began to play softly "Silent Night" as the men lay quietly in their bunks thinking of home, peace, and better times.

We cannot appreciate the arts unless we become involved with them on some level, and one cannot become involved with music without becoming immersed in all of the arts.

On April 30, 1945, the prisoners of Stalag Luft I were freed. Two months later, Clair Cline arrived back home with the beloved violin. "Today, over fifty years later, the violin sits in a display case on the Clines living-room wall in Tacoma," a reminder of the power of music.[29]

We cannot appreciate the arts unless we become involved with them on some level, and one cannot become involved with music without becoming immersed in *all* of the arts. Music, drama, the visual arts, and dance all have the power to uplift, inspire, and edify the human spirit. Our children's ongoing association with the arts will enhance their lives immeasurably. One might ask the question, can our children learn these same values and skills by playing a sport, or being involved in leadership opportunities, or other similar activities? The answer, of course, is yes, but there is something unique about the skills and values that are developed when children study a musical instrument, or otherwise become immersed in the arts on some level. It is simply this: their involvement with the arts will grow with them, as do the skills and the values associated with them, building and flourishing year after year, becoming a part of who they are and how they view themselves. It is rather unlikely that a person will be throwing a football around when they are sixty years old, but they can play in a band or orchestra, or sing in a choral group, throughout their entire life. Instead of dreaming about past glories and honors, they can still be actively achieving musically as they continue to hone and perfect those skills and values that will bring joy and satisfaction into their life and the lives of others.

PART

A NEED FOR ADVOCACY:
MUSIC EDUCATION
IN THE SCHOOLS

CHAPTER 7

A DYNAMIC MOVEMENT: MUSIC'S POWER TO EDUCATE

When we teach a child to draw, we teach him how to see.
When we teach a child to play a musical instrument, we teach her how to listen.
When we teach a child to dance, we teach him how to move through life with grace.
When we teach a child to read and write, we teach her how to think.
When we nurture imagination, we create a better world, one child at a time.

—Jane Alexander, Imagine

In 1988, the International Association for the Evaluation of Educational Achievement conducted a test to evaluate the science proficiency of fourteen-year-olds throughout the world. Seventeen countries participated. The United States came in fourteenth out of the seventeen countries. This is a dismal result considering we spend twenty-nine times more on math and science programs than any other country in the world.

According to the Association, the top three countries were Hungary, Japan, and the Netherlands, respectively. What do these countries offer in their schools that we don't? For one thing—training in music and the arts! Extensive music training is part of the curriculum beginning in kindergarten and continuing through high school. The music programs in these countries are impressive and appear to be the reason for their high achievement in math and science.

Music has been in Hungarian schools for 1,100 years. Their programs are both extensive and comprehensive because Hungarians believe that music is the heart and soul of a child's education. In Hungary, there are two different schools. In the regular schools, students have music lessons twice a week and choral rehearsals once a week. They also offer Music Elementary schools where students are tested in their musical abilities before being accepted. In these schools, music is offered every day and students have the opportunity to learn an instrument. The music curriculum also includes listening skills, improvisation and composition, reading and writing, memorization, and harmonization.[1] Additionally, Budapest has many excellent music conservatories and private music schools to accommodate the budding musicians produced by the public schools. Here, students can receive further training in solfege, orchestra, chamber music, ear training, reading and writing music, and playing selected percussion instruments.

Hungarian educators strongly believe that there is a direct correlation between music, math, and science. They believe that music helps children to think logically and critically, and that the process of learning music builds character and develops the "whole" person.

The Japanese, also recognizing the value of music in the curricula, sought to improve their programs by studying the music system of the Hungarians, whom they considered leaders in the field. They visited Hungary to learn more about their school music programs. A report issued in 1987 by the U.S. Department of Education, *U.S. Study of Education in Japan*, shows the results of the Japanese quest to improve their music and art curricula:[2]

- Each year in grades one through six, students are required to take two class periods a week in music, art, and handicrafts.

- Music includes singing, instrumental performance, and appreciation of both western and Japanese music.

- Development of artistic skills in drawing, painting, printmaking, and sculpture is required.

- In seventh and eighth grade, two courses per week are required in music and fine arts. In ninth grade, one course per week in each of these disciplines is required.

- In middle school, students sing in a chorus and play musical instruments in an ensemble.

- Students learn classical Japanese music; world folk songs; and classical, modern western, and Japanese orchestral and solo music.

- Basic music theory and history are studied, as well as painting, sculpture, and graphic design.

- In grades ten and eleven, students are required to take classes in calligraphy and music.

Frank Hodsoll, former chairman of the National Endowment for the Arts, said of the Japanese system, "I don't think anyone would doubt that the Japanese educational system . . . has produced one of the most productive work forces in the world. And music, art, and literature have been integral to that system."[3]

Schools in the Netherlands also boast strong music and arts programs. In 1968, art and music became mandatory subjects in Dutch secondary schools. By 1976, the arts became a part of the testing system that determined whether students qualified for college. A very specific and extensive curriculum was developed after the tests were devised. (It is usually the other way around: curriculum first, tests second.) The final examination includes a detailed history of the arts, analyzing works of art and music, and a portfolio of the student's own creative works. Finally, students are assigned a comprehensive music and arts subject and given twenty-eight days to produce a portfolio of drawings, notes, and a project.[4]

Demonstrating the strong link between music, math and science, in the 1994 to 1995 school year, seniors in the Netherlands came in first in the general mathematics category and second in the general sciences on the Third International Mathematics and Science Study, billed as the most comprehensive international study of academic achievement, ever.[5] Clearly, one could conclude that the reason for the academic success of these countries is their music and arts programs. Some might still question, though, does music really make a difference in the educational process, and if so, has it been proven through research? The answer, of course, is a resounding, yes!

Some might still question, though, does music really make a difference in the educational process, and if so, has it been proven through research? The answer, of course, is a resounding, yes!

The Evidence

Hundreds of studies have been conducted to show the significant role music plays in brain development and in the education of our children. In the book *Handbook of Music Psychology*, more than 400 studies on music are reviewed in one chapter alone.[6] In 1987, Jeanne Akin wrote *Music Makes a Difference: Resource Guide to Educational Research*, published by the Lafayette Arts and Science Foundation. In this Master's thesis, she compiled many studies that show how music education helps children learn in school. To illustrate how extensive these studies are, here is a partial list:[7]

- Arts education leads to cognitive and basic skills development. (Medeja, 1978)

- Brain research shows that music and the arts develop the intellect. (Sinatra, 1986)

- Physical, mental, emotional, and social development is faster when students learn a musical instrument. (Mueller, 1984)

- Singing sight words to kindergarten children helped them to learn the words much faster than those children learning the words without the teacher singing them. (Blackburn, 1986)

- Kindergarten students' basic skills achievement scores increased when music was added to the curriculum. (Minicucci, 1981)

- Music accelerates learning. First graders learn to read and write within a few weeks when learning lessons to music. (Delehanty, 1982)

- The reading achievement test scores of students rose dramatically when music was included in the curriculum. (Learning, 1980)

- In reading for meaning, music students outperformed non-music students. (Friedman, 1959)

- Students who study a keyboard instrument score higher in mathematics and history than those who do not. (ESEA, 1969)

- Studying a musical instrument can lead to increased learning in mathematics. (Maltester, 1986)

- Listening skills improve for students involved in music education. (Kohanski, 1970)

- Learning a foreign language is accelerated when music accompaniment is used. (Ostrander & Schroder, 1979)

- Grade point average is higher for high school students studying a musical instrument than non-musician students in the same school. (Horne, 1983)

- Forty percent of the Westinghouse Science Talent Search winners were accomplished musicians, showing that music helps the development of additional achievement skills. (State of California, 1986)

- Relaxing music helps children perform better on standardized achievement tests. (Moon, 1985)

- Fifth-graders enrolled in instrumental music classes in public schools in Albuquerque, New Mexico, scored higher in all areas on CTBS tests than those students not enrolled in music. The longer they studied a musical instrument the better they did. (Robitaille & O'Neal, 1981)

When the arts are included in the curriculum, learning is significantly enhanced. As evidence linking the arts to learning continues to mount, some researchers are referring to the arts as the "Fourth R."[8] Eric Oddleifson said, "Teaching arts every day in the core curriculum of elementary schools is the single most powerful tool presently available to educators to motivate students, enhance learning, and develop higher-order thinking skills."[9]

There are striking examples of academic success in United States schools where music and the arts are an integral part of the learning process. In these schools, the arts do not take priority over reading, writing, math, or science, but are skillfully integrated into the basic curriculum, as well as being taught as separate subjects. The result in the majority of cases is increased achievement in all subject areas. Let's look at some of these schools across the nation that are experiencing success with an arts-based program.

- The Davidson School in Augusta, Georgia, is considered one of the top schools scholastically in the nation. It is a fully integrated 50 percent white, and 50 percent African-American school with grades five through twelve. In 1981, music and the arts were added to the curriculum. The students in fifth grade spend one-and-a-half hours a day in instruction in the arts. By the time they enter high school, students spend up to 25 percent of the day studying the arts. The school has a waiting list of hundreds.

- The Ashley River School in Charleston, South Carolina, is a kindergarten through eighth-grade school. This magnet school, which has successfully integrated music and the arts into the curriculum, is an example of the far-reaching effects of music on learning. Nearly one-third of the student body has learning disabilities, yet they maintain a high scholastic record. School officials believe this is because of the music and arts programs offered in the school. It is ranked second academically in the city and the county, despite the fact that it is located in one of the city's poorest areas. Ashley River has a waiting list of 1,200 students. As an outgrowth to Ashley River, the school district started Charleston County School of the Arts (grades six through twelve) for students wishing to continue their arts education along with other academic pursuits.

- In 1992, the Commonwealth of Massachusetts tested all fourth-graders for basic skills and critical-thinking skills. The school that finished the highest in the state was John Eliot School in Needham. Although many of the students attending there are economically disadvantaged, nearly 75 percent of the students study a musical instrument through the school music program. All children in the fourth and fifth grade are in the choir. Principal Miriam Kronish uses artists-in-residence to complement a growing arts program in her school. She states, "When people ask what is the most important subject that we teach, I say it's music."[10]

- Key School in Indianapolis, Indiana, is possibly the best elementary school in the country, according to the National Education Association. Started by an art teacher, this kindergarten through fifth-grade school offers a superior education for all children, using arts as the vehicle.

- Concord Elementary School is located in one of the less affluent areas of Seattle, Washington, yet every student from kindergarten through fifth grade takes part in a dramatic performance each year that includes music. The plays focus on cultural diversity and non-violence and include *Beauty and the Beast*, *The Wizard of Oz*, *The Phantom Toll Booth*, and Shakespeare's *The Tempest*. The school has four stages to accommodate the full schedule of rehearsals and performances. Housed on the grounds of the school is also a set of "America's Hall of Fame" showing historical scenes of the contributions of a diversified collection of American leaders, including Harriet Tubman and Rosa Parks. The fourth- and fifth-grade students run a daily in-house television program, *Eco-News*. Principal Claudia Allen believes that arts have significantly contributed to the increase of test scores. She states she is seeing "incredible achievement, especially in reading skills. Fourth- and fifth-grade students increased their reading scores by two levels on the Macmillan Reading Inventory from fall to winter quarter 1995 to 1996, and California Test of Basic Skills scores have increased by twenty to twenty-five points."[11]

- Kellogg Elementary in Chula Vista, California, is found in a low- to middle-class neighborhood, but its students consistently rank in the top quartile nationally in math, reading, and writing. Not surprisingly, it also is the district's Creative and Performing Arts Magnet School. Teachers report that the students' creative problem-solving abilities are strong and their self-esteem is high. Kellogg has a dazzling curriculum and integrates the arts into all areas. Students receive training in dance, drama, voice, instrumental music, and art from professional artists and teachers. The school boasts a 240-piece band and orchestra, and kindergartners receive keyboard training. All students receive instruction from a professional ceramist, and fourth through sixth grades receive scenic art instruction from a set designer, thus learning the creative process as performers, artists, and technicians. Other subjects are learned more easily at Kellogg because the arts are integrated into the curriculum, with lessons taught by using an art activity as the vehicle to understand the topic. It is an education program that works![12]

- Thomas Jefferson High School for Science and Technology in Alexandria, Virginia, is a magnet school with a national reputation for consistent high achievement. The most prestigious colleges and universities seek its graduates. The school has an extensive art and music program with senior projects such as "Computer Arrangement of Twelfth-Century Choral Music through an Artificially Intelligent Knowledge-Based System" the norm. Principal Jeffrey Jones expresses his philosophy of the importance of educating the whole person: "In order to be a good scientist, one must also be a good humanist. The arts and humanities are as richly evident as the sciences in this school."[13]

- Fort Hayes Arts and Academic High School in Columbus, Ohio, is a fusion of arts magnet and academic magnet, where students take intensive college prep and advanced placement classes and intensive music and art classes. The philosophy of Fort Hayes is that there are many types of intelligence and creativity, and that both are central to life and learning. The school also has received national recognition—*Redbook* selected the Fort Hayes Metropolitan Education Center as one of the fifty best high schools in the country in 1991 to 1992 and 1993 to 1994.[14]

Of the many success stories of schools using arts-based education, perhaps one of the most remarkable is that of the Sacred Heart/Mount Carmel School located on the south side of Mount Vernon in New York. It is an inspiring story of how music and the arts can change the lives of students, and how the perseverance and hard work of educators can dramatically change a community.

Principal Katherine Damkohler was struggling with declines in enrollment and low morale in the community. The school was heading toward closing its doors forever. In fall 1987, Damkohler and her staff decided to integrate art and music into the classrooms, after studying the positive research on how the arts help in the learning process. They began the year with a fledgling music and arts program. Their goal was to expose the students to music and art through simple classroom projects and choral music.

In fall 1991, representatives of Education Through Music, a nonprofit organization that brings the arts into economically disadvantaged schools, approached Damkohler. They wanted to use her school as a test site for integrating music, the arts, and academics. In January 1992, the school and the organization entered into a partnership, and the school was able to add a choral director, dance instructor, and piano and violin classes. Dalcroze Eurhythmics and recorder classes were added to their early childhood program. Damkohler, who holds a master's degree in curriculum planning, wrote the arts into the curriculum without sacrificing any of the basics.

In just one year, the administrators and teachers noticed a positive change in the students. Self-esteem was increasing, and attitudes toward school were changing for the better. Enthusiastic and excited about what was happening, teachers gave hours of after-school time to come up with creative ideas and to share thoughts on ways to infuse music and the arts into social studies, science, reading, and math. But they didn't stop there. The teachers spent their weekends scouring flea markets for art supplies, tape recorders, and books on music. Students and teachers were excited about what was happening at their school. The success was overwhelming. After four years, reading and math scores went from 25 percent of the students performing at grade level to 75 percent performing at grade level and above.

In May 1994, two years after changing its name, Sacred Heart/Mount Carmel School for the Arts won a National Blue Ribbon Award, distinguishing itself out of some 55,000 elementary and middle schools nationwide. At that time, the Juilliard School of Music piloted an outreach program at Sacred Heart/Mount Carmel by bringing graduate students to work in the classrooms. Says Damkohler, "We didn't have the resources to add a new math, reading, or science program—the only real change was the addition and integration of the arts!"[15]

Because of her tremendous enthusiasm for the program, she was asked to join Education Through Music, where she is now the executive director. The organization now serves almost 5,000 children in eleven schools in the greater New York area. It continues to be an enormous success as it touches the lives of children through music and the arts.

The Arts-Integrated School: How Children Learn Through the Arts

One of the biggest breakthroughs in education came in the early 1980s. The work of psychologist Howard Gardner gave educators and parents a greater understanding about intelligence and how children learn. In his book *Frames of Mind*, he introduced his "Theory of Multiple Intelligences." Until Gardner's research, educators believed that children are born with a fixed intelligence that is measured through an IQ test. Not so, said Gardner, there are *many* ways to be intelligent. Originally he identified seven different areas of intelligence and said that these seven areas develop at different times and to different degrees in different individuals.[16] He later identified an eighth intelligence, that of the naturalist. We have within us capabilities of all eight types of intelligence. Contrary to the fixed or predetermined intelligence notion of the past, we have a tremendous capacity for learning a variety of things throughout our lives. The possibilities are enormous in terms of what we can accomplish!

Contrary to the fixed or predetermined intelligence notion of the past, we have a tremendous capacity for learning a variety of things throughout our lives. The possibilities are enormous in terms of what we can accomplish!

The bad news is, schools only reward two of the types of intelligence identified by Gardner: the verbal/linguistic and logical/mathematical. Six other areas are equally important, but are not necessarily acknowledged in school. They include musical, bodily/kinesthetic, visual/spatial, interpersonal, intrapersonal, and naturalist. The good news is that musical intelligence is so powerful that by learning a musical instrument and studying the arts, the other seven types of intelligence can be developed at the same time. Speaking to this idea, Eric Oddleifson says, "Music education at the elementary school level appears to be a necessary ingredient for children to realize their potential in mathematics and reading. Visual arts appear to be necessary for children to realize their potential in science. Similarly, other arts, such as creative writing, dance, or drama, appear to be necessary for development of one's abilities to fully express oneself, whether in writing or in interpersonal communications, both of which are requisite for being an effective member of a highly technological society."[17]

The chart on pages 140–143 identifies the eight types of intelligence and how they relate to music and the arts. (The definition of the "arts" includes the disciplines of music, the visual arts, drama, dance, and creative writing.)

Gardner's work and theories have dramatically shown that music may help children learn more and more readily, beyond the limited contexts in which their musical intelligence is generally put to use.

How do children learn? Primarily by hearing, seeing, doing, or a combination of the three. Lynn O'Brien of Specific Diagnostic Studies showed through research that students who are auditory learners, or those who learn by *hearing* information, comprise only 15 percent of the population. And yet, lecturing is the most popular way of teaching in our 16,000 school districts nationwide. Students who are visual learners are those who learn by *seeing*. They need diagrams, charts, graphs, or pictures to understand the information. They comprise 40 percent of the population. Brain research shows that the visual cortex of the brain is five times larger than the auditory cortex.[18] In other words, it is already established in the brain that a child is able to learn more easily and more effectively by *seeing* a picture of a dinosaur rather than just hearing about one. Those students who need to *touch, feel, experiment,* or *move* to understand information comprise 45 percent of the population. To personalize these types of learning, ask yourself, "Could I learn to use the computer by *hearing* someone lecture on it? Would I understand it better if I drew a detailed picture of a computer and its operations? Or, would I understand the computer best by sitting down and actually working on it?" Most of us would have a difficult time learning how to operate a computer just by hearing about its many functions. But by drawing a detailed picture of a computer, using a computer, or building a mock computer, we would learn to use the computer!

The Eight Types of Intelligence

Intelligence	Definition	
Verbal/Linguistic	Uses words well; enjoys writing, reading; good at entertaining through the spoken word.	
Logical/Math	Love numbers, are logical, able to reason, sequence, see pattern relationships.	
Visual/Spatial	Visualize in pictures and images. Able to create what they mentally see, good at drawing, sketching in detail, understand three-dimensional space.	
Bodily/Kinesthetic	Aware of their body, have control over their body movements. Able to use their hands hands skillfully.	
Interpersonal	Able to work with and understand other people. Good team players. Able to view the world from another's perspective.	
Intrapersonal	Know and understand who they are; aware of their feelings, emotions. They enjoy meditation, contemplation. They are self-disciplined, independent, goal-oriented.	
Musical	Understand and produce melodies, rhythms. Can sing in tune, enjoy music, play a musical instrument.	

How intelligence relates to music and the arts
Students involved in drama learn to express themselves, memorize lines, and speak in front of an audience. Creative writers use the written word to articulate thoughts and ideas.
When learning music students also learn fractions, ratios, pattern relationships, sequencing and repetitions. Children learn to count the correct beats in a measure, identify patterns and repetitions of a musical theme, and understand different forms of music, (rondo form, etc.). Music strengthens understanding of certain concepts of math.
Spatial intelligence is increased when studying a musical instrument. They mentally see in pictures and visual images. Are able to physically reconstruct their visual world. Artists constructing a mural understand spatial relationships to get it proportionally balanced. Drama students use spatial skills in staging a dramatic performance.
Dancing increases physical coordination, dexterity, and development of large and small muscles as children move their bodies to the music. Artists and craftsmen use their hands to create artistic masterpieces. Students playing musical instruments learn finger and arm dexterity and movement.
In orchestra, drama, and dance, students learn the importance of teamwork. They interact with one another and thrive on their involvement with their peers. Orchestra members must cooperate and listen to each other to play successfully together. Drama students work together painting scenery or performing a play. The artist critiques another's artwork, etc.
In the creation process artists are independent thinkers and creators. A musician independently composes music. Artists "find" themselves through individual expression of their artwork. Through the process of studying music and the arts students come to "know thyself."
Helps a child in reading and mathematics. Stimulates creativity, imagination. Helps in learning foreign languages, memorization of facts, retention of ideas. Children think more clearly and more critically by studying a musical instrument.

continued

The Eight Types of Intelligence *(continued)*

Intelligence	Definition	
Naturalist	Are sensitive to the natural world and enjoy spending time outdoors. They notice relationships in nature and see connections and patterns within the plant and animal kingdoms.	

So, how do music and the arts incorporate these three ways of learning? Simply put, children use their hands, feet, eyes, ears, and sometimes mouth as they learn a musical instrument. All of the senses are being utilized as they hear, see, and touch the instrument. Learning a musical instrument involves the entire brain and helps in its total development and organization. The result: the child retains information and can transfer learning to other subjects.

Another example of how the arts incorporate the three ways of learning is found in Anne Green Gilbert's book *Teaching the Three R's Through Movement.* She is the director of Kaleidoscope, a modern dance company of young people, and has shown how music, movement, and dance are the keys to learning. Gilbert taught her third grade class to spell by forming the letters with their bodies. The children expressed the feeling of sentences and punctuation marks through movement. They learned multiplication by moving in sets of threes and fours, discovered the difference between lunar and solar eclipses through planet dances, and choreographed their way across the Oregon Trail. Later, through a federally funded grant, she recorded the progress of 250 students from four elementary schools as they studied language arts using movement, music, and dance. She studied the

---

How intelligence relates to music and the arts

These individuals find the sounds in nature—birds, wind, rushing water, rain, thunder, and so on—music-like. (Many CDs have been made using the sounds of nature.) They find art expressed in nature through the changing of the seasons and the varying size, shape, and colors of plants, animals, clouds, and oceans. Through their lenses, outdoor photographers see art and beauty in the earth's natural surroundings. Artists find the varying patterns of natural objects perfect for creating artistic pieces. Musicians find patterns and themes in a fugue, symphony, and so on.

---

students for twenty weeks and found that these third-grade students increased their MAT scores (standardized tests) by 13 percent from fall to spring, while the district-wide average showed a *decrease* of 2 percent. Gilbert made a most significant observation in the research: She found a direct relationship between the amount of movement the classroom teacher used and the percentage increase in the students' test scores.[19]

Arts-based education is a "win-win" situation because a child involved in music and the arts increases her ability to learn and understand other subjects. Let's elaborate by comparing a traditional approach to the teaching of a social studies unit with an arts-based approach.

In a traditional classroom, children learn about Native Americans by listening to lectures full of facts and figures. Worksheets with fill-in-the-blanks and pictures to color are provided for students to organize and put into neat little notebooks. Over the years, many parents have seen dozens of these books that their children have brought home. Overall, this is a lifeless experience with very little learning. Children need a stimulating environment with active participation in order to learn, process, and understand information. A classroom such as this falls short of providing such an environment.

By contrast, in an arts-based classroom, students learn by using all of their senses. They learn Native American songs and dances. Students weave small rugs on a loom and use interesting materials to create Native American–style jewelry and costumes.

In an arts-based classroom, students learn by using all of their senses.

Native American facts and sign language are learned to the rhythmic beat of a drum. They create dioramas of native life, dramatize legends, and cook traditional dishes. Imagination, creativity, and enthusiastic interest are the basis for this hands-on experience.

"Whew," say teachers. "There is no way we can do all that. It's impractical, there's not enough time, and look at the size of our classes! We definitely don't have enough money and what about the diversity of the kids?" are typical remarks heard from some teachers. To teachers who voice comments like this, I say there *is* a way, as shown by the work of the dedicated Sacred Heart staff.

The arts-based classroom is not some new, impractical brainchild of educators who never set foot in the classroom. For years, dedicated, intelligent teachers have been instinctively teaching to all the senses by providing varied and motivating hands-on learning experiences for their students. Elizabeth Kristensen of Salt Lake City, Utah, received such learning experiences thirty-five years ago in a public school in a class of thirty or more students. She recalls that the class had to *make* their looms before they could weave a rug. Using vegetables, they made dyes and colored macaroni to create native necklaces. Oatmeal boxes were brought from home to make drums. To the syncopating rhythm of a beating drum, the children chanted facts about Native American life. They made salt dough and used assorted beans and rice to create dioramas and relief maps. After learning native dances and songs, the children put together a program that their parents came to see. She remembers that her class learned Longfellow's famous poem *Hiawatha*, and of course, each day the teacher read to them exciting stories about Native American boys and girls. This was not a preschool setting, either—she was in the third grade—and most of her elementary years were filled with experiences like this. There are still many dedicated and wonderful teachers in schools across the nation who provide these kinds of experiences for their students, but they are the exception, not the rule. If you want this kind of teaching for your child, *you* need to provide it for them with activities like hands-on classes offered at many museums.

The studies and stories are overwhelmingly convincing that infusing music and the arts into the curriculum enhances a child's individual learning style, and when children learn through their strengths, learning and processing information is easier and more effective. For example, second-grade teacher Ana Infante in Gardena, California, uses songs and dances—a "reader's theater"—to teach her culturally diverse class how to speak and read in English. She does not consider music and the arts an "extra," but rather an important part of their education. She says, "It's not just singing and dancing. There's a lot of instruction going on. We use the arts as a vehicle for delivering our instructions. By putting it into a script, the kids develop fluency, reading with expression, vocabulary, and vocabulary sequencing."[20]

Marylin Leinenbach, a sixth-grade teacher at Chauncey Rose Middle School in Terre Haute, Indiana, and a Disney American Teacher Award winner uses rap music to teach multiplication tables and musical notes to teach fractions.[21] Randy Grant's third-period American literature and composition class at Fairfax High School in Los Angeles uses opera to teach multiculturalism, racial stereotypes, and history. Recently, his class attended a performance of *Madama Butterfly* sponsored by the L. A. Opera's program for high schools. The students in his class are a diverse group from Russia, the Ukraine, Korea, Guatemala, and El Salvador.[22] Barbara Harris, a teacher of second-graders at Vena

Avenue Elementary in Arleta, California, combines the piano, autoharp, and dulcimer to teach her students history. They learn "Pick a Bale of Cotton" to understand slavery, "When Johnny Comes Marching Home" to learn about the Civil War, and "Yankee Doodle Dandy" when studying the Revolutionary War.[23]

Debbie Meyer is the music specialist at Banting Elementary in Waukesha, Wisconsin, a school that boasts a very sophisticated choral music program for grades four through six. Meyer works closely with the classroom teachers to musically complement the social studies curriculum for students in the first through sixth grades. For example, students in first, second, and third grade study world cultures while learning songs in Japanese, Hawaiian, Spanish, Italian, French, German, Hebrew, Chinese, Latin, and African languages. Fourth graders learn Native American songs and Canadian music to enhance their understanding of Native Americans. Fifth-graders learn songs and dances to complement units on the westward expansion, the Civil War, and the United States. Sixth-graders studying the Medieval and Renaissance periods learn authentic dances from these periods—circle dances, bransle, and estampie dances. They learn "Greensleeves," a popular Renaissance-era tune and, utilizing higher-order thinking skills, compare and contrast Vaughn Williams's arrangement to the original piece. The students learn recorder music by Claude Gervaise and watch Ars Antigua's video *Sounds of a Distant Tyme* to see firsthand early Renaissance music played with authentic instruments of the period. The unit ends with a dazzling Medieval Christmas Concert, in which students, dressed in authentic-style costumes, sing, dance, and play instruments reminiscent of the era. Meyer says, "Using music to enhance what students learn in the classroom, and watching them perform at our yearly concerts, I have seen a remarkable increase in the students' level of confidence, their poise, and their ability to express themselves. I have also seen this carry over into other areas of their education. My goal has been to help my students become persistent risk-takers, to work beyond their grade level 'expectations.' My students and their families readily acknowledge that I teach more than musical skills. I've given them the recipe for living a more meaningful and success-filled life." In 1998, Meyer was honored by Senator Kohl as one of the top 100 teachers in the state of Wisconsin.

> *Learning through music and the arts not only allows the child to develop all of the types of intelligence that lie within her, but also allows the child to express her uniqueness as a person, thereby promoting a strong inner confidence and self-worth.*

Learning through music and the arts not only allows the child to develop all of the types of intelligence that lie within her, but also allows the child to express her uniqueness as a person, thereby promoting a strong inner confidence and self-worth.

How Music and the Arts Help Children with Learning Disabilities

Many children have learning disabilities. Some are unable to read, write, spell, do math, or pay attention in class. The numbers seem to be growing each year. Unfortunately, many of these children slip through the cracks and are still struggling academically when they reach high school and even college. As a parent, I have had firsthand experience with learning disabilities in children. In the discussion of this problem, I prefer to use the term that many experts in the field use, which is learning *differences* and not disabilities. Learning differences indicates to me that the child is not disabled, but rather needs to learn in ways that are not necessarily taught in school.

In my experience, I have found that the arts, particularly music, can make a profound difference in the way these children process information. Our third son, Brandon, was diagnosed in kindergarten with auditory discrimination, visual motor, visual perception, sensory motor, and attention deficit disorder. The difference between his oral IQ and written IQ was thirty-eight points, indicating severe learning "disabilities." Brandon was considered high risk. This meant that as he got older, he could be a candidate for dropping out of school, experimenting with drugs, or worse. Why? Because kids need a measure of academic success. They are in school many hours each day, and they need to feel good about their abilities to learn. He needed to experience some kind of school success to increase his confidence level. But how do you help a child achieve academic success when he can't read, write, spell; doesn't understand even the simplest of math concepts; and sports confuse and frustrate him?

It was a challenge, and as a parent I was worried that I would not be able to meet the challenge. I didn't know the first thing about learning "disabilities," but I was determined to find out and to help him.

We enrolled Brandon in a number of specific programs outside school to help him with these various problems. We also utilized the services of educational therapists and tutors. Each night, a minimum of three hours was spent with the simplest of homework assignments. We used musical games, rhymes, and songs to help him learn the material. Knowing the importance of music to brain development, we continued to play classical music for him day and night and enrolled him in several group music classes. I was convinced that parts of his brain, rather than malfunctioning, were in need of the kind of exercise that one gets from studying a musical instrument.

When Brandon turned eight, he started taking private piano lessons. It was a painstaking process as he and I sat at the piano learning the notes and their location on the keyboard. Each day brought new challenges. He was unable to remember from day to day where middle C was on the piano—or any of the other notes, for that matter. The spatial arrangement of the lines and spaces of the music was most confusing for him. Putting an orange dot on middle C and pointing to the note on the music page, and then pointing to the same note on the piano helped him make the association. Having read stories about Albert Einstein and Thomas Edison, and knowing how music helped their so-called learning challenges, I persevered. As he slowly gained proficiency with his music, his reading, math, and spelling improved, as well.

Brandon is now a junior in high school. Academically, he is doing extremely well. He was on the honor roll the last three years of middle school and his first two years of high school. He just completed Liszt's *Hungarian Rhapsody No. 2* and the first movement of Beethoven's *Moonlight Sonata*. His music teacher, understanding the vast difficulties he has had, remarked to me the other day, "If you were bringing Brandon to me for the first time and I heard him play the piano like he plays now, I would say that you have a very musically gifted child!" Remarkably, his teachers in school do not even recognize that he has learning differences. Although it has been a difficult process, we feel Brandon is a success story. *Many* things have contributed to his success—music being a very important one. Music *can* make a difference!

Stacie Zimmerman, at age five, was diagnosed with learning disabilities in basic reading, writing, and math, had poor motor skills, and was only able to use one eye at a time. School was a daily struggle, but her home was filled with music and her mother taught her piano and singing when she was very young. When she turned eight, she started taking violin lessons. At thirteen, she was again tested at the local university, and the results astounded the psychologists. Her memory, writing, and reading skills were higher than her IQ indicated they should be, her ability to recognize sound patterns was excellent, and most important, she demonstrated an unusually high level of confidence and sociability for a thirteen year old, with or without learning and physical challenges. Additionally, they were amazed that she was able to play the violin and piano—two instruments requiring strong motor coordination. Even the psychologists could see that Stacie's extensive training in music had helped her to overcome many of her learning difficulties.[24]

Mark Jordan, a teacher at Samuel Gompers Elementary School in Chicago, related the following story at a Music Educators National Conference in Chicago.

"One of the teachers was complaining about one of the band kids who was having a problem with fractions. She wanted to pull her from the band program. When I asked if the child could use any aids during the next exam, she said, "Calculators are out!"

I asked, "How about pie pans?"

She gave me a strange look, but said, "Okay."

A long time before, I'd gone to one of the bakers in the city and he gave me a lot of pie pans. So when I teach the breakdown of musical notation, it's the same thing as fractions, but I teach it with the pie pans—a whole note is a whole pan, a half-note is half a pan, and so on. I told the math teacher, if you let this child take the test with the pie pans on her desk, she'll pass. She did, too. With an A!"[25]

Children who have difficulty learning in traditional ways are usually able to learn through exposure to music and the arts. The following are some additional examples taken from studies of how music helps children who have difficulty learning in the traditional ways.[26]

- More than 13,000 educationally deprived children in forty-three schools learned to read when music and other related arts were included in the curriculum. (ESEA, 1969)

- When handicapped children in the Clover Park School District in Tacoma, Washington, were taught basic academic skills through music, they were consistently able to learn more easily. Music helped in teaching them perceptual skills. (Appell & Goldberg, 1979)

- Dr. Lassar Golkin brought music games into schools to help teach academic skills. Children who were unable to learn in a traditional school setting were able to learn the skills set to musical games. (Hillery, 1979)

- Research shows that slow learners who learn to read music also improve in their language reading abilities. Music is so effective in teaching reading that teachers are encouraged to include music in their reading lessons. (Tucker, 1981)

- The hand-eye coordination skills that are necessary to write are enhanced and developed by learning to play a musical instrument. (Wishey, 1980)

- "Different Ways of Knowing" was a three-year program for high-risk elementary students that focused on using the arts to teach. Elementary students with one year in the program gained eight percentile points on standardized language arts tests; students with two years in the program gained sixteen percentile points; and students not in the program showed no percentile gain. Students with three years in the program outscored non-program students with considerably higher report card grades in the core subject areas of language arts, math, reading, and social studies. A total of 920 students in fifty-two classrooms in Los Angeles, south Boston, and Cambridge, Massachusetts, were studied in this program.[27]

- Fifth-grade remedial readers using creative drama as a learning strategy, scored consistently higher on the Metropolitan Reading Comprehension Test.[28]

Music and the arts also can help a child behaviorally, with personal growth, and can be the motivating factor in keeping them in school. In 1995, an interesting report from the U.S.

Department of Education, *Schools, Communities, and the Arts: A Research Compendium*, found that "using arts processes to teach academic subjects results not only in improved understanding of content, but it greatly improved self-regulatory behavior."

Barry Oreck of ArtsConnection and Susan Baum from the College of New Rochelle observed an integration of the arts into major subjects in fourteen New York elementary and secondary public schools. They found that "student behavior improved strikingly in such areas as taking risks, cooperating, solving problems, taking initiative for learning, and being prepared. Content-related achievement also rose."[29]

Jo Ann Hood, a music teacher speaking at the Nashville Forum for the National Commission for Music Education tells of her experiences: "I have found, during my eighteen years of teaching, that music students tend to score better on tests, have better communication skills, and are better disciplined students. They tend to be more prepared for the work force and are more readily hired by businesses. I have also seen several instances where *music kept a student in school who would have otherwise dropped out* [emphasis added]."[30] Keeping young people in school is not only important to their educational future, but it becomes an economic issue as well. For example, in Los Angeles, 85 percent of all daytime crime is committed by truant young people. The yearly cost of truancy to the nation is $228 billion. Later, when these young people get jobs, it costs the business community approximately $30 billion to train these workers in the basic subjects of reading, writing, and mathematics.[31]

An example of music motivating students to stay in school by increasing inner confidence in their academic abilities is illustrated by the following stories.

Allison Baker was the victim of extreme domestic violence that left one parent dead and the other in jail. She was being raised by extended family in a home where she was surrounded by frequent drug users. With the overwhelming stress and pressure, Allison was ready to quit school. Fortunately, her neighborhood school offered an extensive music and arts program as part of the curricula. She found that she loved to dance and became involved in the school's classical ballet program. Her involvement with dance gave structure and meaning to her life. It was through the movement of ballet that Allison was able to express her deepest, most personal feelings. This classical ballet program literally saved her life, and she is the first to tell you so. After graduating with honors from high school, she went on to attend Columbia University, where she enrolled in the premedical program.[32] Music and the arts made a difference!

For several years, Sue Levy was on the scholarship committee at her son's high school. One year, her interest was piqued by the application of a young man whose 2.8 grade point average was much lower than the other students applying for the scholarships. She was curious as to why he even applied. His story is amazing—and once again illustrates the power of music education.

As a sophomore, Travis Johnson was failing every subject. He was very discouraged and was ready to quit school. Although he was a member of the band, he was playing the clarinet—an instrument he disliked. The kids in the low brass section needed a tuba player and talked him into switching instruments. This seemingly minor change was instrumental in his subsequent success—not only in music, but also in his other academic subjects. His experience with the tuba changed his perspective on school and what he wanted to do with his life. While learning to play the tuba, his confidence began to increase, as well as his interest in school. His grades began to soar, he became the student band president, as well as a leader in his other classes, and he began making plans to go to college. Although his GPA was low in comparison to the other applicants, this was a success story that needed to be rewarded. The committee wanted to see him go on to college, and he received one of the scholarships. Later, he became a walk-on tuba player in the marching band at a major university and worked as assistant bandleader at a local high school. Music made a difference!

Music can also make a difference for young people who come from homes where the income and parent education levels are low. In 1998, James Catterall, professor of education and codirector of the UCLA Imagination Project, conducted a study of eighth- through twelfth-grade students that showed a connection between participation in the arts and academic achievement. The study focused on the relationship between sustained involvement in instrumental music and mathematics achievement, and theater arts and human development.

The researchers found that low SES students who took music lessons from eighth through twelfth grade, increased their test scores in math and scored significantly higher than those of low SES students who were not involved in music.

Of particular interest to the researchers were students from low socioeconomic status (SES). The researchers found that low SES students who took music lessons from eighth through twelfth grade, increased their test scores in math and scored significantly higher than those of low SES students who were not involved in music. In addition, low SES students involved in the arts generally scored higher than their non-involved counterparts in reading, history, geography, and citizenship. For example, math scores more than doubled for the low SES students taking instrumental music, and history and geography scores climbed by 40 percent.

Another area of interest to the researchers was in theater arts, which included acting in plays and musicals, participating in drama clubs, or taking acting lessons. Students involved in the theater arts scored higher in reading proficiency, self-concept, and motivation, and demonstrated higher levels of empathy and tolerance for others. In reading proficiency, the scores grew steadily from the eighth to twelfth grade. And by the twelfth grade, nearly 20 percent more of the low SES students involved in theater arts were reading at a high proficiency level than those not involved in the arts. The researchers believed that the results were due to the students spending so much time reading and learning lines as actors. The researchers concluded that music and the arts can be a catalyst for success for students in at-risk situations.[33]

If music has such a tremendous influence on a child's ability to learn, find success in school, overcome learning differences, and change their lives, why was it ever taken out of the schools in the first place? Certainly the studies have been out there long enough to prove the value of music education. Perhaps Frank Vellutino, a professor of educational psychology at State University of New York at Albany, hit on the answer when he said, "We do more education research than anyone else in the world, and we ignore more as well."[34]

The body of music research rarely has been used in most American classrooms. Why? According to Linda Darling-Hammond, professor of education at Columbia University's Teachers College, "In most states, neither teachers nor administrators are required to know much about how children learn in order to be certified."

"What's worse," she adds, "decisions to cut music or gym are often made by non-educators, whose concerns are more often monetary than educational. Our school system was invented in the late 1800s, and little has changed."[35]

We talk about changing curriculum and making more demands on students through higher expectations. Perhaps we should begin by making more demands on the education requirements of teachers. Teachers should be required to know and understand how children utilize the entire brain when learning music and the arts, be able to apply those techniques to their teaching, and become more educated in the arts. Linda Verlee Williams, in her book *Teaching for the Two-Sided Mind* says, "Children come to school as integrated people with thoughts and feelings, words and pictures, ideas and fantasies. They are intensely curious about the world. They are scientists, artists, musicians, historians, dancers, runners, tellers of stories, and mathematicians. The challenge we face as teachers is to use the wealth they bring us. They come with a two-sided mind. We must encourage them to use it . . . so that they have access to the fullest possible range of mental abilities."[36] Music and the arts teach both sides of the mind. Including these in the curricula can help teachers meet this challenge.

During the time of Aristotle and Plato, music was considered one of the four pillars of learning along with geometry, astronomy, and mathematics. In the late Middle Ages and throughout the Renaissance, when every educated person was expected to play an instrument and read musical notation, and some of mankind's most revered works of art were created; music and the arts flourished. In the periods that followed, the world's greatest musical compositions were written by musical giants such as Handel, Bach, Haydn, Mozart, and Beethoven. In this same period, music schools were conducted in orphanages. Orphans, abandoned children, and poor children received a complete music education, and some of these disadvantaged children became the most sought after vocalists and musicians in all of Europe.[37] Nearly every age throughout history has recognized music as essential to the learning process and, thus, an integral part of the education process. In this sophisticated technological age, can we consider it less?

Actor Richard Dreyfuss, the producer and star of the film, *Mr. Holland's Opus*, recognizes the far-reaching impact music has had on children through the ages. In a speech to the American Federation of Teachers, he said:

Mr. Holland's Opus was about a guy struggling to become a school teacher and a good person. But it was also about a larger debate within American society over what is valuable and important to us as a people. What touched people in the film, why they responded so strongly to it, points to certain fundamental values in America, certain aspirations and longings that are not currently being fulfilled, that we, in an odd way, have walked away from. Sure, parents want their kids to be able to go to college and get a good job, but that is not enough. They want teachers who help their kids to understand life and its meaning. They want them to understand who we are and how we should express our character in words and actions. And I believe people, as they watched this movie, unconsciously recognized the importance of a complete education, from math, science, and history, to art and music. Perhaps we've all misunderstood the reason we learn music, and all the arts, in the first place. It is not only so a student can learn the clarinet, or another student can take an acting lesson. It is that for hundreds of years it has been known that teaching the arts, along with history and math and biology, helps to create "The Well-Rounded Mind" that western civilization and America have been grounded on. America's greatest achievements—in science, in business, in popular culture—would simply not be attainable without an education that encourages achievement in all fields. We need that "Well-Rounded Mind" now. For it is from creativity and imagination that the solutions to our political and social problems will come.[38]

In 1991, the National Commission on Music Education, Growing Up Complete, presented a report to Congress and the Bush Administration that discussed the intrinsic value of arts in a well-balanced education. The report, *Growing Up Complete: The Imperative for Music Education* said, in part:

All manner of persons—philosophers and peasants, candle-makers and kings—have for centuries sought to understand the profound connection between music and emotional life, its power to both challenge and comfort, to enthrall and enthuse, to calm and arouse. Music can make us laugh, weep, and shout for joy; it can bring us to our feet or drive us to our knees. The fact that, in vast numbers of our schools, an educated understanding of this dimension of life is left to either lip service or chance is deeply disturbing. It is a form of dehumanization by default.[39]

$\mathscr{M}$ARCHING FORWARD: ANSWERS FOR A CHALLENGING TWENTY-FIRST CENTURY

The business leaders of tomorrow will need what the arts can give them. They need to see and hear and feel the world. They need to lead with vision and passion. And these are the characteristics our young people develop when they are encouraged to participate in the arts.

—Richard Gurin, former president and CEO, Binney & Smith

In the mid-1980s Motorola, Inc., began a Statistical Process Control (SPC) training program for their entire employee base. Their goals were to improve the quality of products, processes, and services offered by the company. A few weeks after the training was complete, it became apparent that the employees were not applying what they had been taught during the training process. After further investigation, it was discovered that the employees lacked basic reading and math skills needed to meet the company's goals. During the next five years, Motorola spent nearly $30 million on remedial education for thousands of their employees. They estimate that more than half of those workers received their education in the United States. Today, Motorola, Inc. no longer teaches basic skills to their employees. It is simply too expensive. Instead, they employ a screening process that tests future employees in basic seventh-grade math and ninth-grade reading skills. On the average, only one out of every two prospective employees passes the entry-level test of basic skills. The few who do pass are then interviewed to determine interpersonal skills, given a drug test, and another test to determine their proficiency in critical thinking, problem solving, and higher-level thinking skills. The result: only one out of every ten people qualifies.

"The problem we will face in the future," according to Brenda Sumberg, director of education system alliances at Motorola University, "is that skills in problem solving, critical thinking, team skills, and lifelong learning will be absolute requirements for employees to have in order for United States companies to remain competitive in a global marketplace." She continues, "Many students coming out of school lack these proficiencies. The competitive advantage is no longer software or hardware, but mindware, which is the ability to organize and reorganize patterns of thinking. It is estimated that people will change jobs between eight and ten times during a lifetime and, even though it may be with the same company, the requirements of their present job could change that often. We need lifelong learners, those who are willing and capable of learning new skills as the job requires."[1]

Motorola, Inc. is not the only corporation or business experiencing challenges in finding qualified employees. The *Wall Street Journal*, in a special article on the growing problems of education, reported that New York Telephone Company had openings for several hundred full-time positions; of the 117,000 applicants, fewer than half qualified to take the basic employee exam and, of those, only 2,100 passed. A bank manager for Security Pacific Corp. lamented that each year they interview people for entry-level teller jobs who can't add or subtract well enough to balance their own checkbooks.

"I'm almost taking anyone who breathes," he told a *Wall Street Journal* interviewer.[2] Pacific Bell has to screen up to seven applicants to find one high school graduate with the reading and math skills required to be a telephone operator.[3] Perhaps one of the reasons why businesses are having difficulty finding qualified workers becomes apparent when one considers a recent report released by the California State University (CSU) school system showing that more than two-thirds of the students entering the CSU system need remedial instruction in math or English. In some cases, three out of four freshmen needed remedial classes in math and English.[4]

Many believe that this is a serious problem that will undermine our ability to compete as a nation in a global marketplace unless effective educational changes are begun immediately.

Perhaps one of the reasons why businesses are having difficulty finding qualified workers becomes apparent when one considers a recent report released by the California State University (CSU) school system showing that more than two-thirds of the students entering the CSU system need remedial instruction in math or English.

Dr. Arthur Costa, president of the Association for Supervision and Curriculum Development warns, "We're facing a critical time in history. For our nation to survive, we have to realize that what's coming up is the smallest work force we've had in a long time; we've had a big population dip and our industries have a much smaller pool of talent. This small group is one of the most under-trained, with the largest number of dropouts. At the same time, industry has the greatest demand for problem solvers and thinkers, entrepreneurs, and craftsmen—creative people whose products are so excellent and whose thinking is so forward that we can match the other countries for survival. We're at a time of great competition for creativity and thinking—we've got to develop these skills in all our students."[5]

Finding Solutions

So, why aren't the schools developing these necessary skills in our students? What are the problems with the current methods employed in our present educational system that are producing the current under-trained work force? Examining these problems will answer these questions and help find a viable solution to this national dilemma.

First of all, to improve instructional practices, teachers need to be qualified to teach. A special report in the *Los Angeles Times* on "Why Our Schools Are Failing," stated that in California, more than 31,000 classrooms are taught by teachers who do not have teaching certificates and are still in the process of learning how to teach.[6] Individuals looking for career changes found it almost as easy to get a job teaching school as it was to work at a fast-food restaurant and that no experience was necessary.[7] Second, schools need to improve the instructional practices used to teach the basic education skills of reading, writing, and math. Their present methods are simply not doing the job, as evidenced by Motorola's plight to find qualified people and by national test scores. In addition to these problems, our schools need to take seriously the teaching of higher-order thinking skills, such as creativity, innovation, and problem solving—all important skills that are so essential for students who will need to function successfully in the future.

Another problem is that current instruction methods target primarily left-brain learning. As children learn reading, writing, and arithmetic, they are exercising the logical and rational parts, or the left side, of their brains. But there is more to learning than merely thinking rationally and logically and coming up with the one "correct" answer. Challenges at work are not "true or false," "fill in the blanks," or "circle the correct answer." In today's world, there is never just one way to solve a problem or one way to respond to a situation, and workers need to use imagination and imagery, parts of the creative-thinking process, to solve challenging problems. Confirming the importance of creative thinking, Mary Alice White of Teachers College says, "It is quite possible that linear thinking, as opposed to imagery thinking, has been one of our handicaps in trying to solve pressing worldwide problems. The mode of thinking we need . . . must help us to visualize the connections among all parts of the problem. This is where imagery is a powerful thinking tool, as it has been for scientists, including Einstein."[8]

Ms. White's statement points out yet another problem—the practice of fragmented instruction. This kind of instruction gives students bits and pieces of information; a little history, a little English, a little math, but for the most part there is no connection between subjects. Peter Senge, an expert on the "learning organization," says, "From a very early age, we are taught to break problems apart, to fragment the world. This apparently makes complex tasks and subjects more manageable, but we pay an enormous price. We can no longer see the consequences of our actions; we lose our intrinsic sense of connection to a larger whole. . . . After a while, we give up trying to see the whole altogether."[9]

To understand and see the whole or big picture, students need to connect information, look for patterns, and then apply that knowledge to the past, present, and future events. *All* subjects in school contain connecting patterns, and students need to be able to see how all knowledge is like a puzzle with each piece being important and interrelated to the finished "big" picture. Being able to find patterns, as well as details, and apply them to big-picture problem solving and reasoning not only equips students for their future work, but also helps to make sense out of education for students, especially those who often lament, "How is learning this ever going to help me?" Speaking to the importance of patterns, Priscilla Vail, author of *Smart Kids with School Problems* and *Clear and Lively Writing* says, "The ones who have kept alive their ability to play with patterns, to experiment—they will be the ones who can make use of what technology has to offer. Those whose focus has been on getting the correct answers to get a high score will be obsolete."[10]

In the past as well as the present, the main responsibility of education has been to teach our children the skills necessary to be able to live, grow, and compete in the world, to enjoy life through their talents and abilities, and to be prepared for the future workplace. But our workplace is changing rapidly, and the education system is not keeping up. The 200-year history of the Industrial Age, where the emphasis was on manufacturing and trade, is over. We are now in the Information Age, working with information and technology coming toward us at warp speed. As in the past, workers of the twenty-first century still need to be competent in reading, writing, and math, but now more than ever, they need to be flexible thinkers and skilled in evaluating, analyzing, and synthesizing knowledge. Team workers, good communicators, and strong decision makers are a must in this increasingly complex society. Companies today need individuals with imagination, those who seek and find solutions to problems, innovative personalities with creative ideas, strong critical thinkers, and people with a wide range of higher-order thinking skills.

This leads to another question: What can our schools do to produce students proficient in these areas? Certainly, there is a need for many schools to look at the way their basic skills are taught, to employ more effective teaching methods, and to hire more qualified and better-trained teachers, but they need only look at schools that are producing competent students. They will find proficient teachers who are using a variety of effective strategies appropriate for their different classes to meet their clearly stated objectives. They will find in these teachers' classrooms, students who are being held to a higher standard, students who are actively involved in their learning process, and students who know exactly what is expected of them and what they will be held accountable for. No magic bullet solutions, here, just the basic foundation of any good educational system—competent, dedicated teachers trained in teaching methods developed from the knowledge of how children learn best. Most importantly, however, schools need to recognize that there is something missing from the curricula of many schools today. That "something" is the conduit needed to connect basic skills with higher-order thinking skills, to connect learning to both right and left sides of the brain, and to connect those "bits and pieces of information," now taught in isolated parts as separate subjects. What, then, is missing in our school system today that can help our students meet the demands of the business world tomorrow? Appropriately, many prominent business leaders feel they have the answer to this question. Here is what four have to say.

According to Richard Gurin, former president and CEO of Binney & Smith, "After a long business career, I have become increasingly concerned that the basic problem gripping the American workplace is not interests rates or inflation; those come and go with the business cycle. More deeply rooted is . . . the crisis of creativity. Ideas . . . are what built American business. And it is the arts that build ideas and nurture a place in the mind for them to grow. Arts education programs can help repair weaknesses in American education and better prepare workers for the twenty-first century."[11]

Likewise, William Kieschnick, former president and CEO of Atlantic Richfield Company, believes that "Leadership, decision making, planning, and professional achievement in the institutions of the world are becoming increasingly complex as our societies mature. Whether you are a leader or a professional in an art museum, oil company, or state government, the odds are that the execution of your assignment is fraught with challenges with the need for innovative ideas, and with ambiguity." He further notes, ". . . successful experiments in art [and music] promote and coexist with innovation in other activities."[12]

Dan Lacy, corporate vice president for communications at Ashland, Inc., says, "It's a given that today's employee has to have basic skills. But superior skills are needed to survive competitively in the global context. Acquiring them has to begin as early as possible in a child's education, and we see that it comes through arts education. We are not doing justice to our economy or our children if they don't get that in the K through 12 context."[13]

And finally, Jane Polin, manager of the G.E. Fund, has this to say regarding education and the arts: "We see a tremendous need for workers who are creative, analytical, disciplined, and self-confident. And we believe that hands-on participation in the arts is one of the best ways to develop these leadership abilities in young people."[14]

Sheila James Kuehl, California legislator, graduate of Harvard Law class of 1978, and the second woman ever to win Harvard's famed Moot Court competition, recently asked a group of San Fernando Valley, California, entrepreneurs and executives what the state government should be doing for them. Kuehl recounts, "Naturally, I figured they'd ask for some kind of tax cut. But they didn't. They're in the multimedia and computer business, one of our fastest growing sectors. You see their names at the end of a movie, during those endless credits. But what they wanted from government absolutely floored me: 'We need more students who study art in school. We need workers who can use all their creative tools.'" Kuehl explains that today's multimedia recruiters are often forced to import computer artists from abroad because so few are being trained in the arts and graphic and computer arts here. It is a well-known fact that Korean and Japanese students are exposed to music and the arts throughout their educational experience. She ended by saying, "California must maintain its current status as a center of world trade for the United States and the Pacific Rim—and as the center of multimedia arts and entertainment for the entire world. Given the globalization of commerce and the technological transformation of the arts, our children must be given the opportunity to work and thrive on the cutting edge."[15]

Perhaps it seems too simplistic to think that by merely adding music and the arts to the curricula, the schools will turn out students ready to accept and meet the challenges of the workplace in the next century. But when you consider the information gained through the scientific studies on brain development, you can see that this simple idea provides the method by which the complex process of developing optimal brain function can be achieved. The research speaks loudly and clearly—learning must include activities that exercise the whole brain for students to reach their full individual potentials. The parts of the brain that our schools fail to develop are the creative areas, which we use for the imagination, for postulating innovative ideas, and for dealing with complexity and ambiguity. Creative abilities eventually lead us to generate new ideas and discovery, vital qualities that our nation was built on and will continue to be needed in the next century. Yes, as simple as it may seem, when a child receives a comprehensive sequential education in music and the arts, the creative areas of the brain are stimulated and higher-order thinking skills develop naturally. Couple this with teaching methods that are effective in teaching the basics— reading, writing, and math—and watch the test scores soar! And the best part is, the learning process is much more exciting and fun than reading workbooks and filling out worksheets.

> *Perhaps it seems too simplistic to think that by merely adding music and the arts to the curricula, the schools will turn out students ready to accept and meet the challenges of the workplace in the next century. But when you consider the information gained through the scientific studies on brain development, you can see that this simple idea provides the method by which the complex process of developing optimal brain function can be achieved.*

Several years ago, while Jan Whitesides was attending her son's orientation for the new school year, the teacher began touting the new critical-thinking books that the students would be using to teach them "higher-order thinking skills." Not sharing her enthusiasm, she thought to herself, "Another boring workbook and more boring worksheets to teach *critical-thinking and problem-solving skills?*" It didn't make sense to her then, nor does it now. What method would you rather see a child engaged in to develop problem-solving and critical-thinking skills: constructing and painting a mural, playing in a band or orchestra, being a part of an opera production—or sitting at a desk reading a critical-thinking workbook? We all become proficient in higher-order thinking skills by *doing* and *experiencing,* and music and the arts, by nature, are *doing* and *experiencing.*

SCANS: The First Steps

In 1991, as a result of the growing concern for educating our future workers adequately, representatives from education, business, labor, and the government met to discuss the needs of the future workplace. From this meeting a publication, *What Work Requires of Schools,* was published by the Secretary of Labor's Commission on Achieving Necessary Skills (SCANS).[16] The report stated that students, to meet these needs, must achieve these specific skills:

• Have the ability to use resources

• Have interpersonal skills

• Be able to manipulate information

• Use appropriate technology

• Understand systems

The foundation of these skills is proficiency in the basic skills—reading, writing, mathematics, speaking, and listening—as well as thinking skills; that is, being able to think creatively, make decisions, solve problems, see things in the mind's eye, and know how to learn and reason. Also, the development of the personal qualities of individual responsibility, self-esteem, sociability, self-management, and integrity is needed. You will see in the following examination of the SCANS skills that all of them can be acquired through music and arts education.

ABILITY TO USE RESOURCES

The ability to use resources is defined in part as workers being able to allocate time, materials, and space.

Although there are other activities, such as sports, that will teach a child how to allocate and organize time, materials, and space, music is a consistent ongoing activity that continually perfects these skills. Students involved in music and the arts learn very early the importance of balancing their time effectively. A music student needs sufficient time to practice his instrument each day; meet rehearsal schedules; go to music lessons; and fit in other activities of community, home, school, and friends. They learn the necessity of careful planning, which enables them to juggle many assignments at once.

Additionally, students involved in drama or dance learn how to organize, divide, and choreograph space on the stage as they plan and prepare for a performance. Mural artists must be able to organize a variety of materials as they design and proportion space in creating large murals that will be viewed by many in the community. These qualities of organization and planning of one's time and space when developed in childhood become skills in adulthood, which will carry over to their future jobs.

INTERPERSONAL SKILLS

Interpersonal skills are defined as the ability to work in teams, teach others, and work well with people from culturally diverse backgrounds.

For the most part, it takes the talents of many to accomplish most "great" ideas. Very few ideas are realized through the efforts of one person, so being able to work well with others, share and communicate opinions, and collaborate on issues become essential assets in the work force today. Teamwork is being able to see another's point of view—realizing that two, three, or four heads are better than one. It is also the ability to set aside one's ego in order to see alternate approaches to a situation or problem. A music and arts education trains children in teamwork skills. Whether you are singing in the school choir, playing in the band, painting a group mural, or performing on stage, you are engaging in teamwork skills.

Because most teams work toward a standard of excellence, mediocrity is never acceptable. They want the finished product to reflect excellence, attention to detail, and the work of both an individual and group effort. And there is nothing like the competitive, supportive nature of a team to keep everyone working at their highest capacity. For example, students in a high school drama class need to individually know their parts *and* work closely together to achieve a polished theater performance that flows. Students in the band or orchestra must listen carefully to one another to achieve a harmonious and balanced sound. It takes team effort, cooperation, and communication for an orchestra to achieve performance-level competency. There is an intense team effort that is expended when a school produces an opera. Singers, musicians, artists, dramatists, dancers, and stagehands work as a unit as they develop an operatic masterpiece. As this process evolves, students learn about the power of communicating and cooperating as a team, that there is strength in numbers, and that it takes rigorous hard work and perseverance to achieve a standard of excellence. These lessons become valuable personality assets, no matter what the student chooses to do in life.

Additionally, music serves as a powerful universal language that crosses all race barriers because it draws on the culture and history of nations all over the world. In the next century, the United States will be a country of "majority-minority," meaning the minority population will become the majority population.[17] An education in music and the arts will bridge the gaps between nationalities and will give people a greater understanding of one another as they learn, understand, and appreciate the cultural and artistic talents of other people and countries.

MANIPULATION OF INFORMATION

Manipulation of information is defined in part as acquiring and evaluating data, interpreting and communicating, and using computers to process information.

Today in the work force, it is imperative to stay abreast of information that changes daily. Bruce O. Boston, author of "Educating for the Workplace Through the Arts" in *Business Week*, talks about a new job that has been defined in corporate America— chief knowledge officers (CKO)—who are being hired by companies to help them maintain a competitive edge.[18] As the name implies, their job is to keep the company aware of the latest knowledge and technology in the world. Once again, this job requires creative thinkers; lifelong learners; and people with the ability to analyze, synthesize, evaluate and interpret information, understand and relate important facts, and solve problems. The following true story from *Innovation and Entrepreneurship* by Peter Drucker illustrates how the innovative thinking of a musician and his ability to evaluate and interpret new information turned a company into multimillion-dollar enterprise.

In the mid-1920s, Hoffman-LaRoche was a small, struggling company that made a few textile dyes but was overshadowed by huge German dye makers and other large firms. About this time, vitamins were discovered. The scientific world could not quite accept the whole concept surrounding vitamins and questioned their necessity. Although no one wanted the patents for these new substances,

Hoffman-LaRoche took a gamble and purchased them. The company then hired the Zurich University scientists who had discovered the vitamins, offering them several times what they were currently making as professors. The company then invested all possible funds into the manufacturing and marketing of the vitamins. Seventy years later, Hoffman-LaRoche owns almost half of the world's vitamin market, amounting to billions of dollars in sales each year.

The man behind the success of the venture was a family member of LaRoche—a musician with an orchestra he could not support. According to Drucker, "In creating something truly new, something truly different, non-experts and outsiders seem to do as well as the experts, in fact, often better. Hoffman-LaRoche did not owe its strategy to chemists but to a musician who had married the granddaughter of the company's founder and needed more money to support his orchestra than the company then provided through its meager dividend. The company, in picking the vitamins in the early twenties exploited new knowledge. The musician who laid down its strategy understood the 'structure of scientific revolutions' a full thirty years before a philosopher, Thomas Kuhn, wrote the celebrated book by that name."[19]

In the process of studying music, this young musician developed both his creative (right) and logical (left) sides of his brain, thus enabling him to draw on all of his mental capabilities. Hence, he understood:

- The complexity and uncertainty of solving problems that involve calculated risk

- The power of new and innovative knowledge (by picking vitamins to market he was testing new knowledge)

- How to see the "big" picture of what was happening (he envisioned the success before it happened)

- The importance of visionary thinking—seeing the potential of vitamins when even scientific experts of the time did not see it[20]

Each year more and more companies are spending millions of dollars to foster and ignite creativity and imagination in their employees, which will enhance their capabilities in manipulating information. They find those who are the most creative are those who are willing to think in different, unpredictable ways. Creative people naturally "think outside the box" by looking for ideas in areas beyond their comfort zone and "color outside the lines" by eliminating those rules that no longer work or apply. Because learning music requires using the entire brain, children involved in the arts exercise those areas of the brain that allow them to have the confidence in their ability to take calculated risks, come up with new ideas, and look for innovative ways to accomplish tasks.

Also included within this competency is the ability to use computers to process information (the key word here is *process*). *Atlantic Monthly* reports that, by the year 2000, 60 percent of the nation's jobs will demand computer skills and pay an average of 10 to 15 percent more than jobs requiring no computer work. But the article also quotes Joseph Weizenbaum, a professor emeritus of computer science at MIT, as stating that even in his technology-heavy institution, new students can learn all the computer skills they need "in a summer."[21]

Unfortunately, schools are choosing to hear only of the future demand for computer-literate workers and are outfitting computer labs at a frenzied pace, often at the expense of dropping music and arts programs. Each year, millions of dollars are poured into the latest computer technology in school districts nationwide. Millions more are spent as the computers break down or become obsolete. Despite this futile outpouring of funds, schools continue to bemoan the fact that they need better and more sophisticated systems for their students in order for them to compete in the work force. The fact is, computers were *never* meant to be the answer to education's problems. They were developed for the purpose of *processing* and manipulating large amounts of data and information in businesses. Yet, examples abound of the venerable position given computers in schools.

When it comes to schools purchasing the latest in computer technology, the money miraculously appears, but when a music or arts program needs money to stay alive at a school—a program that is known to be a crucial part in developing higher-level thinking skills (and which, it is also known, a computer is not)—the money is nowhere to be found!

In Redondo Beach, California, the local high school purchased laptop computers for all 463 incoming freshman. The cost: $1 million. The school said that even if it can't get outside help to cover the expense, not to worry, they have it figured into the budget.[22] Allen Glenn, dean of the University of Washington's education school, had this to say about laptops: "Laptops are like the new electronic tablet notebook—they have good potential as a writing tool and a place to store information, but as far as how you really integrate laptops into actual lessons, in a way that will help students understand their problems, that's still up for grabs."[23]

When it comes to schools purchasing the latest in computer technology, the money miraculously appears, but when a music or arts program needs money to stay alive at a school—a program that is known to be a crucial part in developing higher-level thinking skills (and which, it is also known, a computer is not)—the money is nowhere to be found! An example is Kittridge Street Elementary School in Los Angeles. *Atlantic Monthly* reported that the school dropped its art, music, and physical education programs and then spent $333,000 on computers.[24]

Certainly the administrators of these schools have good intentions to provide their students with the benefits of modern technology to enhance their education, but it is important to carefully review the findings of research, reports, studies, and experts, which *clearly* point out that computers are not education's panacea. To the contrary, research shows that music and arts programs in our schools are needed to produce students competent in the skills to succeed in the future work force of our nation. For example, Drs. Gordon Shaw and Frances Rauscher, in a follow-up to their groundbreaking studies we discussed in Chapter 2, found no significant increase in spatial reasoning when children were exposed to the computer each day, as compared to a 34 percent increase when the students were exposed to a piano keyboard daily. Also as mentioned in Chapter 2, although a later study using a specifically designed computer program for increasing spatial intelligence showed a 100 percent increase in spatial intelligence, Dr. Shaw still believes that over the long term, the music lessons will have a greater impact. *Newsweek* reported that both music and physical education programs feed the brain and make it easier for kids to learn.[25] A recent study cited in *Atlantic Monthly* states, "One small, but carefully controlled study went so far as to claim that Reader Rabbit, a reading program now used in more than 100,000 schools, caused students to suffer a 50 percent drop in creativity. (Apparently, after forty-nine students used the program for seven months, they were no longer able to answer open-ended questions and showed a markedly diminished ability to brainstorm with fluency and originality.)"[26] The article further points out that corporations and businesses find that employees who use computers a lot "grow rusty in their ability to think." The reason—because computers use only two senses—hearing and sight, and children and adults need an integration of all their senses to learn, understand, and connect information. And Larry Cuban, a professor at Stanford University and an authority on the history of technology in American education, says, "Anyone who tells you computers are more effective than anything else is either dumb or lying." Cuban also states, "Schooling is not about information. It's getting kids to think about information. It's about understanding and knowledge and wisdom."[27]

If a school wants to be unique, different, and a model for other schools, it will stay away from the "herd" mentality. Just because putting together sophisticated computer labs seems to be the "in" thing to do in education, it is not reasonable justification for the great expenditure needed to do so. As business leaders do, schools must check the bottom line—will this expenditure increase test scores? The answer is no, the research shows. If a school absolutely must have the latest in technology, consider these ideas. Provide computer programs that require imagination and creative thinking, such as computer animation; video production activities; school web sites with each grade responsible for a part; or programs that help create presentation boards, graphs, or charts for reports or for interfacing with other schools. Most of these projects are conceived through storyboarding, video shooting, pre-drawing and planning—all three-dimensional hands-on creations—*before* they are transferred to the computer. These types of activities will require students to think, evaluate, and interpret vast possibilities and ideas as they create something truly exciting and, at the same time, gain marketable skills for whatever they choose to do in the future.

USE OF APPROPRIATE TECHNOLOGY

Use of appropriate technology is defined as selecting equipment and tools, applying technology to specific tasks, and maintaining and troubleshooting technologies.

Technology has been a part of the arts since the beginning of time. But the place the arts holds in the technological world is, more often than not, misunderstood. Some feel that as man was able to make better things through improved skill and pace, it gave him more time to pursue creative and artistic endeavors. But to the contrary, history shows us that the arts generated the improved skills and that, in turn, led to the advancement of technology. Many anthropologists believe that it was solving creative problems that ultimately led to inventions with utilitarian purposes. For example, early man learned that clay could be used to make art objects such as bison, deer, foxes, or bears. Later, he discovered that baking the clay turned it into a hard material that eventually led to the making of ceramic pots and dishes used for food storage, preparation, and serving. Knives, dating back to Cro-Magnon times show that, perhaps, they were first created as objects of beauty before they were used in a practical application.[28]

Musical instruments were made for producing sound to allow man to extend his sound production capabilities beyond what could be projected by his voice. From this came the science of acoustics, furthered by the Greeks in their dramatic performances. In studying the development of man's skills, it becomes apparent that art and technology cannot be separated.

Today, the arts and technology continue to be a team. With the computer technology of Musical Instrument Digital Interface (MIDI), students are able to write and orchestrate their own music. The use of interactive media combines art and technology, thus creating highly sophisticated special effects and animation. This artistic technological medium has become an enormous opportunity for students to express their creative and inventive ideas, while demonstrating to them the vast possibilities of technology combined with their own imaginations. For example, high school students from Plano, Texas; Naperville, Illinois; Union City, California; and Redondo Beach, California, combined the arts and technology and produced a play, complete with music, dancing, and script through video conferencing and e-mail. In March 1998, at Redondo Union High School, the 100 students from the four high schools across the country came together and performed *Changing Terms*, which they believe is the first musical produced over the Internet.[29]

For the past two years, one of our sons has been involved with Vidkidco, an educational media production program that provides hands-on technical means for young people ages twelve to eighteen to produce innovative media arts (video, computer graphic animation, and multimedia) works. It has proven to be an incredible program, teaching him and allowing him to experiment with sophisticated technologies and artistic mediums that most sixteen-year-olds only dream about. Through the use of computers, storyboarding, and three-dimensional mock-ups, the class created media animations using the same innovative competencies that businesses will need from future employees.

The compact disc market is another example of the interrelationship between technology and art. Compact discs were originally produced as a way to create excellent sound quality in a musical application. They are now being linked with computers as they store information for hundreds of uses. Philip Elmer-Dewitt, science and technology writer for *Time* magazine, said, "Without the CD music market, data CDs would not exist. . . . Every time Bruce Springsteen and Stevie Wonder sell a compact disc, it's good news for the data side."[30]

Ten years ago, Steven Spielberg could not have created *Jurassic Park*, with its phenomenal special effects, but with media arts pushing for more complicated computer technology, the creation of *Jurassic Park* became a reality, with other technically brilliant movies following it. Students educated in the arts will have no trouble understanding, utilizing, and applying the vast possibilities of technology in their future occupations.

UNDERSTANDING SYSTEMS

Understanding systems is defined as understanding social, organizational, and technological systems, monitoring and correcting performance, and designing or improving systems.

Many years ago, the University of Washington required a course called "Creative Dramatics" for elementary teacher certification. It was recognized as an effective teaching/learning strategy or system that brought almost any subject to life for students. Because of budget cuts, the program no longer exists, but while it was in place, it provided students an opportunity to work within such systems through the medium of artistic expression. For example, in a drama lesson the students both listened and read stories and poems, analyzed a painting, or listened to a piece of music. From this, they organized themselves into groups as they planned a dramatic presentation around a particular art form. Designing a plot, creating characters, setting, dialogue, and action were all a part of the presentation. Other students who were not in the play, critiqued and monitored the performance, suggested changes, and gave the artists a chance to improve. Afterward, the students changed roles. As you can see, social, organizational, and technological skills were all brought into play.

Dee Dickinson, author of *Learning Through the Arts*, explains the success of the program: "Clearly this process is a highly collaborative one, develops quick-witted spontaneous thinking, problem solving, poise and presence, concentration, and both conceptual and analytical thinking skills. Making a piece of theater with students encourages, in fact demands, cooperation, compromise, and commitment." She further states, "Formal theater demands additional skills, including the coordination and creation of sets, costumes, props, lighting design, scripts or script-writers, and possibly musicians and dancers. Memorization of lines and action are essential to the process, and great dramatic literature may enrich the actor's memory throughout life."[31]

Within all of these systems, a certain amount of conformity to basic rules and standards is necessary; however, within that framework, the flow of imagination and new ideas, which are essential to success, is unrestricted. If a person can imagine it, they can make it happen. Imagination causes people to seek and find solutions to problems, as well as to recognize and act on presented opportunities. August Kekule's dream of six encircling snakes led to the discovery of the benzene molecule. Scientists say that, "the benzene molecule is so complex that no amount of logic could have conceived it." It was Kekule's imagination that gave him the idea that led to this scientific breakthrough.[32]

There are many examples in our history of designing systems through the use of imagination. Alexander Graham Bell created the design for the telephone by imitating the ear.[33] Through the use of his imagination, Einstein worked out formulas to explain what his mind was experiencing and, as a result, came up with one of the most significant theories of all time. Military designers borrowed Picasso's cubist art to create more effective camouflage patterns for tanks. Tim Berners-Lee, the visionary inventor of the World Wide Web, used his imagination and expanded a system that was initially set up as a way for physicists to store and access information in a hyperlinked environment over the Internet. It was the addition of pictures (a strong visual medium!) that caused it to take off among a wider audience and thus our present-day information highway, or World Wide Web, was created in just three short years![34] (Berners-Lee also happens to be a pianist!)

As in the "Creative Dramatics" program, children who are involved with music and the arts projects where imagination reigns will develop proficiency in social, organizational, and technological systems. Paul Griffiths, a journalist for the *New York Times*, wrote that "a child involved in musical performance is confronted with challenges that will be of lifelong benefit: how you present yourself in public, how you argue a case, how you interpret a document, what evidence you accept and what you will question, where you draw the line between what you are told and what you want, and how you work with others toward a common goal."[35]

Stephanie Perrin, head of the Walnut Hill School in Natick, Maryland, sums it up succinctly when she says, "If you want a motivated, organized, hard-working, flexible, smart, creative worker, able to work well alone or in groups—hire a young violinist!"[36]

The SCANS report has given our nation's schools a mandate to produce students proficient in the five skills just examined. Hopefully, school administrators will realize that providing a comprehensive sequential music and arts program is the way to do it. Many business leaders recognize this and are working with local schools, arts organizations, and arts professionals to bring these programs to students where budget cuts have all but eliminated them. Several states across the nation have held conferences to discuss how best to implement arts programs into their schools, and how the business community can help.

Businesses Taking the Lead

In 1994, more than 300 business leaders and arts educators attended the Arts Education for the Twenty-First Century American Economy conference in Louisville, Kentucky. The attendees, invited by the American Council for the Arts, discussed how the arts make a significant contribution to business and how students educated in the arts can help the future economy. Since then, additional forums and conferences have been held in other states. In 1996, the Connecticut Alliance for Arts Education was held, then South Carolina's Arts in the Basic Curriculum, followed by the Pittsburgh Cultural Trust, and the Bronx Development. The goal was universal: bring business leaders, arts educators, and arts organizations together to discuss the importance of arts education and how, by working together, they can educate our students in the arts.

In 1995, the Goals 2000 Arts Education Partnership (now called the Arts Education Partnership) was formed through a cooperative agreement among the National Endowment for the Arts (NEA), U. S. Education Department (USED), National Assembly of State Arts Agencies (NASAA), and Council of Chief State School Officers (CCSSO). The partnership promotes the role of arts education in school reform and in assisting all students to achieve high levels of success in school, life, and work. More than 100 national education, arts, business, and civic organizations have joined the partnership. The collective goal is to ensure that the arts become a vital component of every child's education. The partnership recognizes the role that business can play in making this become a reality. In March 1999, the Arts Education Partnership released a report focusing on ninety-one school districts nationwide that were identified by state and national education and arts organizations as having outstanding arts education throughout their schools. (Although hundreds more school districts were identified, the report includes only ninety-one.) Thirteen factors were identified as "Critical Success Factors for Achieving District-wide Arts Education." The first factor was the community, which included, in part, businesses, local civic and cultural leaders, and institutes that are actively engaged in the arts, politics, and instructional programs in the district. For the report, school districts provided information demonstrating the important role businesses play in support of the arts within their particular districts. Dick Deasy, director of the Arts Education Partnership, believes that businesses are key players in seeing that the arts are included in our school's curriculum. He states, "When business comes to the table, the issue is taken seriously. Business people increasingly realize that the arts are evidence of a school's commitment to high standards of excellence for every child—the fundamental idea behind Goals 2000. So business is a key player—and a key partner—in our efforts to provide a solid education in the arts to every child in America."[37]

The National Coalition for Education in the Arts (NCEA) has looked at communities that use the talents of local musical performing groups, artists, arts agencies, and other arts organizations and institutions for programs in their schools. They found hundreds of examples in local communities throughout the United States that have added enriching, hands-on music and arts experiences and exposure programs that include a variety of workshops; artist-in-residencies; musical, orchestral, and operatic performances; and visits to galleries, theaters, and museums. Although these programs provide a positive experience for the students involved and have well-planned educational objectives, they do not provide students with learning that comes when music and the arts are infused into the curriculum and taught as separate subjects. However, they do expose students to enriching musical programs, provide an opportunity to see and experience creativity at work, and help them to strengthen their connections to the community and possible future jobs. Corporations, understanding the importance of music and arts education for students of the future work force, play a critical role in helping to fund programs for the schools that are brought into the classroom by various arts organizations. The following is a small sampling of some of the arts organizations that share their talents with their local schools and communities and the corporations or businesses that help fund such programs.

TEXACO

Texaco is keenly aware that an education in the arts is a major factor contributing to a child's academic success. Of all the arts, the role of music is of particular interest to them, hence they have created a music education grant program known as "Early Notes: The Sound of Children Learning." Under this program, the Texaco Foundation supports education partnerships with university schools of music and nonprofit arts and community organizations, school-based music programs, music in the earliest school years (pre-kindergarten through second grade), and significant research in the field of cognitive development through music education.

Texaco funding is intended to stimulate creative changes in curriculum and improve community and parental involvement with the schools. Through "Early Notes: The Sound of Children Learning," Texaco has supported music organizations such as 42nd Street Fund, Eastman School of Music, Education Through Music, Inc., Houston Grand Opera Association, Levine School of Music, Louisiana Philharmonic Orchestra, Metropolitan Opera Association, Music Intelligence Neural Development, and University of South Carolina Music Development Center. The foundation's support does not end there. In a major new initiative called "TEMPO: Texaco Eastman Music Partnership Opportunities," the Texaco Foundation and the Eastman School of Music have joined forces. They have crafted a project with two equal objectives: to enhance the development of musical knowledge and skills, and to enhance student performance in regularly assessed educational areas. The foundation says, "By coupling the financial resources of a successful energy company and the musical and educational resources of a preeminent school of music, the Texaco Foundation-Eastman project aims to locate and support the highest quality collaborative initiatives between school music programs and community music resources. The goal is to prepare children for the demands of an increasingly diverse culture and workplace and advance education reform."

For over sixty years, Texaco has supported the arts through radio broadcasts of the Metropolitan Opera, reaching 95 percent of the American public and many millions around the world. Through this program and the others mentioned above, Texaco has poured in millions of dollars to enhance music education and awareness around the globe. In 1998 alone, Texaco spent approximately $3.8 million in support of the arts.

In summing up Texaco's commitment to the arts, Anne Dowling, president of the foundation, states, "We at Texaco have a special understanding of the power of music due to our decades-long affiliation with the Metropolitan Opera. This commitment inspires us to dedicate our corporate philanthropic resources to improving the quality of music education in public schools—especially those serving inner-city and disadvantaged children. Music and the arts help children grow and learn in multiple ways, and they are vital to educating our nation's children."

H. J. HEINZ COMPANY

In 1996, celebrating 100 years of ketchup being the nation's favorite condiment, the H. J. Heinz Company gave the National Endowment for the Arts the largest corporate gift that the agency has ever received. The $450,000 grant, paid in $150,000 increments over three years, was to be used to support children's arts programs that were cut back or were in danger of being eliminated. This generous gift came at a critical time, as the NEA's budget was cut 39 percent by Congress. As a result, the NEA was forced to cut its support of hundreds of children's music and arts programs throughout the nation. Jane Alexander, former NEA chairman, stated, "This generous donation is a shining example of how public-private partnerships can improve the lives of all Americans. . . . Art will not only open doors to [children's] creativity and imagination, but will help give them the problem-solving and communication skills they'll need to meet the challenges of the twenty-first century."[38] In the first year, thirty organizations with a focus on children's arts programs received $5,000 each from the Heinz monies. The organizations represent nine different arts disciplines and bring hands-on programs to children in fifteen states across the United States.

Wolf Trap Foundation

TRW/Wolf Trap Institute for Early Learning Through the Arts is a program sponsored by the Wolf Trap Foundation for the Performing Arts, which is housed on the grounds of the United States' only national park for the performing arts, near Washington, D.C. The Wolf Trap Institute works with children across the United States between the ages of three and five. The goal is to engage children in rich performing arts activities that include music, drama, and creative movement. Wolf Trap believes that active participation in music and the arts can serve as the foundation for future learning. The program was the subject of a four-year study conducted by Harvard Project Zero that documented significant evidence supporting Wolf Trap's positive effect on learning and teaching in preschools. Professional performing artists are trained by Wolf Trap in early childhood practices and placed in various classroom settings for either a one- or seven-week residency. The program offers teachers, caregivers, and parents practical experience in Wolf Trap's approach to infusing music and the performing arts into the daily curriculum. This part of the program is important because when the artists and musicians leave a school, the program can then continue under the guidance and direction of the trained teacher.

Wolf Trap receives funding from foundations, corporations, school systems, Head Start, and private and public institutions. Since 1995, TRW has committed more than $1 million to the Wolf Trap Institute to implement stART smART, a partnership for young children. TRW has played an active role in bringing this program into areas where the corporation's plants, offices, and facilities are located. The company has established partnerships with local schools in more than ninety TRW communities across the country and in key international locations.

In 1995, the Wolf Trap Institute received from the NEA the first award ever presented to a program focusing on young children. It also was named in a national report from the President's Committee on the Arts and Humanities, *Coming Up Taller*, as a model arts program and way to reach at-risk children. In 1997, the Business Committee for the Arts presented the Innovation Award to TRW for its stART smART partnership with Wolf Trap.[39]

YOUNG ASPIRATIONS/YOUNG ARTISTS

Young Aspirations/Young Artists (YA/YA) was started ten years ago by New Orleans artist Jana Napoli, who, after seeing a group of high school students hanging around a vacant lot with nothing to do, decided to put that creative energy to good use. She put paintbrushes in their hands and challenged them to turn their hidden artistic talents into entrepreneurial skills. Young Aspirations/Young Artists is now a nonprofit organization that offers opportunities to interested students from New Orleans public and private schools to become self-sufficient artists with professional experience and business skills. YA/YA receives funding from the NEA, the Philip Morris Companies, the Stewart Mott Foundation, the State of Louisiana, the City of New Orleans, the Arts Council, and others. According to Napoli, the initial goal behind YA/YA was to "give students confidence and success in expressing their artistic talents and to find an international market to sell their artwork." They have been successful at both.[40] In the beginning, Napoli spent $30,000 a year of her own money to keep the program running. Their first show—student drawings of neighborhood buildings—brought in $1,800 that went right back into the organization. The success of these first drawings gave her students the encouragement needed to thrust them into thinking creatively about other ways of expressing their artistic talents, as well as providing something at which they could be successful. "I wanted something they couldn't fail with," she states. As a result, they started painting unique designs on furniture, which gave them national and international acclaim. The contracts and commissions started rolling in. In the past few years, students of YA/YA have designed a chair that was included in the Hammacher-Schlemmer catalog, painted a large mural in the New Orleans Centre shopping mall, designed two limited-edition watches for Swatch for its 1995 spring collection, and established a thriving art gallery. By their sixth year of operation, YA/YA had sold more than $250,000 of artwork. Students understand that being a part of YA/YA is a privilege; they must maintain a "C" grade point average, and a "B" average if they want to travel with the organization. They are taught basic techniques, business training, portfolio development, and office and leadership skills. Students are paid through commissions and internships. Design contracts and artwork income are paid directly to the students on a percentage basis. Over the last ten years, YA/YA has expanded and provided a model for other programs for interested students and has given its alumni opportunities to teach at other organizations that are patterned after the original. Napoli's legacy has been realized because, through her vision, she has changed lives, banished stereotypes, and given young people goals and aspirations for the future through the medium of the arts. Student Rondell Crier, summing up his experience and success at YA/YA states, the work "depicts the things you find in life: pain, interest, love, the questions you have in life, the demands people put on you. You can find that all in here."[41]

The Milwaukee Symphony Orchestra: Arts in Community Education Program (ACE)

The Milwaukee Symphony Orchestra, Wisconsin's largest cultural organization, uses music and the arts as a tool to enhance learning throughout the standard school curriculum in its Arts in Community Education (ACE) program. ACE currently serves

8,000 children in twenty-five schools in grades kindergarten through eighth in Milwaukee and seven other surrounding school districts. Throughout the year, each grade level experiences three to four in-school ensembles, as well as custom-designed thematic concerts performed by the full orchestra at the Symphony's primary concert venue. ACE focuses on a single theme at each grade level appropriate to the social and intellectual development of the students. For example, the theme for the first-graders' program, "Musical Tales," focuses on events, thoughts, emotions, and imagination, as the students are developing language arts skills. In second grade, "Musical Detective" encourages problem solving and critical-thinking skills. The fifth grade's "ACE Inventors" investigates connections between the arts and sciences. Higher grades have themes tailored to fit the needs of the individual schools.

All 500 teachers are given in-service training. These sessions, along with curricular resource materials, help teachers utilize ACE techniques on a daily basis to enhance learning in the classroom. Parents receive a newsletter with tips and information on how to encourage a child's musical experiences at home and how to utilize the musical community. Because of its success, the program was featured in the June 1996 NEA publication *Beyond Tradition: Partnerships Among Orchestras, Schools, and Communities*, in which ACE's assessment program was named the best model for the field. The program receives funding from sources that include the G.E. Fund, Harley Davidson Foundation, Miller Brewing Co., Rockwell, and Union Pacific Foundation.

THE MUSIC CENTER OF LOS ANGELES

The Music Center of Los Angeles has, for almost two decades, been committed to music and arts education in the schools. Recognizing that music and the arts enhance reasoning, stimulate

the imagination, and complement the work of classroom teachers, they strive to bring both educational and enjoyable programs
to more than 850,000 students throughout Southern California.
They offer a variety of programs, such as Music Center on Tour,
which encompasses more than 150 different offerings, each
being artistically beautiful, as well as educationally sound. Presented by a variety of professionals, the programs introduce
students to the rich history of music and hands-on artistic workshops that build skills in a range of areas. All of the programs enhance the core curriculum. Individually Designed Arts Packages
are programs creatively tailored around a central theme or curriculum focus and include hands-on participation by students
through a series of music and arts workshops. ART Partnerships
are programs offering in-depth sequential instruction in music
and the arts that span several months and meet the needs of the
school curriculum. Artsource™ integrates the arts into the curriculum by providing teachers with more than fifty different
units to choose from. Each Artsource™ unit features an artist or
company presenting works from a broad range of styles and cultures. In 1996, selected units of Artsource™ were adopted by the
state of North Carolina. The materials reflect universal themes
common to history and social science curricula and include
three lesson plans and supplemental audio, video, and slide materials. The funding to subsidize all these programs for the
schools is provided by of individual, corporate, and foundation
gifts to the Music Center Unified Fund. The goal of the Music
Center is to make the education of the arts accessible and affordable for all.[42]

ArtsConnection

ArtsConnection, founded in 1979, is New York City's largest
and most comprehensive arts-in-education organization providing professional programs in the performing and visual arts to

children in the New York City public schools. The organization reaches a total audience of 300,000 children and teachers annually and works in 120-plus public schools in all five boroughs. ArtsConnection believes that, through the arts, children can develop curiosity, love of learning, imaginative thinking, a positive self-image, and a respect for their own and their neighbors' cultural heritage. It is supported by public funds, numerous foundation and corporations, including G.E. Fund, Philip Morris Companies Inc., Wasserstein Perella, and the *New York Times*, to name a few. ArtsConnection is recognized as a national model by numerous public agencies because of the extensive work it does to bring the arts to children and adults in New York City. ArtsConnection provides numerous arts programs for the community and families—the following list includes only the comprehensive in-school programs and services:

- Thematic Arts Seasons are semester-long units built around a central theme such as Shapes and Sounds, Rhythms of the Earth, Communities: Traditions Then and Now, Storytelling Across Cultures, and Roots of American Music, Word/Play Language Arts. Incorporated within these themes are visual arts activities, music, dance, and theater. Seasons of Workshops and Performances are individual, collaboratively designed programs in more than 120 schools citywide. They include staff development sessions, artist/teacher planning meetings, curriculum materials, and invitations for families to attend events on-site at the ArtsConnection Center and other New York cultural institutions.

- The Young Talent Program identifies talented fourth-, fifth-, and sixth-graders and provides them with instruction in music, dance, or theater; trips to professional studios, and academic tutoring. Through an annual summer institute and ongoing workshops, teachers and administrators receive professional instruction to reintroduce the arts as a part of the core curriculum and to support school improvement through the arts.

- The Student Art Program creates juried exhibitions of professionally framed student artwork for exhibition in the offices, conference rooms, and dining facilities of the program's corporate sponsors.[43]

YOUNG AUDIENCES OF GREATER DALLAS

Young Audiences of Greater Dallas is an arts-in-education organization for children that brings performing artists into schools, libraries, museums, juvenile facilities, and community centers throughout north Texas. Young Audiences was founded on the belief in the transforming power of the arts and focuses on creative development, problem solving, and abstract thinking. Its programs range from classic western disciplines—including opera, classical music, theater, and ballet—to culturally specific programming. Young Audiences began in New York in 1952, and now has more than thirty chapters nationwide. In 1997 and 1998, Young Audiences of Greater Dallas presented 1,095 performances; 8,242 workshops; and 643 artist residencies to more than 250,000 children throughout north Texas. Although Young Audiences works extensively with schools, it boasts a program called Creative Solutions that uses the arts to help young people between the ages of thirteen and seventeen who are involved in the Dallas County Juvenile Justice System. This highly successful program offers a nurturing, nonthreatening environment for exploration and expression—things that are critical to rehabilitation. Now in its sixth year, it has served more than 8,000 at-risk youth. Its goal is to provide participants with an outlet to freely express their opinions and emotions in a creative, nonjudgmental environment; to enhance their ability to work together as a team; to help improve problem-solving skills; to promote creative thinking; to give participants an opportunity to make a positive contribution to their community through a public performance and/or an art exhibition; and to provide them with opportunities to experience success. In 1995, fifteen teens on probation worked with a local playwright and wrote and produced their own play, *The Flight to Turn Around*, which played a four-performance run at the Dallas Horchow Auditorium. In 1997, the teens presented *Time to Focus* at the Horchow Auditorium. Another project used the talents of twelve young artists, who painted two triptychs representing justice to decorate walls on four floors of the George Allen Courts Building. Attorneys from the Dallas Bar Association and two professional artists contributed more than 300 hours to help the kids with the projects, as well as helping them compile portfolios of their artwork and write resumes. Nearly 75 percent of the participants said that, through Creative Solutions, they learned important teamwork skills that helped them interact with other kids. It has also helped them express their feelings in positive ways, increased their self-esteem, and improved their relationships with family and peers. Creative Solutions embrace Young Audiences' mission in both philosophy and action. Over the past five summers, the program has proven to be a powerful tool for transformation. In addition to parents and probation officers, the clients themselves attest to the impact of this program with statements like, "I have turned my life around and Creative Solutions helped." The mother of one boy simply said, "It's like I got my son back."[44]

The Benefits Beyond Better Grades

Apart from the obvious educational benefits derived from music and the arts, they offer yet another advantage—the arts boost the economy and provide future employment opportunities for students. The National Assembly of Local Arts Agencies (which is now part of Americans for Arts Education) did a study to determine the economic impact of nonprofit organizations in the United States. Almost 800 arts organizations in twenty-two states were studied over a three-year period. The organization concluded that music and the arts are an industry that generates thousands of dollars to the nation's economy. It estimated the following:[45]

- The annual contribution of the arts to the national economy is $36.8 billion, which jumps to $314 billion when the commercial arts sector is added.

- The number of jobs supported by the arts nationally is 1.3 million.

Rexford Brown of the Education Commission of the States said, "Out of a classroom of thirty children, maybe ten will be employed in an arts-related occupation someday."[46] When one-third of a classroom is projected to have a future job in the arts, that discipline should be considered most significant!

Apart from the obvious educational benefits derived from music and the arts, they offer yet another advantage—the arts boost the economy and provide future employment opportunities for students.

In 1994, the California Arts Council published *The Arts: A Competitive Advantage for California*. This report gave the economic impact of the arts industry on California, how the arts enrich the quality of life in California, and how they help in the creation of new jobs. The council's report also included the following:[47]

- Spending on the nonprofit arts directly and indirectly supports more than 115,000 full-time and part-time jobs in California and adds $1 billion to the California economy.

- People working in the arts in Los Angeles County earn an average of $38,000 a year.

- The first automotive design studio of any automaker in the world employing more than 400 people was opened in the 1970s by Toyota Motor Corporation and was located in California to be near a nonprofit arts institution—Pasadena's Art Center College of Design.

- The design and manufacture of musical instruments, with accompanying electronics and accessories, is a $500 million industry in California.

One might think that, because California is the hub of the media arts, naturally the arts would boost the state's economy, but a similar study in South Carolina showed a parallel impact of the arts on that state's economy, even without the significant presence of the media arts. The South Carolina study's findings included:[48]

- The cultural industry provides a direct source of income for individuals and business totaling $380 million.

- Spending by the cultural industry leads to spending by other businesses in the state, and this indirect spending represents $640 million in state economic output.

- The cultural industry has an impact on statewide earnings. In 1992, the cultural industry was responsible for $229.9 million in earnings and 17,631 jobs for South Carolinians.

- Ninety-nine percent of the chief executive officers questioned say that the availability of cultural activities in an area is an important consideration in choosing a new location.

- South Carolina leads the nation in discipline-based arts education as part of every child's basic school curriculum. The state's Department of Education says that salaries and fringe benefits combined with other arts education data produced a direct expenditure of $73,678,000.

An extensive education in music and the arts will give students an exciting plethora of job opportunities, as well as preparing them and making them more marketable for future employment, whatever it may be. Prominent business leaders and chief executive officers are keenly aware that having employees who are literate in the arts adds value to their businesses. The Music Educators National Conference asked prominent chief executive officers of major companies to share their feelings and commitment to the arts in education. Here are some of their responses.[49]

- Robert E. Allen, former chairman and chief executive officer of AT&T Corporation: "We live in an age increasingly ruled by science and technology, a fact that only underscores the need for more emphasis on the arts. . . . A grounding in the arts will help our children see; to bring a uniquely human perspective to science and technology. In short, it will help them as they grow smarter to also grow wiser."

- Willard C. Butcher, former chairman of the board of The Chase Manhattan Corporation: "I firmly believe that there is place for the arts—music, dance, drawing, painting, writing— in the school curriculum. In the elementary grades, the arts are a valuable component in broadening a child's mind and talents. In secondary school, the arts provide a sense of history, connecting the past to the present. When a student reaches college, a liberal arts education teaches not just clear but creative, innovative thinking. That's the kind of individual I'm interested in recruiting for Chase: one who can think conceptually, write well and—perhaps most importantly— bring a creative outlook to the conference-room table."

- Kenneth T. Derr, former chief executive officer of Chevron U.S.A.: "Every part of a vital society depends on creative thought. . . . A large corporation such as ours can thrive best in a society in which young people are vital and quick and creative."

- David T. Kearns, chairman and chief executive officer of Xerox Corporation: "The purpose of education is not simply to inform but to enrich and enlighten, to provide insights into life as it has been led and as it may be led. No element of the curriculum is better suited to that task than arts education. . . . The arts take us beyond pragmatic concerns of the moment and give us a glimpse of human possibility."

- William E. LaMothe, former chairman of the board and chief executive officer of Kellogg Company: "Business also benefits from education in the arts. Successful companies in our emerging global economy need more than technicians. Appreciation of music and related arts bridges the gap among societies and offers young people valuable lessons in cooperation and sensitivity to others."

- Edward H. Rensi, former chief operations officer, president and chief operating officer of U.S.A. McDonald's Corporation: "We must encourage our youngsters in such pursuits as music education. In addition to learning the valuable lesson that it takes hard work to achieve success, no matter what the arena, music education can provide students with a strong sense of determination, improved communication skills, and a host of other qualities essential for successful living."

- John Sculley, former chairman and chief executive officer of Apple Computer, Inc.: "The creative arts provide us with a unique and vital perspective about our world. . . . I want to work with people whose imaginations have been unleashed and who tackle problems as challenges rather than see them as obstacles. An education enriched by the creative arts should be considered essential for everyone."

To ensure a successful future for our children in the next century and help our nation maintain a competitive edge in a global marketplace, nothing less than an education in the arts will suffice. When we ponder the significance of the arts to the future of our nation, it is impossible to view them as frills or easily expendable subjects. In 1994, John Goodlad in *A Place Called School* concluded, "The arts are not an educational option; they are basic." And—we can add—they are basic to the survival of our nation.

PART

A CULTURAL HERITAGE

CHAPTER 9

♪TRIKING A CHORD: PRESERVING OUR CULTURAL HERITAGE

For some strange reason, when it comes to music and the arts, our world view has led us to believe they are easily expendable. Well, I believe that a nation that allows music to be expendable is in danger of becoming expendable itself.

—Richard Dreyfuss, 38th Annual Grammy Awards

On December 20, 1965, a newly formed agency of the government awarded a check for $100,000 to the American Ballet Theater, saving this national treasure from extinction. Playwright Alfred Uhry claims that *Driving Miss Daisy* would have never gotten out of the garage if not for the support of this organization. Since its inception in 1965, the National Endowment for the Arts (NEA) has kept the arts alive in the United States, supporting scores of artistic institutions and individual artists at a crucial time in their existence. The following list is just a sampling of the awards won by artists over the years whose work was supported by the NEA:

- The Pulitzer Prize—Laurel Ulrich won this award in 1990 for *A Midwife's Tale: The Life of Martha Ballard, Based on Her Diary, 1785-1812.*

- The National Book Award—Charles Johnson won this award in 1990 for his novel, *Middle Passage.*

- The MacArthur "Genius" Award—Fred Wiseman, a prolific documentary filmmaker whose works are shown across the United States.

- The Academy Award—Barbara Kopple won for her documentaries, *Harlan County, USA,* and *American Dream.*

- The Emmy Award—for *Dance in America* and *Metropolitan Opera Presents Live from the Lincoln Center.*

- The Tony Award—Jane Alexander won for *Great White Hope.*

The NEA has awarded $2.9 billion for approximately 110,000 fellowships and grants to thousands of American artists and arts organizations in all fifty states. It has put thousands of artists into our nation's schools through artist residencies, school performances, and master classes, frequently providing the only exposure to the arts for millions of American children and leading the way in arts education reform.[1]

Recent figures show that before the NEA was established, only 20 million Americans attended arts affairs annually, as opposed to 76 million today, and many people credit this organization with playing a key role in cultivating this interest.

Recent figures show that before the NEA was established, only 20 million Americans attended arts affairs annually, as opposed to 76 million today, and many people credit this organization with playing a key role in cultivating this interest.[2] This is only a small sampling of the far-reaching impact this federal organization has had on American culture and, yet, many Americans know little or nothing about this agency.

Government and the Arts

September 29, 1965, was an historic day for our nation. For 140 years, leaders in government and the arts community had debated the role government should take as a supporter of arts and culture in America. It was the culmination of years of hard work by countless individuals, groups, and the government, when President Lyndon B. Johnson, members of Congress, and a group of artists and administrators gathered at the White House for signing of legislation establishing the NEA. As a new public service agency, its purpose was to further the artistic and cultural aspects of this country. In that first year, with a budget of $2.5 million, six active programs began in our nation: music, dance, literature, visual arts, theater, and education. The NEA also was able to fund twenty-two institutions and 135 individuals. Since its creation, the NEA has helped to dramatically increase the number of arts organizations in America.[3] For example:

- The number of nonprofit theaters has grown from 56 to 425.

- Professional orchestras have more than doubled in number to 230.

- Opera companies have grown from 27 to 120.

- Dance companies have grown from 37 to 400.

- Public arts agencies in small towns and cities have grown to more than 3,000.

Although the NEA has worked hard to keep our cultural heritage alive in America, many misconceptions about its role in the government still persist. To help Americans appreciate the function of the NEA in the nation, communities, and individual

lives, the agency offers the following facts to assist in understanding its role.[4]

- The NEA is a great investment. The National Endowment
  for the Arts costs each American about *thirty-six cents per
  year*. With this modest investment, the agency helps enhance
  the quality of life for Americans through a breathtaking array
  of cultural activity: from the best in theaters and touring
  dance companies, to folk festivals and music concerts, from
  museums and orchestras, to arts programs in our nation's
  schools that reach millions of students each year.

- The arts help build communities. The arts make communities
  better places to live and work. The NEA helps support community festivals, rural chamber music, arts centers, galleries,
  and the arts in libraries, town halls, children's organizations,
  and other social and civic institutions where families can experience the arts. Arts endowment-sponsored programs build
  bridges of understanding among diverse groups of Americans.

- The NEA helps leverage private support. The NEA provides
  a "stamp of excellence" that leverages private support. NEA
  grants confer national prestige that cannot be duplicated on a
  state or local level. Each NEA dollar is matched by at least
  1:1 and is a funding catalyst, attracting many more dollars
  from local and state agencies, corporations, foundations, and
  individuals. National panels of private citizens select grantees
  in a rigorous, democratic review process.

- The arts stimulate local economies. The arts attract tourist
  dollars, stimulate business development, spur urban renewal,
  attract new businesses, and improve the overall quality of life
  for our cities and towns. On a national level, the nonprofit
  arts generate an estimated $37 billion in economic activity
  and return $3.4 billion in federal income taxes to the U.S.
  Treasury each year.

- The arts mean jobs. More than 1.7 million Americans are employed in the not-for-profit arts industry. Since 1970, the number of artists employed in the U.S. has more than doubled.

- Without public support, the not-for-profit arts would become the sole province of the well-to-do. The NEA helps to make the arts affordable to the average American, who otherwise would be faced with the prospect of skyrocketing, unafford-able tickets. Accessibility to the arts has been widened by the NEA's patronage to arts groups in every corner of the nation.

- The NEA brings the arts for young people. Each year, the NEA opens the door to the arts to millions of school children, including "at-risk" youth. As discussed in previous chapters, the arts help instill self-confidence and discipline, provide creative outlets for self-expression, and help prepare America's future high-tech workforce.

- The NEA helps bring the arts to more Americans. The number of arts organizations has risen dramatically since its founding in 1965. In 1965, there were but five state arts agencies. Today, every state has one. The NEA has helped deliver the arts to every congressional district in the nation. The increase in audience attendance for the performing arts has been significant. The annual attendance for the performing arts now exceeds that of all professional sports combined.

- The NEA nurtures promising artists. From 1965 to 1995, the NEA funded thousands of writers, composers, film and video producers, visual artists, choreographers, designers, play-wrights, and directors, scores of whom subsequently received Obies, Emmys, Tonys, Pulitzers, and other prestigious awards. In 1996, Congress suspended most of the NEA's ability to award individuals, leaving the literature fellowships as the re-maining openly competitive fellowship category, in addition to the "by-nomination-only" National Heritage Fellowships and American Jazz Masters.

- The American people want the arts. A recent Lou Harris poll showed that 57 percent of the American people believe that "the federal government should provide financial assistance to arts organizations such as art museums, dance, opera, theater groups, and symphony orchestras." Additionally, 61 percent said they "would be willing to pay five dollars more in taxes per year to support federal government efforts in the arts."

Each American citizen's investment of thirty-six cents per year has made possible the growth of American culture in the following areas:[5]

- Symphonies and chamber music
- Artists in the schools
- Children's festivals
- Museum and gallery exhibitions
- Operas
- Dance on tour
- Book festivals and poetry readings
- Literacy programs
- Concerts in the park
- Mobile art galleries
- Jazz festivals
- Children's museums
- Puppetry theaters
- Fourth of July festivals

- Local Shakespeare festivals

- Folk festivals

- At-risk youth projects

- Historic revitalization

- Arts on television

- The Mayors Institute on City Design

The Funding Debate

Considering the phenomenal impact the NEA has on our nation's cultural heritage and the education of our children in the arts, it was disconcerting to many when, in 1997, Congress voted to cut the NEA budget by 39 percent. Writer Robert Hughes in "Pulling the Fuse on Culture," said of the Republican leadership, "It wants the federal government to give no support at all to music, theater, ballet, opera, film, intelligent television, literature, history, archaeology, museum work, architectural conservation and the visual arts. It intends to abolish federal funding for the National Endowment for the Arts, the National Endowment for the Humanities, and the Corporation for Public Broadcasting. And it wants to do it tomorrow." This move was even more disturbing considering that the government was spending less than *five hundredths of 1 percent* of its national budget on *all* forms of cultural subsidy—the NEA, the National Endowment for the Humanities (NEH), and the Corporation for Public Broadcasting.[6]

The leadership behind such a move obviously forgot several important government documents that established a need for the arts, including the SCANS report, which was completed in 1991 and established skills criteria for the future work force, and Goals 2000, which was signed into law in 1994 and mandated including arts curricula in our schools' programs. Just three short years after the signing of Goals 2000, our government voted to nearly annihilate the very government agencies (NEA, NEH, etc.) that help to support arts and culture in America, *and* Goals 2000, *and* SCANS. It makes one wonder if the left hand knows what the right hand is doing! Hughes confirms this and says, "Hypocrisy reigns. The right complains (with reason) about the dumbing-down of American education and then wants to kill one of the essential means of its spread and improvement, the National Endowment for the Humanities [and Arts]. It laments the depravity of network and cable TV, especially in the stew of commercial gunk it serves up to children, then wants to cut all federal funding for PBS, the only source of decent educational programming for children and of intelligent documentaries for grown-ups."[7]

This cut came as a result of Congress wanting to sever all ties between American government and American culture because of fewer than forty grants supported by the NEA in its thirty-three-year history that were deemed controversial or un-American. Two widely publicized examples were Robert Mapplethorpe's controversial homosexual photos and Andres Serrano's photo of a crucifix in urine. According to Hughes, Mapplethorpe neither asked for nor received one cent from the NEA to make the photos—a museum received the money to show his work. One might ask, do we dissolve every government agency that makes a dubious decision? If so, there's a good chance all government agencies will disappear. One senator who adamantly and eloquently spoke in the NEA's defense was Senator Orrin Hatch from Utah. Interestingly, in 1899, Utah was the first state in the nation to establish a state arts council. Utah continues to be a consistent and active supporter of all the arts, as evidenced by the yearly Sundance Film Festival held in Park City; the internationally acclaimed Mormon Tabernacle Choir; the Utah Symphony Orchestra, which is one of the busiest performing orchestras in the nation; and numerous other music and arts organizations throughout the state. Utah obviously had a vision of the importance of the arts long before the rest of the nation did, and its present leaders continue to see its vision. At the same time, Utah is well known for being one of the most, if not *the* most, conservative states in this country. Undoubtedly, it has had its fair share of controversial art conceived in the name of "creative expression," yet the arts, in all their varying forms, continue to thrive there.

The question needing an immediate answer from government officials anxious to axe the NEA is: What about the tens of thousands of grants the NEA has supported that have positively influenced American lives for the better? This issue has glaring similarities to the 1970s, when music and the arts were eliminated from the schools' curricula by administrators who ignored the research demonstrating the value of music and the arts in developing the mind and their ability to reach all children. Money guided those decisions instead of what was best for the education of our children. And now we have a group of politicians doing essentially the same thing. They have left the cultural heritage of the greatest nation in the world hanging in the balance. They, too, have ignored the research regarding the value of the arts in the lives of *all* individuals. Mistakes are made, but whatever happened to reform, change, and evaluation—or do we stupidly "throw the baby out with the bath water?"

If music and the arts had never been taken out of the schools, we could now be spending that money in refining the programs rather than fighting to reinstate them!

In all of this, we have somehow lost a sense of what's important. The fight to get music and the arts put back into the schools has required tremendous work by many different organizations and thousands of individuals, not to mention the millions of dollars spent. If music and the arts had never been taken out of the schools, we could now be spending that money in *refining* the programs rather than fighting to *reinstate* them! Carolynn Lindeman, past president of both the California Music Teachers Association and the Music Educators National Conference states, "Music programs in the schools take years to rebuild after they have been cut."[8] If the NEA is dissolved, or drowns because of its measly budget, it will take millions of dollars and maybe another 140 years of fighting to bring it back. It seems strange that instead of looking at ways to avert problems, we would rather spend the money on fixing them after they happen. Case in point—the *Los Angeles Times* reported that "California's annual state budget for the warehousing and maintenance of prisoners is $3.6 billion and growing." The state ranks first in this category and fortieth among all states in public funding for education.[9] Perhaps if more money were spent on education, particularly music and arts education, the numbers in our prisons would be lower, considering how dramatically the arts reach high-risk kids. Ridiculous, you say. Maybe, but consider what art teacher Beth Thielen, who teaches at the California Rehabilitation Center in Norco, has found. She sees many lives in prison change because of the influence of art. The tragedy in all of this is that some of the resources that eluded these prisoners on the outside are now available to them in prison. According to Thielen, "We're willing to pay for in prisons what we won't pay for in neighborhoods: the job training, the counseling, the *art* classes. It's ironic, it's perverse [emphasis added]."[10]

Misconceptions About the NEA

It is important for people to understand the misconceptions regarding government involvement in the arts. First of all, some people think the government should not be supporting the arts, but all great nations throughout history have done so and continue to do so. As mentioned earlier, taxpayers of this country only spend about thirty-six cents per person each year to support the arts. In Canada and France, each person pays thirty-two dollars, and in Germany, it is twenty-seven dollars per person.

Throughout its history, the Russian government has solely supported arts and culture, which has always been a source of national pride. But with the Soviet Union's collapse in 1991 and the ensuing economic difficulties, the government no longer supports the arts. For many Russians, it is a tragedy and serious crisis because they feel the arts are what identify them as a civilized nation. Alexander Krauter, Moscow State Symphony Orchestra's general manager, says, "State officials don't understand that if they let Russia's culture die, all they'll be left with is a nation of bandits."[11]

When the NEA was created, Congress noted, "An advanced civilization must not limit its efforts to science and technology alone, but must give full value and support to the other great branches of scholarly and cultural activity in order to achieve a better understanding of the past, a better analysis of the present, and a better view of the future."[12]

Second, some think that the support of the arts in America is a frivolous expenditure, but to the contrary—and as pointed out in earlier chapters—they significantly generate money for the growth of the economy, as well as provide jobs for thousands of people.

Third, some people believe that the loss of government money will be picked up by the private sector when, in fact, the opposite is occurring. Unfortunately, corporate support of the arts has been declining, and leaders from the philanthropic sector have made it very clear it is impossible for them to pick up the slack.

Fourth, some people feel that the states are better suited to support the arts. However, the NEA has explained that it provides "the way and means for national culture to continue and support for projects that serve the whole nation and help Americans share their diverse cultures with one another."[13]

Finally, some believe erroneously that the NEA is an "elitist" organization that serves only the upper class. In fact, just the opposite is true. It has made the arts available to far more individuals from all economic classes as it reaches Americans of every race, ethnicity, and geographic region, and includes millions of children across the states. Without the NEA, the arts could very well become affordable for only the wealthy.

What You Can Do

Parents should be aware that the NEA provides many wonderful programs for children. As we mentioned earlier, within its Arts in Education Program, 14,500 artists work with 4,700 children in schools across America. Since Goals 2000, the NEA also has been actively involved in putting the arts back into the curriculum for children from kindergarten through high school. But disturbingly, we are already seeing the effects of these 1997 budget cuts. With the rising production costs of quality symphonies, ballets, musicals, and other productions, tickets to some of these events have started to skyrocket. Museum hours are being shortened, and many outreach programs are being cut back or, worse, eliminated. In the years to come, this problem could become more serious as the cultural opportunities decrease instead of increasing. Parents can help change this tide by becoming involved and speaking out. Here are some suggestions:

- Write your congressperson and senator to express your concern over the cuts to the NEA budget. Let them know your strong feelings regarding music and the arts, and also tell them that you are willing to pay more than thirty-six cents to help support arts and culture in America.

- Volunteer your time to your favorite music or arts organization. According to Independent Sector's 1996 study, *Giving and Volunteering in the U.S.*, individual giving and volunteering in the arts rose at a faster pace between 1993 and 1995 than did total giving and volunteering in the nonprofit sector. The number of households contributing to arts, culture, and humanities rose by 55 percent in 1993. And, in 1995, 11.8 million Americans volunteered their time to arts organizations, which was a 36 percent increase from 1993. Computing the time volunteered into a dollar amount showed an impressive value of $201.5 billion. This increase indicates that American households are becoming more and more interested in supporting the arts in their communities.[14]

- Volunteer your business skills to your favorite cultural organization. Nonprofit organizations are in critical need of volunteers who can provide business expertise in areas such as finance, marketing, strategic planning, and information systems. To see how you can become involved contact Business Volunteers for the Arts (see Resources section). Founded twenty-two years ago in New York City, this organization helps in volunteer management consulting in more than thirty cities nationwide. The collective value of their donated services exceeds $10 million per year. These are men and women, aged from the mid-twenties to seventies, and include senior business executives in Fortune 100 corporations, young aspiring managers, and individual entrepreneurs who have a passionate love for the arts and want to give their time and talents to help their local arts organizations.[15]

- Talk to your employer, and ask if they offer a matching gifts program. Coca-Cola offers this program to its employees, both current and retired. Any employee can give a donation to a symphony orchestra, ballet, opera house, or other arts organization of their choice, and Coca-Cola will match that amount, up to $4,000 per year. (This means your symphony orchestra could get $8,000 in your name, in one year!) This is a wonderful way to support your favorite music or arts organization and at the same time involve your employer in supporting the arts. If your business or corporation does not currently have such a program, ask if you can start one for the company.

- Subscribe to your favorite music and arts organization. According to a recent study by three Swedish researchers, if you want to do something that will make you feel healthier and live longer, go to a musical concert or your favorite symphony.[16] Additionally, you will be helping preserve our national arts and culture heritage.

One of the most powerful reasons we need the support of music and the arts by our federal government is for our children and future generations. If not, culture in this nation will become a lost treasure. How will our children pass on what they do not know, understand, and have experience with? It is imperative our children experience this heritage, taste its significance, feel the peace it can bring into their lives, and discover how the arts help to identify them as human beings. Robert Coles, psychiatrist and professor at Harvard University, talked about a twelve-year-old girl he met while doing his residency at Children's Hospital in Boston. He was involved with many children struggling with life-threatening illnesses. This young girl was a ballet dancer of great promise, but she had contracted polio and had lost the use of her legs. She could not walk and most certainly would never dance again. It was devastating to her family, but she, surprisingly, did not become discouraged and simply said, "I'll begin learning to paint." Although Dr. Coles felt she did not understand the full extent of what had happened to her and would in time be devastated by this blow, he learned otherwise. "This young lady showed me, one day, a sketch she'd done, a picture of a horse,

One of the most powerful reasons we need the support of music and the arts by our federal government is for our children and future generations.

bearing a straight-backed rider in obvious control, on its way down a road lined with sturdy trees, and too, some bushes, some hedges. The sun shone above, lighting up a clear sky. On either side of the road, beyond the trees, stretched inviting meadows strewn with flowers—a carefully and skillfully rendered postcard scene." He expressed his delight with the picture to which the young girl replied, "The polio got my legs, but I'll make my hands dance now." Such a statement by one so young caused him to stand in silent awe. He said, "She had shown me what 'art' meant to her, enabled in her—beauty glimpsed and appreciated, a direction or purpose in life explored. In a sense she had already discovered what some of us spend a lifetime seeking—a way of affirming her particular humanity."[17]

The arts have the power to do this. We must make them available for the children in our homes, schools, and communities by establishing a strong national arts heritage, which can only happen through government support.

Jane Alexander, former chairman of the NEA, said, "Children who have the arts at home and school understand that our lives are indeed poems in the making, songs unsung, a dance of days, and a symphony of years."[18]

CHAPTER 10

*V*OICES IN UNISON: SUPPORTING THE ARTS IN YOUR COMMUNITY

While there can be no greater introduction to music than through singing or playing an instrument, the fact remains that the overwhelming majority of our pupils will be neither singers nor players. Whatever contact they will have with music in their adult life will be as listeners. We therefore have to teach them how to listen if we are to make them true music lovers.

—Joseph Machlis

In *Megatrends 2000*, it was predicted that "during the 1990s the arts will gradually replace sports as society's primary leisure activity."[1] It was also predicted that in the next century, people will attend museums, ballets, symphonies, and operas more than ever before and as a result, many new jobs will open up.

It is thrilling to anticipate and be a part of this renaissance and resurgence in the arts, and to know that many new and wonderful art forms will emerge as a result of expanding knowledge and technology. Exposing your children to the musical fare of the next century will be both fun and exciting, but until we arrive at the next decade, there is a plethora of musical activities and concerts to experience now. Whether you live in a big city, the suburbs, or in a rural area, musical opportunities are not far

217

away. The number of choices you have will depend on where you live, but whatever your choices, take advantage of as many concerts as possible. Expose your children to a variety of musicals, symphonies, grand operas, chamber music concerts, ballets, and choral music recitals. Each can provide a wonderful and memorable experience for your family.

In this chapter, we discuss some of the musical programs available in communities around the world; what to expect from each; how to prepare your children before, during, and after a concert; and ideas to make it a lasting and positive experience.

Finding Events in Your Community

Musical events in your community are more common than you might think. The following list offers suggestions on how to find them:

- Check your local newspapers daily, particularly on the weekends. Look for programs that are especially designed for children. As your child gets older (around fifth or sixth grade) critically consider *all* the musical programs offered.

- Listen to the classical radio stations for any advertisements on upcoming programs. Some stations may even offer special deals or discounts.

- Check community colleges and universities for what they offer in the way of children's musical programs. Often, they will offer a children's series that will be both affordable and excellent in content. For many years, we took our sons to a children's classical music series offered at our local community college. The programs were wonderful, affordable, and best of all—close! (In Los Angeles, "close" is a big deal!)

- Check with the religious organizations in your area. They usually sponsor guest performers and musical groups throughout the year, particularly during holidays. These concerts tend to be reasonably priced, the right time length for children, culturally expanding, and very entertaining. Offer your child a broad sampling of music from different cultures, religions, backgrounds, and nations. For example, take your child to hear the music of churches other than your own— such as gospels, cantors, Gregorian chants—or to cultural festivals in your community where she'll hear music from diverse peoples.

> *If you are on a tight budget, search for affordable or free concerts in your community.*

- Network with other parents who expose their children to musical concerts. Find out what they have enjoyed and why. Ask your children's private music teacher and school music teacher about concerts they would recommend. Generally, these people are up to date on enjoyable children's programs that are offered in your area.

- Check the bulletins, advertisements, and flyers at your local library. You will find this to be an excellent source for concerts presented by local talent. Summer concerts held at community parks are a great way to see and experience local performers.

- Become concert subscribers with matinee tickets. Not only are you committing your family to a certain number of concerts a year, but you also are communicating to your children that music and the arts are important, and that attending concerts is a part of the family routine and a fun family affair. By consistently exposing your children to classical concerts year after year, you are starting a tradition that will influence generations to come both educationally and culturally.

If you are on a tight budget, search for affordable or free concerts in your community. Even though Kevin and Tracy Bergen of

Torrance, California, are on a budget, they still find ways of taking their four children to musical concerts. Here's what they do:

- When their piano teacher performs a free recital at the local college, the Bergen children attend. It gives them an opportunity to hear wonderful music and, at the same time, see their piano teacher in a performance setting.

- They call local colleges and universities, find out what they are offering musically, and attend the rehearsals, which are free.

- During the summer, their city offers an outdoor concert series on a weekday night for free. The Bergens have enjoyed all kinds of music at these concerts—jazz, country, bluegrass, big band, and classical.

- Tracy calls the local elementary schools and inquires about school music assemblies. She puts those dates on her calendar and takes her two younger children to those—once again for free.

- Through a flyer at the local library, they discovered a series entitled "Musical Circus" held at the Pasadena Civic Auditorium. Five free events are offered yearly on Saturday mornings at 8:30 A.M. and include actually seeing, touching, and playing the instruments of the orchestra and a half-hour recital, usually featuring the guest soloist for that evening's performance. Tracy says, "These are wonderful events that children as young as three can enjoy." Through attendance at this series, the Bergens found out that children could attend the symphony for only three dollars apiece when accompanied by a full-paying adult. They buy one adult ticket and two children's tickets, and the parents trade off taking the children throughout the year.

No matter what your financial constraints are, you can always find something to fit your budget—so don't let cost hold you back from exposing your children to the arts!

Preparing Your Children for Concerts

Whether you have subscribed to a series of concerts or purchased tickets for a single concert, the next step is to prepare your children for what they will experience. The following are practical suggestions that will help make the experience memorable.

LISTEN TO THE MUSIC

Whether you are taking your child to a ballet, opera, symphony, or musical, get a copy of the music that will be performed, either at the library or CD store. About two weeks before the concert, start playing the music for your child. You can do this while they are getting ready for school in the morning, during the day, or while they are going to sleep at night. Point out the interesting parts of the music, the lively parts, the slower parts, and the instruments playing each. Ask them what they like and don't like about the music and why. After listening to the music for a few days, bring out some rhythm instruments and let them beat out the rhythm of the music, or let them dance and move to the music.

Another fun activity is have your child sit at the kitchen table; provide her with paper, markers, crayons, and paints; and encourage her to "draw what she hears." It is exciting to watch your child's imagination flow. You will be amazed at the creative artwork your family will produce. Hang the pictures up on your bulletin board and entitle them: "Our Interpretations of the Music from *The Nutcracker*" (or *The Magic Flute* or Vivaldi's *Four Seasons*). By doing these activities, your child will become very familiar with the music and, as a result, enjoy the concert more.

GET TO KNOW THE COMPOSER AND THE PERIODS OF MUSIC

Talk to your children about the composer, the period in which he or she composed (Baroque, Classical, and so on), and some interesting facts about his or her life. An excellent children's book about composers is *Lives of the Musicians: Good Times, Bad Times (And What the Neighbors Thought)* by Kathleen Krull. It gives meaningful facts and stories about the composers, as well as humorous happenings in their lives. As you take a few minutes each day to read stories about the composers to your children, the composers will become real people for them and not just names on a page.

Also, introduce your children to the four periods of music—Baroque, Classical, Romantic, and Twentieth Century—by letting them listen to familiar music that is played in the particular style of these eras. Two highly recommend recordings that will help you are *Heigh-Ho! Mozart* and *Bibbidi Bobbidi Bach*. They are a compilation of Walt Disney songs recorded in the style of individual composers from the various musical eras. You will hear "Can You Feel the Love Tonight" (from *Lion King*) in the style of Tchaikovsky (Romantic period), "Little April Showers" (from *Bambi*) in the style of Handel (Baroque), and "Heigh Ho!" (from *Snow White and the Seven Dwarfs*) in the style of Mozart (Classical). When your children hear these familiar songs repeatedly, they will begin to recognize the various styles and nuances of each composer and the musical era. While listening to these CDs, you might find the following information helpful regarding each of these musical eras.

Baroque

The *Baroque period* lasted from approximately 1600 to 1750, with the main composers of this period being Bach, Vivaldi, and Handel. The music of this era was very ornate, very orderly, flowery, and had lots of emotional contrasts of feelings (high/low, loud/soft, fast/slow). The composers of this era conveyed through their music a wide range of emotions: passion, heroism, sacrifice, reverence for religion, and feelings of ecstasy.

Classical

The *Classical period* was marked by music that was for the masses and not just the royalty or wealthy. It lasted from approximately 1750 to 1820. The main composers of this period were Mozart, Haydn, and Beethoven. The musical forms of the symphony, sonata, and string quartets were used extensively during this era.

Romantic

The *Romantic period* lasted from approximately 1820 to the end of the century. The expression of emotions and feelings is typical of this era, with the composers being inspired by the flora and fauna of nature, sunrises, sunsets, the sea, and thunderstorms. The composers of this era included Schubert, Schumann, Mendelssohn, Chopin, Liszt, Brahms, and Tchaikovsky.

Twentieth Century

The *Twentieth Century period* comprises the music of Mahler, Debussy, Strauss, Stravinsky, and Shostakovich. This music is varied—with some composers seeking to create a mood or atmosphere, some wanting to express the inner feelings of man, and still others wanting to incorporate the folk tunes from their countries, but one thing is for sure—most just wanted to do things their own way!

GET TO KNOW THE ORCHESTRA

Part of your pre-concert preparation should include becoming familiar with the instruments of the orchestra, and the musicians who play those instruments. Check out books from the library that show your children pictures of each instrument of the orchestra, so they can see what they look like. If possible, take them to a music store, so they can actually see, touch, and hear some of these instruments. This would be a good time to play

Benjamin Britten's *A Young Person's Guide to the Orchestra,* as it will help them become familiar with each instrument's distinctive sound. Then when you play the CD for the upcoming concert, have your children listen carefully for each instrument.

Check out a general music book from the library that will show your children where everyone in the orchestra sits. When the musicians are seated on stage or in an orchestra pit, they form a large half circle. Each group of musicians is seated in a specific area, with the violins to the left of the conductor, the violas in the center, and the cellos to the right of the conductor. Behind the cellos are the double bass; and behind the violas are the piccolos, flutes, oboes, bassoons, English horns, and clarinets. Behind the violins is the harpist. In the back row (going from left to right) are the percussionists, then the horns, the trumpets, the trombones, and finally the tubas. There are usually 100 musicians in a symphony orchestra and, on the day of the performance, they are dressed in formal attire. There are many wonderful books available to use in explaining the orchestra and each orchestra member to your child. Some favorites include *The Philharmonic Gets Dressed* by Karla Kuskin, *Alligators and Music* by Donald Elliott, and *Meet the Orchestra* by Ann Hays.

The life of the musician is not always glamorous or exciting; in fact, it can be very stressful at times. Professional musicians give enormous amounts of time, effort, and dedication to their art. They want the music to sound beautiful and flawless for their audiences. To do so, they must put in long hours of practicing and rehearsal time with the other musicians. Most orchestras typically have seven to nine rehearsals each week where each rehearsal is two-and-a-half hours long. This doesn't include the time they spend practicing their instruments each day, or the amount of new music they must learn in a week. Within seven days, they can perform up to four different concerts, which translates into a lot of music that needs to be learned. When people go to hear a symphony, they usually do not realize the dedication that has gone into making the performance sound perfect and polished. It is usually an "eye-opener" to find out the amount of time expended to accomplish what they do. One famous pianist, after performing a concert, was told by a woman, "I would give my life to play like you." To which he replied, "I have, Madam."

GET TO KNOW THE CONDUCTOR

Prior to taking your children to a concert, explain to them some of the responsibilities of the conductor. Early orchestras did not have conductors. The first violinist did the job; he started everyone together and saw to it that everyone finished together. As the music became more complicated, a leader was needed, and the role of the conductor was born. Jean-Baptiste Lully was one of the first conductors during the Baroque era. He would stand in front of the musicians pounding out the beat on the floor with a heavy staff. Once as he was beating out the time, he mistakenly pounded his foot instead of the floor. Unfortunately, the wound proved fatal because his foot became infected with gangrene. Today, this is obviously not a hazard because conductors no longer pound out the beat of the music with a staff. They employ their arms, hands, and baton movements to communicate to the orchestra the rhythm of the music.

The conductor is a very important part of the orchestra. He is literally the leader of the group—guiding each musician through the music; controlling the delicate balance of speed, volume, and note length of the musical score; and getting everyone to play with a sense of musicality. Musicality is the ability of the musicians to play with emotional expression, creativity, knowledge, and technical ability. To have this come off well takes enormous skill on the part of the conductor. He must be a confident tour de force! All of the musicians must be able to read his every gesture, his body language, face, eyes, and baton movements, as each has meaning and importance to the success of the music. Stored in his brain is the entire score of the piece, as well as every part, nuance, and musical interpretation for each instrument. He must be able to bring in the violins, clarinets, trumpets, and percussionists at just the right time, with the right volume, expression, and feeling that causes the music to drive us to tears. When you are at a symphony, carefully observe the conductor. He or she is as interesting to watch as listening to the music itself. A fascinating story is told of Felix Mendelssohn, who, when conducting the premiere performance of Bach's *The Passion According to St. Matthew,* discovered at the podium that he had the wrong musical score! But, because the show must go on, Mendelssohn lifted his baton and began to conduct Bach's *Passion.* Every so often, he would turn the pages of the score, so as not to alarm the musicians, but in reality he conducted the entire two-hour score from memory and with no noticeable mistakes! It was a phenomenal success, and only the most talented of conductors could pull off such a feat successfully.

GET TO KNOW THE STORY

If you are going to an opera, musical, or ballet where a story is involved, check out books from the library and read the story to your children. Explain the plot, the characters, and the setting. The more information and preparation you can give them the better, for obvious reasons—we enjoy that which we understand and can easily follow. A few years ago, we took our boys to the stage production of *Beauty and the Beast.* Even though they had seen the Disney movie, we still checked out the fairy tale from the library to read. We found more than one version of *Beauty and the Beast* and ended up having fun comparing different variations on the same theme. If you see the ballet *Cinderella,* you will find over 400 written versions of that fairy tale! Before we saw *Phantom of the Opera,* we read the book and listened to the music many times. It was a spectacular production, and even though our youngest was only in the second grade at the time, he loved it because of our preparation. If you have lots of creative energy, you can even "act out" the ballet, opera, or musical at your house with each member of the family playing one or more parts. Resurrect the costumes from your Halloween supply and improvise! Who knows, it may be the beginning of a new career for your family! Over the years, as you take your children to these productions, you will end up with a marvelous collection of books on ballets, operas, and musicals that will become a treasure trove and can be used for future generations.

PLAN A BACKSTAGE TOUR

Prior to the performance, call and arrange a backstage tour. Many places will do this, especially if you have a large group of children. These tours can be a valuable educational experience and will make the performance come to life on many levels. One of our sons, Ryan, had the opportunity to go on a backstage tour for *Phantom of the Opera*. A mother in his class called the theater and arranged a tour for the whole class, which turned out to be a fascinating experience for everyone. Ryan came home very excited, and he shared with us intricate details of how this spectacular opera was choreographed and produced. We learned that there are usually fifteen backstage people to run the lights, scenery changes, and so on, in most productions, but with *Phantom* there were so many special effects that it took more than sixty backstage people to see that everything came off perfectly. The fabrics for the masquerade ball came from Europe, and the weekly cleaning bill for all of the gorgeous costumes was enormous! Although there was only one person playing the part of the Phantom, there were others dressed up as the Phantom to help create certain special effects and illusions. Two weeks later when we went as a family to see *Phantom*, Ryan's extra information helped everyone to appreciate and understand what went into the production of this musical. A few years later, another son went on a backstage tour of another musical. He saw how the backstage people change the scenery, but he also learned how a sound system works. All of the principal actors' voices are pumped through a PA system back to a computer that analyzes the pitch, volume, and sound levels of the voice. Corrections are made so that on the night of the performance, the singing and speaking voices of the actors sound perfect. Even on the night of the performance, if adjustments are necessary, they can be made right on the spot, so that the voices sound flawless—and all because of the wonders of technology! Backstage tours can be very informative and educational for your children. For that reason, do not be afraid to *ask* if backstage tours are available—the worst thing they could tell you is no, but it is definitely worth a try!

Going to the Concert

The next step is actually going to the concert. It is important to make this event special and fun. The following ideas will help ensure that it is both.

- As far as what your children should wear, the rule is comfort! I've been to many concerts in Southern California and, believe me, I've seen *everything!* Dress your child in comfortable clothes, such as slacks and a polo or dress shirt for boys and a soft dress or nice pants for girls. Boys in tight ties and girls in scratchy, fluffy dresses can be very uncomfortable. We all want our children to be comfortable throughout the concert, but we should also want them to know that this is a special occasion and wearing something a little nicer communicates respect for the event and the performers.

- Let your children know that you expect proper concert etiquette from them. This means that during the performance, they must be absolutely quiet out of respect for others who have paid money to see the performance and want to be able to enjoy it without hearing interfering noise of any kind. In most concert halls, the acoustics are incredibly sensitive, and even a sneeze, cough, or whisper can resonate throughout the hall. Also, instruct your children on the appropriate time to clap for the musicians, as well as the time not to clap, such as in between movements. Many *adults* make the mistake of clapping too soon, so follow this rule of thumb—don't clap until you see the conductor put his hands and arms down to his side and all the musicians have put down their instruments. A wonderful book written for children on this very subject is *When Can I Clap, Daddy?* by Margaret Keith.

- Arrive on time. Most places have strict rules on late seating, and if you arrive late you may not get seated until the intermission, which is only fair to the other people around you. By arriving early, you do not feel rushed, you can get to the restroom one last time, and you will have an opportunity to look over the program and point out any last bits of interesting information about the performers or musical numbers to your child.

- During intermission, if you are at an opera, ballet, or musical, take your child down to see the orchestra pit. It is always interesting for a child to see where the music is coming from. This is also a good time to evaluate if your child can last through the second half of the performance. I remember when we took our oldest son to his first big concert. He was barely four and we took him to see the Austrian Boys Choir (not a great choice for a first concert). By intermission, he had had enough and was ready to leave. So, that is exactly what we did. We decided that by leaving early and not forcing him to stay until the end, we could still leave with a good feeling—and that was our main goal. So, when you buy those expensive tickets, remember that you may see only half of what you have paid for. That is another important reason to invest in children's series, they tend to understand a child's limited attention span and produce concerts that are just the right time length.

After the Concert

After the concert you can either make a beeline for the nearest exit, or stay and go backstage to meet the artists. We've done both. We have taken our children to places where, after the performance, the artists come out into the foyer to shake hands with the children, sign autographs, and pose for pictures. When booking tickets, ask if they offer this wonderful perk. Post-concert is also a great time to go to dinner, lunch, or dessert because everyone is usually famished (or at least they think they are). While you are eating, discuss what everyone liked best about the concert, the performers, the music, and so on. If you saw a ballet, opera, or musical, talk about the actors, the story, the scenery, and the music.

If there is a performance that you take your children to year after year—such as the *Nutcracker, A Christmas Carol,* or a favorite musical—compare performances from year to year. What changed, what is the same, which of all the performances did they like better, and why? What is their opinion of the artistic abilities of the principal performers or musicians? Did they like their performance better this time or not as well? Why or why not? What made this performance more special or unique than the others? By asking open-ended questions, you will get your children thinking, analyzing, comparing, and expressing ideas about their musical experiences.

Some friends of ours took their children to see *Phantom of the Opera* twice, each with different men performing the role of Phantom. It was very interesting for the parents to hear everyone's opinion on which Phantom they liked better and why. Another memorable activity you might want to add to your list of family traditions is to write down each of your children's feelings about the concert in a special family journal saved just for musical experiences. It is fun to look back and read everyone's thoughts and feelings about the concert and to see how your children grow and mature in their ideas and responses as the years progress. This book also can be a great place to put programs and pictures of each event as a visual memory. As the years go by, your family will enjoy reliving those special musical memories.

Good Concert Choices for Children

Not all concerts are appropriate for children. Consider the following before buying tickets.

THE SYMPHONY ORCHESTRA

Most symphony orchestras provide children's programs that introduce them to the wonder and excitement of live orchestral music. For children to learn from and enjoy these presentations, they should be visually colorful, short, lively, and entertaining. You will find that many of these geared-for-children programs are centered on a theme with appropriate classical music that complements the subject. For instance, if the theme is animals, the orchestra may present Saint-Saëns's *Carnival of the Animals*. If the theme is seasons, the orchestra might play Vivaldi's *Four Seasons*, or if the theme is musical stories, it might perform *Peter and the Wolf*. Orchestras also like to introduce music from other countries or music from a particular ethnic group to help children understand and appreciate the songs and music from other countries and people.

If your community has a symphony orchestra, find out if it offers children's concerts and the appropriate age they recommend a child to be. Some orchestras present concerts that can be appropriate for children as young as three. For the past seventy years, the Los Angeles Philharmonic has offered a series of five concerts for the very young (three to five years old) and another series for the five to twelve age group. These hugely popular concerts use different themes for each season and introduce them with lively, colorful presentations.

Today, many symphony orchestras, realizing how visually oriented children of the nineties are, use interactivity and hands-on experiences. You will find the use of video enhancements, screens around the hall where close-ups of the instruments can be shown while they are being played on stage, as well as crafts and activities that will make the experience memorable. Most of these concerts last anywhere from thirty minutes to one hour, which is perfect for a young child's attention span.

Actually seeing the symphony orchestra "up front and personal" can be thrilling to young children. They are able to see and observe (and many times talk to) the musicians playing the pieces that they have previously only heard on a CD. It adds a whole new dimension to their musical experience, and suddenly they realize how music is produced by a whole group of people working together.

CHAMBER MUSIC

Chamber music is music that is written for small, intimate groups of instruments or vocalists and is performed in rooms rather than in theaters or large public areas. It usually comprises somewhere between two and ten performers, and there is no conductor. Considering this definition, a family of musicians could conceivably perform chamber music and, as a matter of fact, many of the "privileged" of Europe did just that. Haydn is credited with establishing the string quartet as the crowning chamber music form. Nearly all of the composers wrote some chamber music, but originally most of the chamber music was written for only the wealthy of Europe. It was not until the nine-teenth century that chamber music was written for the masses.

Today, chamber music is performed more than any other kind of music because the musicians love the small, intimate set-tings, where they can be close to their audience and at the same time engage in a wonderful discourse among their fellow players. It is fun to take your child to experience chamber music for this rea-son. The cozy setting makes it easier to talk and mingle with the musicians afterward. They are usually extremely friendly and anx-ious to answer questions and talk about their musical experiences.

Pianist Leif Ove Andsnes said this about chamber music, "Playing chamber music feeds my solo performing," he said, "You get so close to others you're playing with—it's like a marriage, musically and personally."[2] Before going to hear chamber music, anticipate that your children will be able to talk with the musi-cians afterwards, so think about some questions they could ask. For instance, what part does music play in their lives; is this a hobby or their regular occupation; how long have they been playing with this group; how long do they practice each day; and what have they sacrificed to reach this level of music profi-ciency? If you have a child who is wavering and wants to quit playing his instrument, take him to hear chamber music and let him talk to the musicians. It might be just the right experience he needs to help him over a difficult period and inspire him to continue with his musical studies. Among some favorite pieces of chamber music that are suitable for children are Schubert's Piano Quintet in A-major (the *Trout*), Mozart's Quintet for Clarinet and Strings, Dvořák's String Quartet in F (*American*), and Brahms's Trio for Violin, Horn, and Piano.

CHORAL MUSIC

If you have ever sung in a choir at church, a chorus at school, or a choral group in the community, you know how rewarding and fun it is to be a part of these singing ensembles. I remember one Christmas when I was fourteen years old, singing Handel's *Messiah* with our church choir. It was a wonderful experience, and those songs will be etched forever in my memory. Even today, when I hear choruses sing *Messiah*, it gives me goose bumps. Apparently, many people feel the same way because during the holidays, many music centers throughout the United States offer to the public an opportunity to be a part of a massive sing-a-long choir performing *Messiah*. If your community offers an opportunity like this, take advantage of it with your entire family. Whether you are a participant or spectator, it is a thrilling experience and can add a memorable tradition to your holiday season.

Seek out opportunities in your community for your children to hear choral music, and keep in mind that most of it will be of a religious nature. In preparing them, do the same activities you would to prepare them for any other kind of concert. First, get the music and let them listen to it, repeatedly. You want them to become familiar with both the words and the music because the words give additional meaning to the music. Second, tell your children a little of the history behind choral music and what exactly choral music is. Choral music is music with words and is performed by a combination of solo singers, choruses, and orchestras. It is usually associated with religious or sacred music and has been around longer than orchestras—in fact, centuries longer. Recorded history states that a "School for Singers" existed during the time of Pope Silvester's reign more than 1,600 years ago.

Choral music includes oratorios, cantatas, and chants. An oratorio is a very large work of music and can last several hours. It is written for a chorus, orchestra, and vocal soloists, and usually tells a story from the Bible. Probably the most famous oratorio ever written is Handel's *Messiah*. Bach also wrote several spectacular oratorios, including *The Passion According to St. Matthew*, which is referred to by his own family as "the Great Passion."[3]

A cantata is a short oratorio. Bach wrote more than 200 cantatas—including one that was meant as a joke, the *Coffee Cantata* or Cantata no. 211. It is about a father and his daughter who love coffee (also Bach's favorite drink) and was written as a result of coffee just being introduced into Europe by the Turks.[4]

Chants are melodies that have been around since Pope Gregory the Great (540 to 604 A.D.), and legend has it that he received them from the Holy Spirit. Today, these chants are known as Gregorian chants.

Choral music also can be found in symphonies. In Beethoven's Ninth Symphony, he uses a chorus for the "Ode to Joy." Hector Berlioz used anywhere from 300 to 900 singers in his "Mass for the Dead" (or what is jokingly referred to as "Mass To Wake the Dead") from *Symphonie Fantastique*.[5]

When introducing your children to choral music, choose programs that are short and have a variety of different songs such as school choruses, choirs of various religions, and community choirs singing a variety of songs. By doing so, you will help them become familiar with this wonderful art form, gain an understanding and appreciation of it, and instill within them a desire to experience a whole oratorio or cantata when the time comes. Some favorites to include are "Jesu Joy of Man's Desiring" (Cantata no. 147) by Bach, *Messiah* by Handel, the final chorus of *The Passion According to St. Matthew* by Bach, and *Requiem* by Mozart.

When introducing your children to choral music, choose programs that are short and have a variety of different songs such as school choruses, choirs of various religions, and community choirs singing a variety of songs.

BALLET

Ballets are enchanting stories told through colorful dancing and music and are enjoyed by boys and girls. Many years ago, the dancing was the most important part of a ballet, and the music was used for the background. Then famous composers such as Peter Tchaikovsky began writing ballet music that was as beautiful as the dancing. Today, we go to see a ballet as much to hear the music as to see the dancing. In fact, the music is usually so breathtaking that it can be enjoyed on its own.

Music in a ballet is considered programmatic, which means that the music itself tells a story, and each note corresponds to the action on the stage. One of the most popular ballets that children of all ages enjoy is Tchaikovsky's *Nutcracker Ballet*. The story, similar to a fairy tale, is about a young girl named Marie who discovers that the nutcracker she received from her godfather for Christmas is real. Through a series of exciting events, he proves to be a young man who has been put under a spell by an evil mouse king. Throughout the story, Marie and the nutcracker visit many lands, including the land of the Sugarplum Fairy and Toyland. The *Nutcracker Ballet* is both beautiful and visually exciting and is a "must" for all children to see and experience. It is usually presented in December around holiday time, but the music should be included in every child's CD collection and enjoyed year round. With the videotaped version of Mikhail Baryshnikov and the American Ballet Theater performing the *Nutcracker Ballet*, you can throw a "Nutcracker Party" any month of the year complete with decorations and refreshments.

Before going to the ballet, explain to your child that the ballet dancers tell a story and express their feelings through their hand movements, gestures, and dancing. Each movement of the dancers communicates the story to the audience. Besides the *Nutcracker*, some other wonderful ballets to take your children to include *Sleeping Beauty* (Tchaikovsky), *Swan Lake*, (Tchaikovsky), and *Cinderella* (Prokofiev). For older children, try *Firebird Suit*, (Stravinsky), *Romeo and Juliet*, (both Prokofiev and Tchaikovsky), and *Petrushka* (Stravinsky).

GRAND OPERA

Grand opera is considered the most perfect of all the art forms because it includes the visual arts (scenery and costumes), singing, (vocalists), music (orchestra), drama, literature (the story), and dancing (corps de ballet). Grand opera has no spoken parts—everything is sung. The singing is composed of arias—songs that express the deep feelings and emotions of the character; recitative—chanting the words instead of singing them; and leitmotif—a series of musical notes or a theme played each time a certain character comes on stage. Because it takes four times longer to sing something than it does to say the same thing, operas tend to be *lonnnnng!* In fact, the word "opera" means work—and work it is, particularly for the vocalists whose voices must hold up for four or more hours.

Opera can be a wonderful experience for a child, but there are specific ideas and suggestions that will help your children understand this art form better before they are exposed to it.

Once again, the first thing to do is get the music from the opera and play it every day. Next, get the book that tells the story, and read it to your children, explaining any parts they might not understand. A wonderful children's book about opera is *Sing Me a Story* by Jane Rosenberg. Operas can get very confusing because there are so many characters. To help your children keep all the characters straight (and if you are feeling industrious) make paper dolls of the characters and let them act out the scenes.

Look for an opera company in your community that performs opera geared to children. For instance, the Houston Grand Opera in Texas offers a wonderful children's opera series called "Opera to Go!" This professional touring company produces fully staged portable operas in English for students in kindergarten through seventh grade. It also offers opera geared to high school students and opera matinees for children from ages nine to fourteen.

L.A. Opera in Los Angeles, California, offers operas for children. In February 1999, it performed the first world premiere of an American opera in its history—Roald Dahl's *Fantastic Mr. Fox*. Productions such as these are a perfect way to introduce a child to the opera format. When your children get older, you can take them to opera written by the classical masters. Opera companies are realizing that to capture children's attention and help them understand this artistic medium, exposure needs to be gradual. Expecting a child to sit through hours of singing in a foreign language is not the way to endear a child to opera. Most children end up bored and hating every minute of it. When I was ten years old, my grandmother took me to my first opera. It was Richard Wagner's *Tännhauser*—a terrible choice for a young child's first opera experience! It was so long—four-and-a-half hours—that I just about died from boredom, and I decided I would never go to see another opera again! (But I did.) So, when choosing an opera for your child to see, remember, "less is more."

Remember, too, that most of the grand operas are not written in English, and they are not translated into English because the poetic meaning of the words gets lost in the translation and the words don't fit the music. But, one *musical* that has all the elements of grand opera (arias, recitative, corps de ballet) is exciting, spectacular, *and* is sung in English is Andrew Lloyd Webber's *Phantom of the Opera*. Your children will love it, and so will you. The purists do not consider it grand opera, but it will start your child on the path to enjoying "pure" opera later on.

Esa-Pekka Salonen, music director of the Los Angeles Philharmonic, recently announced that he would be taking a year-long sabbatical in the year 2000 to compose his first opera. Although he will not disclose the subject or proposed title, he did say that it would be written to an English-language libretto, which is very exciting![6]

It is important to know that many operas deal with immorality, violence, and murder—or everything that you find in the popular movies of today! The difference is, at the end of some operas, mainly Mozart's operas, one of the characters comes out on stage and lets the audience know that there is always a price to pay for evil or wrongdoing.

There are some delightful operas to introduce your children to that they will enjoy. Some favorites are Mozart's *Magic Flute*, Menotti's *Amahl and the Night Visitors*, Humperdinck's *Hansel and Gretel*, Prokofiev's *The Love for Three Oranges*, and Ravel's *L'Enfant et Les Sortileges*.

If you want your family to experience opera, but you can't afford it or it is inaccessible where you live, consider tuning into the Metropolitan Opera radio broadcasts. This program, generously sponsored by Texaco, has reached millions worldwide over the past sixty years.

Texaco has also sponsored over seventy Metropolitan Opera telecasts on PBS. The shows have become an award-winning series, with incomparable views of the Met's lavish productions. With the help of English subtitles, they have played a major role in increasing the public's awareness and enjoyment of opera.

Jeannette Peck vividly remembers the radio broadcasts from when she was a child, cleaning her grandmother's house every Saturday. "My grandmother sat in a chair next to the radio mesmerized by the music and story. I remember times when she started to cry, and seeing my concern, she explained to me that it was the beauty of the music that caused her emotions. Each Saturday she talked to me about the opera and explained the characters and story. My grandmother was my first link to opera, and those broadcasts were my *only* link to actually hearing opera as a child."

MUSICALS

The main difference between an opera and a musical is that opera is entirely sung and usually tells a serious story, while musicals have both singing and dialogue, and the story line tends to be light and even comical. Most of the Broadway plays are classified as musicals.

Musicals tell a love story through singing, dancing, colorful settings, and costumes. This art form grew out of the old American minstrel shows popular in the 1840s. *Showboat*, produced in 1927, brought together the traditions of the European operetta with distinctive American themes and folk elements. It became a classic of the American stage, and the American musical as we know it today was born. Some of the best musicals have been adapted from works of literature. For instance, Rogers and Hammerstein's *Carousel* was based on a play by Ferenc Molnar, *South Pacific* was from stories by James Michener, and *My Fair Lady* was from George Bernard Shaw's play *Pygmalion*. Musicals are a delightful way to introduce your children to longer stage productions—and because they are so lively and entertaining and the music is so appealing, children love them.

In preparing your child for a musical, the same rules we discussed earlier apply. Get the music for them to listen to, and make certain they are familiar with the story. If you have exposed your children to symphonies, short operas, chamber music, and choral groups, they will be able to easily sit through a musical by the time they are seven or eight. Some musicals that children enjoy include *Annie*, *Oklahoma!*, *Fiddler on the Roof*, *Sound of Music*, *Seven Brides for Seven Brothers*, and *Joseph and the Amazing Technicolor Dreamcoat*. When they get older, expose them to musicals with a more sophisticated story line such as *Cats*, *Sunset Boulevard*, *Evita*, and *Les Miserables*. *Les Miserables* is a powerful musical story of love and forgiveness—and once you see the stage production and read the book by Victor Hugo, it will become one of your favorites. Both before and after seeing this moving performance, take the time to discuss and analyze this unforgettable story and its characters with your children.

If our children are to enjoy these various art forms when they are adults, as well as derive the benefits to the intellect and the psyche that arts education brings, they will need to have someone show them the way when they are young. That someone can be a parent, teacher, caregiver or anyone who knows that a child's soul and mind are enriched by the beauty of the cultural and educational experiences they are exposed to. Hungarian composer Zoltán Kodály is certainly one who knows. He said, "Music is the manifestation of the human spirit, similar to language. Its greatest practitioners have conveyed to mankind things not possible to say in any other language. If we do not want these things to remain dead treasures, we must do our utmost to make the greatest possible number of [children] understand their idiom."

If our children are to enjoy these various art forms when they are adults, as well as derive the benefits to the intellect and the psyche that arts education brings, they will need to have someone show them the way when they are young.

Exposure to these various art forms over many years will make them living treasures for our children.

FINALE: BUILDING A LEGACY—
A PARENT'S RESPONSIBILITY

We are so much like violins
Frames, with sensitive strings
The touch of the hand
That holds the bow
Determines the music it brings.

—Edna Machesny[1]

N ow that you have read this book, you may feel the urge to
rush to the nearest music store and buy every CD suggested
in the Resources section, or immediately start your child in
music lessons. But before you do any of the above—stop and
carefully read and think about this chapter. (It may be the most
important one in the book!) As parents, we want our children to
respond with enthusiasm and delight to those musical experiences, activities, and lessons we provide for them, as we feel
these opportunities will bring them fulfillment now and later in
life. Many times we become frustrated and even angry when
they do not react the way we envision they should or openly
rebel against those things we value. (Welcome to parenthood!)
Therefore, the goal of this chapter is to give you three specific
ideas that when implemented *consistently* will be so powerful
that the musical experiences, activities, and lessons you give
your children will have the potential to be successful now, and
in the future.

These ideas work. They will literally be the keys to starting musical traditions, or any other traditions in your home . . . so carefully read, ponder, apply, and reap the rewards. Before I present these ideas, however, a little background on how I formulated them is in order.

Without a doubt, the most inspiring and memorable experiences of my life have been the birth of my five sons. No other event comes close in terms of emotions and pure joy. I have captured forever in my mind the memory of gazing down with wonder and awe at each son right after birth and being amazed at the miracle of life. For those brief moments, the huge responsibility that lay before me did not enter my mind or occupy one single thought. But that didn't last long and, now, twenty-two years later, I know and understand all too well the enormously challenging, time-consuming, and, yes, rewarding responsibility that comes with raising children. It has been difficult, but as with *all* challenges that life presents us, I have learned many things along the way. Unfortunately, children do not come with an instruction book—one unique to their personality—and so the "art of raising children," in reality becomes "on-the-job training!"

A few years ago, a news release from Los Angeles related the story of a blind father who rescued his tiny daughter from drowning in the new swimming pool that had been installed in the neighborhood. The father heard a splash as his daughter, who could not swim, fell into the pool. It was evening, and he became frantic, knowing that there was no one but him to save his child. He got on his hands and knees and crawled around the outside edge of the pool, listening for the air bubbles that came from the little girl as she was drowning. Through his heightened sense of hearing, he followed the sound of the air bubbles, and in one desperate attempt and with overwhelming love in his heart, he jumped into the pool and grasped his precious daughter and brought her to safety.[2]

Parenthood is fraught with challenges, and many times we really are "blind"—groping to find the best way to "save" our children and to do the right thing because of our love for them and because of our desire to see them evolve into happy, well-adjusted adults. Dr. Mihaly Csikszentmihalyi, psychologist at the University of Chicago and author of *Flow*, confirmed the power of love in raising healthy children in a twenty-year study he conducted. He found that the most gifted and happiest of individuals are those who come from families that communicate high expectations and have clear rules, but also offer early opportunities for meaningful choices within a *warm*, *loving*, and *supportive* environment.[3] (Emphasis added.)

For my husband and I, the last twenty-plus years have been spent studying the concepts of child rearing and examining our priorities, methods, motives, and goals regarding this task. Along the way, we have made many mistakes that forced us to stand back and look for better ways and approaches to situations and to rethink ideas and expectations. By doing so, we have learned to carefully consider our children's feelings and interests when choosing family, school, community, and church activities we hope will help mold them into well-rounded, independent, and confident human beings. But through this experience called "parenthood," we also have discovered one very important element in raising our children that, when missing, anything else we did with them and for them became almost inconsequential. This element, oftentimes a difficult task, was establishing and maintaining a personal relationship with each of our sons. We found that our sons responded to the things that were important to us (good music, literature, the arts, and so on) when we worked at getting to know and appreciate them as people with thoughts, feelings, and opinions, *first*. As parents, we can give our children all the material possessions in the world, afford all the lessons, or expose them to all kinds of exciting experiences—but if they do not know and feel that we care about them simply for being who they are, and that we love them despite inappropriate and embarrassing behavior at times, the best formulated plans and goals can backfire. When they get to be teenagers, there is always the possibility they will rebel against the very things that are important to us if we haven't shown through our actions that we value them first as human beings. It is as though our children are saying to us, "Don't tell me how much you know until you show me how much you care."

We live in one of the most exciting times in the history of this world, a time filled with countless electronic conveniences. We have access to more information than ever before in myriad forms: books, magazines, television, radio, telephone, short wave, satellite transmissions, audio and video recordings, movies, computers, facsimile machines, cellular telephones, pagers, and CDs. Although the possibilities of all these inventions make our lives easier in one sense, they can complicate matters in our relationships with our children as our attention is stretched in many different and varied directions. With all of these outside influences and demands on our time, raising children becomes a delicate balancing act, and sometimes we can't help but fall off the beam—as shown by many reports and studies of parents too busy to raise their children with proper guidance. In 1995, the Carnegie Commission presented an alarming picture of a society that neglects and discounts adolescents. American parents were seen as preoccupied and dismissive, unable to cope with the problems of their children. These were adolescents from both poor and economically advantaged homes, who only saw their parents while they were taking them from swimming lessons to dance class to tutoring.[4] Sadly, many parents believe that these many activities make up for the time they cannot, or will not, spend with them on a personal level. Children need to have more from their parents than the cost of yet one more lesson or activity.

All we have to do is read the newspapers to know there are serious problems with the youth of today, but if we carefully analyzed the reasons why, we would find that the greater problem lies with the parents. In the past, the kids with difficult problems usually came from impoverished or disadvantaged homes, but not so today. Studies show that whether kids succeed or fail, socioeconomic status of the family makes no difference—the difference lies in parents showing a genuine interest in their children by giving them both quantity and quality time. Lauren Greenfield spent four years photographing kids from Los Angeles. The result was a book entitled *Fast Forward, Growing Up in the Shadow of Hollywood*. The pages show kids with every advantage in life—money, fame, and material possessions—but dramatically illustrate what can happen when children are given everything but parental involvement: early experimentation with drugs, sex, and/or gang affiliation, and a haunting look of oldness. Despite all of their indulgences, these young people are very much alone, left only with the "things" money can buy. Robert Jones in, "Fast Forward Kids," sums it up by saying, "They jump from one indulgence to another, spending ever more money, trying to fill the alone-ness."[5] An educator friend of mine concurred and said, "You can never get full on things you don't need and, all else obtained, the emptiness remains."

Material possessions, or "things" ultimately do not make children *or* adults happy or fulfilled, and when we lose the things in life that really mean something—like a warm relationship with our children—nothing else matters. Even MGM's Louis B. Mayer, the once powerful, wealthy king of Hollywood knew money couldn't buy everything. As he lay dying in his hospital bed, he despairingly said, "Nothing matters. Nothing matters."[6] Likewise, Thomas Griffith, an editor for *Time* magazine some years ago, in writing about our era, said, "We are so caught up in the complexity and clamor of our way of life that we do not realize how much all of these powerful efforts to attract or divert us are a tax on our spirit: they do a double harm, in the triviality of what they offer and the fatigue which they engender, that keeps us from doing something more profitable with our time. Even to screen out that portion of our culture that we do not want becomes an effort of will. Simplicity of life is no longer ours to begin with, as it was in the days of remote farms and of school lessons written on the back of a shovel. In a world of congestion, shattering noise and an infinity of seductions, we must, in the midst of a carnival, find and insist upon our own decent simplicity."[7]

Over the years, I have tried to observe what it is that parents and children of successful families have in common. My definition of "successful" families is families that are emotionally balanced, as opposed to extraordinarily talented. *All* families have numerous talents, but not all have emotional stability. In my search, I have found that although parents of emotionally functional families are busy trying to balance home, work, family, church, and community, they take the time to do those simple acts such as talking and listening to their kids, expressing their love for them, and making them feel special and valued. They understand the importance of prioritizing, putting their children as one of their top priorities, and knowing full well that "no other success can compensate for failure in the home."[8] They take primary responsibility for their children, aware that they will not learn all they need to learn in school, and that the home is the first and most effective place for them to learn the lessons of life. They see themselves as the master teachers in their children's lives and realize that *their* example is the most effective teaching tool. They do not acquiesce their parental responsibilities to the next-door neighbor, the school, or the state or federal government; they consider themselves the primary caretaker and take their responsibility as parents seriously. In short, their lives and the lives of their children are filled with mutual purpose and direction.

Sounds like a family right out of a fairy tale, right? Not quite. There are many such families throughout the world, but for whatever reason, we just do not hear about them very often.

But one woman who single-handedly built a successful family based on these qualities is Sonja Carson—one of my heroines. She was married at thirteen, had two children by the time she was fifteen, and was then deserted by her husband—who left her to raise two young sons in poverty. Despite being a single mother with overwhelming challenges, Sonja took her responsibility of parenting seriously and had a strict law of expectation for her sons. They were expected to do well in school, read a book each week, study their math facts daily, and could only watch two TV programs a week. And they did all this with her constant support, help, encouragement, and love. In spite of her strong parental presence, one day her son, Ben, then fourteen, tried to resolve an argument at school by stabbing a classmate with a knife. A metal belt buckle the boy was wearing saved his life, and essentially saved Ben's, too. Instead of blaming her financial situation, the school, no husband in the home, or lack of opportunities, she put the responsibility where it belonged—on her son. Sonja sat him down and with gentleness and firmness, let him know his behavior was intolerable, and in life more can be accomplished with kindness than with violence. Today, Ben Carson is the director of pediatric neurosurgery at Johns Hopkins Hospital and a world-renowned surgeon. Sonja's other son, Curtis, is a successful engineer. Both are accomplished musicians and are raising successful families of their own. What made a difference for Curtis and Ben was the example of their mother, who took the necessary time to build a loving relationship with them and who let them know they were important and valued. She keenly understood the importance of providing emotional stability for her sons. Sonja Carson's motto for raising children is, "Every mom knows that a child isn't going to hear too much of what she says. It's what she does that is important."[9]

The importance of providing emotional balance is not just psychobabble, but an actual physical reality. As mentioned earlier, evidence in the brain showing the importance of emotional stability has been scientifically demonstrated. Although the limbic system represents only 15 percent of brain mass, it is very powerful and very important. Why? It controls our emotions and feelings and, because of this, has the ability to override any of our intellectual functions. We all know that when we are emotionally distraught, those feelings cloud everything else in our lives and can, at times, immobilize us from reaching our potential. In other words, the small things in life count—big time! Dr. Marian Diamond found in her studies on the brain that our "emotional well-being may be more essential for survival than intellectual." In her book *Enriching Heredity*, she talks about Nathaniel Hawthorne's story of *Ethan Brand* and how essential emotions are in the development of the "whole" or complete person. She says:

> His main character is searching for the unpardonable sin. He concentrates to such an extent on his intellectual pursuit that he becomes emotionally starved. He eventually becomes dismayed and throws himself into his fiery kiln. When others discover the remains, all that is left is his charred rib cage enclosing a cold marble heart. He had discovered the unpardonable sin by neglecting to integrate the warm, emotional heart, in a metaphorical sense, with his intellectual pursuit.[10]

Using both quality and quantity time in constructing a loving, warm relationship with your child is paramount. Deborah Fallows, author of *A Mother's Work*, understands the importance of developing this relationship. She says, "To meet my standard of responsible parenthood, I have to know [my children] as well as I possibly can and see them in as many different environments and moods as possible in order to know best how to help them grow up, by comforting them, letting them alone, disciplining them, enjoying them, being dependable, but not stifling. What I need is time with them—in quantity, not [just] 'quality.'"[11] By spending the necessary time during a month building this relationship with your child, you will be rewarded with your child's emotional well being and stability—a most important and powerful element essential for a successful parent-child relationship.

I have asked many parents of successful families what specific ideas they use to establish and maintain a personal relationship with their children. From the varied answers, I compiled the three most often-repeated suggestions. As you consistently implement these ideas with your children, you may find the following happening in your home: mutual respect and consideration among family members growing, contention diminishing, and your children more responsive to your counsel, particularly in situations where it is most important that they listen to you and heed your advice. Barbara Bush, when addressing a Wellesley College graduating class said, "Your success as a family, our success as a society, depends not on what happens at the White House, but on what happens inside your house." With that in mind, carefully consider these powerful ideas that can change a struggling relationship into a strong parent-child bond, and how you can implement them into your family.

Date Nights

Once a month take each one of your children on their own "Date Night." This does not have to be an expensive activity. It can be as simple as playing at a park, going on a walk, visiting the library, or going to the ice cream store. The main purpose is to have one-on-one time with your child and to interact and have fun with him away from his other siblings. Date nights communicate to your child that he is important enough to have special time alone with his parent or parents. One important rule to remember is no criticism or preaching. Do not bring up issues that are sensitive—grades, homework, sports performance, not practicing a musical instrument, or any other subject that can create negative feelings and ruin the atmosphere of the evening. The most important goal is to have fun, laugh, and enjoy one another's company. Be sure to put all the date nights on the calendar by the first day of the month, if not, the month slips away before you know it.

Family Night

Each week, set aside a specific day and time for the purpose of spending one hour together as a family. Make it the same day and time each week, so members of the family can plan for it on their schedules. Don't allow any other activities to interfere. Some possible suggestions on what to do during the month are:

- Week 1, Religion Night: Share and discuss with your children your religious beliefs. They have a right to know what you believe and why. This may also be a good time to formulate a Family Mission Statement, design a Family Flag, write a Family Cheer, Motto, or newsletter, make Family Goals and plan Family Vacations.

- Week 2, Game Night: Bring out your collection of board games, and for the next hour play as many different games as possible. Please stay away from computer and other electronic games! Board games are more fun and require more social interaction. Games are such a fun way for families to interact that some schools are opening up the cafeteria for families to come and play games together in the evening. Michele Clayton, a third-grade teacher at Lealand Elementary in San Pedro, California, started a "Family Night" because "we need to play together—inside, outside, and upside-down! . . . The more involved parents are, the more successful children are . . . They have better verbal skills, they learn quicker, and they cooperate better with other people." She feels that many of these skills can be developed through playing games, so each week at Leland Elementary, eighty families fill the school cafeteria to play games together.[12]

- Week 3, Culture Night: Use this night to expose your children to music, art, literature, poetry, history, government, and other countries. This is a great time to incorporate the musical ideas discussed in this book—attend a musical concert; study the lives of composers; listen to a symphony, sonata, or concerto; or compose a family song. Visit an art or science museum, paint a still-life, or draw a caricature of each family member. Read a book, write poetry, or compose a short story together, or write them individually and then share them with each other. Study another country, and assign each family member to research an interesting fact about the country. One person can draw the country's flag, one can relate some intriguing facts about the people—their customs, music, and food. Another child can plan an imaginary trip complete with cost and itinerary. Invite a family or individual from another country to come to your home and share their customs with your family. Afterward, serve a dessert from that country. Make the world come alive for your children with these hands-on activities and turn learning into a family affair.

- Week 4, Sport Night: Exercise is good for the body *and* the brain! Invite other families, and meet at the local park for a game of baseball, flag football, or basketball. Take the family ice skating, sleigh riding, bowling, miniature golfing, billiard playing, or swimming at the beach. At home, play tag, jacks, hide-n-go-seek, or red rover, and do not forget that it is always fun to attend a professional sporting event occasionally.

- Week 5, Family Service Projects: In many states across the nation, high school seniors are required to give a certain number of hours of community service before they graduate. Many of the students have commented on their life-changing experiences as a result of unselfish giving. When children take opportunities to give of themselves, their time, talents, or even their finances, they learn early in life that happiness comes when we give to others. A religious leader was asked by a mother, "What is the most important thing I can teach my children?" He replied, "Teach them to deny themselves." This is sage advice considering most of the problems in marriages today and in the world are rooted in self-centered behavior.

Many presidents throughout the ages have talked about how volunteerism has made our country great and how it strengthens communities and enriches lives. Families can strengthen their local communities and improve their own lives as they voluntarily give service in their neighborhoods. Choose those activities that are appropriate for the ages of your children. For instance, when your children are young, make goodies for a neighbor, a shut-in, someone with special needs, and drop them off anonymously on their porch. Write notes and letters, or have your children draw pictures for someone who is lonely. As they get older, take them to a hospital, retirement home, or rest home to visit shut-ins. Volunteer at an animal shelter and help groom and care for the animals. Join other families and give musical performances for the elderly around the holidays. Go to a local park or community facility and pick up garbage and debris. Mow an elderly neighbor's lawn or shovel snow. Offer to baby-sit free of charge for a young mother in need. Teach your children to give service within the family unit, as well. They need chores and responsibilities that are not tied to an allowance because it is important for them to do their part as a contributing member of the family. Check your local newspapers for additional ideas for service projects in your community. Youth Service America is a wonderful organization that offers thousands of volunteer opportunities for young and old alike.

Check out their web site at www.SERVEnet.org. By entering your zip code, you can find organizations in your area that are looking for help. It is important to remember that giving of oneself is *never* convenient—sacrifice is a big part of service—so, if you're waiting for the perfect time to fit service into your schedule, it will never happen!

A weekly family night will bond children and parents to one another and give children a heightened sense of belonging, security, and self-worth. The gains are so great that they are worth any sacrifice to make it happen!

Personal Interviews

Each week set aside a specific day and time to have a personal interview with your child. Parent-child interviews are a very powerful way to strengthen your relationship with your child because they give you an opportunity to listen to their concerns, worries, how school is progressing, and their friendships; understand their feelings; and teach and counsel when necessary. It is a perfect time for parents to help the child set goals. For the child to feel comfortable to freely discuss any problems, fears, concerns, or experiences, this time together must be void of criticism.

Spend a few minutes at each interview expressing your love to your child. To reinforce this, every few months you could give your child a paper that answers the following statements "I Love You Because," "I Like You Because," "I Admire You Because," "I Have Fun with You When," "I Respect You Because," and "I Find You Humorous Because." Try to make goals for the week—including those areas where both child and parent can improve. Use this time to teach your child basic principles on how to live good lives so that their decisions in life will be based on these principles and not on circumstances. (Remember the example of Yo-Yo Ma's father, who wanted his children to be good people first and musicians second.) Most importantly, take the time to apologize to your child for any behavior you regretted during the week. Doing this simple act conveys to the child that even Mom and Dad make mistakes, and no one is too big to say "I'm sorry!"

As you conduct these weekly interviews, you will become in tune with your children as they confide and express their innermost feelings. Opportunities to teach will arise naturally as you encourage your child to share his or her experiences. It will amaze you how open and receptive he or she will be to your counsel and advice. Noted author and psychologist M. Scott Peck wrote this regarding the far-reaching influence a parent has when they take the time to communicate with their child: "The parents who devote time to their children even when it is not demanded by glaring misdeeds will perceive in them subtle needs for discipline, to which they will respond with gentle urging or reprimand or structure or praise, administered with thoughtfulness and care. They will observe how their children eat cake, how they study, when they tell subtle falsehoods, when they run away from problems rather than face them. They will take the time to make these minor corrections and adjustments, listening to their children, responding to them, tightening a little here, loosening a little there, giving them little hugs and kisses, little admonishments, little pats on the back."[13]

We started interviews with our children in 1980, stemming from a lecture we attended. The speaker had conducted personal interviews with his children for many years. He shared with the group that, as parents conduct weekly interviews, not only will they establish a strong bond of love and trust with the child, but, when serious situations arise, their children will listen and heed parents' advice, even when they are teenagers. This one element alone can have very significant ramifications, and years later we had an opportunity to put this to the test. Some of our son's friends were pursuing a very destructive path, one we didn't want our son to be a part of. He was sixteen, in high school, and a typical teenager. We talked to him about where this path was leading, his responsibility, and the consequences involved. For the next six months, our comments fell on deaf ears as we watched the situation get worse, despite our best efforts to help him make the necessary changes. At one particular interview, we asked him to do something that would be very difficult—give up these friends and find new ones. It was not an easy request. These young men had been lifelong friends. With great difficulty and in his own time frame, he made the break. Some people may say we were just lucky, but I feel luck had nothing to do with it. Interviews work. They work for you as a parent, and they work for the child. Interviews give you a time to *analyze* your present parenting goals, to *discover* new and better ways to approach each individual child, and to *change* and *refine* your methods of parenting to complement the uniqueness of each of your children. I can say with certainty that if you consistently, week after week, interview your children with love and kindness, when the day comes that they need to listen to you on important, life-threatening issues—they will.

The formula for starting musical traditions in your home includes: a *compass* to give direction, a *map* to guide the way, and a *plan* to make it all happen. The pages of this book have given you the compass—you now know and understand the powerful direction music can make in your child's life. You have the map—practical ideas, suggestions, and examples to guide you in this endeavor. And you have the plan to make this all happen—the ideas to use to mold and shape a relationship between you and your child. This formula will ensure success in making music a strong force in your home and in the lives of each family member and, by doing so, you will be a part of making classical music, in all its beauty, a tradition in our nation and a legacy for future generations.

Classical Music
for Your Children to Enjoy

In choosing classical music for young children, choose orchestral works over single-instrument selections and fast, lively, entertaining pieces over slow, sedate music. There are hundreds of wonderful classical pieces of music that your children will enjoy, but when introducing them to a symphony, play the movement that is livelier first. This method of exposure will draw them into the music and get them excited about what they are hearing. After they are familiar with the lively movement, introduce them to the entire score.

The following is a list of classical music geared specifically for children. Take this list with you to your local library and check out some of the CDs before purchasing them. By doing so, your family can hear and experience the music first, before deciding which ones to purchase for your collection.

JOHANN SEBASTIAN BACH

Brandenberg Concerto No. 2, Third Movement

Brandenberg Concerto No. 4, First Movement

Keyboard Concerto in D Minor, 1052 (Schieff, pianist)

Fugue in G Minor, "The Little"

Gavotte

Cantata No. 147, Choral Prelude: "Jesu, Joy of Man's Desiring"

Suite No. 2 in B Minor for Flute and Strings

Rondeau

Toccata and Fugue in D Minor

The Passion of St. Matthew, final chorus

LUDWIG VAN BEETHOVEN

"Für Elise"

Symphony No. 1, Third Movement

Symphony No. 5, First Movement

Symphony No. 6 in F, Op. 68, First Movement ("Pastorale Symphony") (You can also see the first movement of this symphony performed on Walt Disney's *Fantasia.*)

Symphony No. 9, in D Minor, Op. 125, "Choral," Second and Fourth Movements ("Ode to Joy")

Violin Concerto in D, Last Movement (Eventually play this entire piece for your children. It is beautiful!)

HECTOR BERLIOZ

"March to the Scaffold" from *Symphonie Fantastique,* Op. 14

"Dream of the Witches Sabbath" from *Symphonie Fantastique,* Op. 14

"Damnation of Faust," Op. 24 ("Rakoczy March")

Roman Carnival Overture

GEORGES BIZET

L'Arlesienne Suite, No. 2—Carillon, Farandole, Minuetto

Carmen, Prelude, Act I, Entr'acte III

Children's Games

"Soap Bubbles"

"The Top"

"Toreadors" (from *Carmen*)

LUIGI BOCCHERINI

String Quintet in E Major, Menuetto ("Celebrated Minuet")

JOHANNES BRAHMS

Hungarian Dance No. 5 in G Minor

Cradle Song

Concerto for Violin and Cello, Last Movement

Symphony No. 4, Third Movement

BENJAMIN BRITTEN

The Young Person's Guide to the Orchestra

Simple Symphony, "Playful Pizzicato"

Serenade, Prologue

FRÉDÉRIC CHOPIN

Waltz, Op. 64, No. 1, "Minute Waltz"

Prelude in C-Sharp Minor, Op. 28, No. 10

Polonaise in A Major, Op. 40, No. 1

"Raindrop Prelude"

Nocturne in E-flat, Op. 9

AARON COPLAND

Rodeo, "Hoedown"

The Red Pony

Old American Songs

Appalachian Spring, "Variations on Simple Gifts"

Billy the Kid, "Street in a Frontier Town"

Symphony No. 3, "Fanfare for the Common Man"

CLAUDE DEBUSSY

Children's Corner Suite: "Jimbo's Lullaby," "Golliwog's Cakewalk," "The Snow Is Dancing"

Gardens in the Rain

Pagodes

La Mer, "Play of the Waves," "Dialogue of the Wind and the Sea"

"Clair de Lune" from *Suite Bergamasque*

Preludes, Book 1, Voiles

ANTONIN DVOŘÁK

Slavonic Dance, Op. 46, No. 1, and No. 8 in G Minor

Humoresque, Op. 101

Symphony No. 9, (*New World Symphony*), Third Movement

Symphony No. 6, Third Movement

SIR EDWARD ELGAR

Enigma Variations—Nimrod

Pomp and Circumstance, March No. 1

GABRIEL FAURÉ

Dolly Suite, "Berceuse"

Pavane

CHARLES GOUNOD

Faust, "Soldier's Chorus"

"Funeral March of a Marionette"

EDVARD GRIEG

Peer Gynt Suite No. 1: "Anitra's Dance"

Peer Gynt Suite No. 1: "Morning"

Peer Gynt Suite No. 1: "Ase's Death"

Peer Gynt Suite No. 1: "In the Hall of the Mountain King"

FERDE GROFE

Grand Canyon Suite, "On the Trail"

Grand Canyon Suite, "Cloudburst"

Death Valley Suite, "Desert Water Hole"

GEORGE FRIDERIC HANDEL

Water Music, Alla Hornpipe

Music for the Royal Fireworks

Xerxes, Largo

Solomon, "Arrival of the Queen of Sheba"

Messiah, "Hallelujah Chorus"

JOSEPH HAYDN

Symphony No. 45, "Farewell," Last Movement

Symphony No. 94, "Surprise," Second Movement

Trumpet Concerto in E-flat Major, Finale

Cello Concerto No. 2 in D Major, Last Movement

String Quartet in C, "Emperor's Hymn"

GUSTAV HOLST

The Planets, "Mars," "Jupiter"

ENGELBERT HUMPERDINCK

Hansel and Gretel, "Brother, Come and Dance with Me,"
"Nibble, Nibble, Mousekin," "Prayer," "Prelude," "Susie,
Little Susie," "Tra-la-la"

ZOLTÁN KODÁLY

Hary Janos Suite, "The Viennese Musical Clock"

FRANZ LISZT

Hungarian Rhapsody No. 2

FELIX MENDELSSOHN

A Midsummer Night's Dream, "Scherzo," "Wedding March"
Symphony No. 4, "Italian,"
Spring Song

JEAN JOSEPH MOURET

First Symphonic Suite, Rondeau

WOLFGANG AMADEUS MOZART

Symphony No. 40, First Movement

Symphony No. 41, "Jupiter,"

Eine Kleine Nachtmusik (A Little Night Music)

Horn Concerto No. 4, Last Movement

Piano Concerto No. 1, Andante

Clarinet Concerto in A Major, Last Movement

Quintet for Clarinet and Strings in A Major, First and Fourth
Movement

Rondo alla Turca

The Sleigh Ride

The Magic Flute

The Marriage of Figaro, Overture

Requiem, "Dies Irae," "Requiem aeternam"

MODEST MUSSORGSKY

Night on Bald Mountain

Pictures at an Exhibition: "Ballet of the Unhatched Chicks," "Promenade," "The Old Castle"

JACQUES OFFENBACH

Tales of Hoffman, Barcarolle

JOHANN PACHELBEL

Canon in D

NICCOLÒ PAGANINI

Perpetual Motion

SERGEI PROKOFIEV

Peter and the Wolf

Lieutenant Kije Suite, "The Birth of Kije," "The Wedding of Kije," "Troika"

Summer Day Suite, March

Love for Three Oranges, March

Classical Symphony, First Movement

Classical Symphony, Gavotta

Romeo and Juliet, Ballet Suite

GIACOMO PUCCINI

Madam Butterfly, Un bel di Vedremo

Turandot, "Nessun Dorma"

MAURICE RAVEL

Mother Goose Suite, "Conversations of Beauty and the Beast," "Laideronette," "Empress of the Pagodas"

String Quartet in F, Last Movement

Bolero

Le Tombeau de Couperin, Minuet

OTTORINO RESPIGHI

The Birds, Preludio

The Pines of Rome, Last Movement

NICHOLAS RIMSKY-KORSAKOV

The Tale of Tsar Sultan, "Flight of the Bumblebee"

Scheherazade, First Movement

Russian Easter Overture

Mlada, Cortege

GIOACCHINO ROSSINI

Barber of Seville, Largo al factotum

Barber of Seville, Overture *William Tell Overture*

The Thieving Magpie Overture

CAMILLE SAINT-SAËNS

Carnival of the Animals

Franz Schubert

Symphony No. 8 "Unfinished," First Movement

Symphony No. 9 "The Great," Third Movement

The Erlking

March Militaire No. 1

Four Ecossaises, No. 1

Piano Sonata in A, Rondo

Trout, Quintet

Robert Schumann

Album for the Young, Book 1: "The Happy Farmer," "Soldier's March"

Album for the Young, "The Wild Horseman"

Scenes from Childhood

Dmitri Shostakovich

The Gadfly

Jean Sibelius

Finlandia

Bedrich Smetana

Dance of the Comedians

Ma Vlast, "The Moldau"

The Bartered Bride Overture

John Philip Sousa

"The Thunderer March"

"Semper Fidelis"

"The Liberty Bell"

"Washington Post"

"The Stars and Stripes Forever"

JOHANN STRAUSS

"Radetzky March"

"Tritsch Tratsch Polka"

"The Blue Danube"

"Wine, Woman, and Song"

RICHARD STRAUSS

Also Sprach Zarathustra

"Vienna Blood Waltz"

Till Eulenspiegel's "Merry Pranks"

IGOR STRAVINKSY

The Firebird, "Berceuse," "Infernal Dance"

Petrushka, "Coachmen's Dance," "Russian Dance"

Pulcinella Suite, "Tarantella"

The Rite of Spring (Watch and listen to this music on Walt Disney's *Fantasia*.)

PETER ILYICH TCHAIKOVSKY

The Nutcracker

1812 Overture

Sleeping Beauty

Romeo & Juliet, Overture

Swan Lake

Serenade for Strings in C Major

Symphony No. 4, Fourth Movement

Symphony No. 6, "Pathetique," Third Movement

Violin Concerto, Third Movement

GIUSEPPE VERDI

Il Trovatore, "Anvil Chorus"

Rigoletto, "La Donna e Mobile"

Rigoletto, "Questa o quella"

La Traviata, "Libiamo ne'lieti"

HEITOR VILLA-LOBOS

Bachianas Brasileiras No. 2, "The Little Train of the Caipira"

ANTONIO VIVALDI

The Four Seasons

Concerto for Guitar in D Major

Concerto in C for Two Trumpets

Oboe Concerto in D Minor, First and Third Movement

RICHARD WAGNER

The Flying Dutchman Overture

Die Walkure, "Ride of the Valkyries"

The Mastersinger Overture

Tannhauser, Overture, "Arrival of the Guests at Wartburg"

Lohengrin, Prelude

Favorite Classical Lullabies to Play for Your Unborn and Newborn (CDs and Cassettes)

The recording studio is given in parentheses.

Baby Symphony: Sweet Dreams (Madacy). Designed to soothe infants.

Baby Symphony: Sweet Fantasies (Madacy). Instrumental sounds recorded with few notes for baby's comprehension.

Baby Symphony: Tender Moods. (Madacy). Classical recordings that appeal to infants.

Bach & Baby Series (Youngheart). Baroque music to stimulate your child's mind. Series includes: *Bedtime, Traveltime, Playtime,* and *Bathtime.* Recommended for twenty weeks gestation and up.

Bach at Bedtime: Lullabies for the Still of the Night (Philips).

Bach for Babies (Philips).

Beethoven at Bedtime (Philips).

Billboard Presents, Family Lullaby Classics (Rhino Records).

Brahms at Bedtime: A Sleepytime Serenade (Philips).

Celtic Lullaby (Ellipsis Arts).

Classical Kids Presents, Lullabies (BMG Music).

Daydreams & Lullabies (Children's Group).

Dream Angels, Orchestral Lullabies (Rising Star).

Dreamsisters in Beautiful Dreamer (Molen Conola Productions). A Parents Choice Honor Award winner in 1995.

Fiedler's Lullaby: Boston Pops (RCA Victor).

Globalullabies (Music for Little People).

G'morning Johann (Music for Little People).

Goodnight Guitar (Applewind Recordings Inc.). Classic guitar lullabies.

Kids Classics, Lullabies (EMI Classics).

Love Chords (Children's Group). Classical music selections to play for your unborn child by Sandra Collier and Thomas Verny. Includes a twenty-four-page book.

Lullabies for Little Dreamers (Rhino Records).

Lullaby: Arthur Fiedler/Boston Pops (BMG Classics).

Lullaby Berceuse (Music for Little People).

Lullaby Series: Classical Music (Twin Sisters).

Mozart for Mothers-to-Be, Tender Lullabies for Mother & Child (Philips).

Perchance to Dream. (Delos). Features pianist Carol Rosenberger.

UltraSound: Music for the Unborn Child (BMG Music).

Musical Stories About Composers (CDs and Cassettes)

"Classical Kids" is a wonderful series for children. It weaves enchanting stories with real drama and superb music from the lives of the composers. (Appropriate for children preschool to sixth grade; produced by Atlantic Recording Corporation.) The titles include:

Beethoven Lives Upstairs

Hallelujah Handel

Mozart's Magic Fantasy

Mozart's Magnificent Voyage

Mr. Bach Comes to Call

Tchaikovsky in America

Vivaldi's Ring of Mystery

Another worthwhile series about music and composers is:

> *An Introduction to the Classics: The Stories of the Composers in Words and Music*

The series is published by VOX Music Masters, a division of Essex Entertainment, Inc. You can request a free catalog by writing to 560 Sylvan Avenue, Englewood Cliffs, NJ 07632.

The tapes and CDs tell the stories of the lives of the composers from the Baroque, Classical, Romantic, and Twentieth Century. They are lively and entertaining, give facts about each composer, and play selected pieces of their music. This is a wonderful way for children to become familiar with the composers and their music. I have played these tapes for my own children for twenty-two years, and I highly recommend them.

Excellent Classical Titles for Children (CDs and Cassettes)

The recording studio is in parentheses.

Baby Dance (Warner Brothers).

Baby Needs Baroque (Delos International).

Baby Needs Beethoven (Delos International).

Baby Needs Mozart (Delos International).

Bach & Baby Series (Youngheart). Baroque music to stimulate your child's mind. Series includes: *Bedtime, Traveltime, Playtime,* and *Bathtime.* Recommended for twenty weeks gestation and up.

Beethoven for Babies, Brain Training (Philips).

Bibbidi Bobbidi! Bach (Delos). Favorite tunes in the style of great classical composers.

Classical Baby: Mozart (Wea). Series includes *Sleepy Time and Awake Time.*

Classical Child Series (Metro Music, Sophia Sounds). Series includes *Classical Child Is Born*, *Classical Child Dreams*, *Classical Child at Play*, *Classical Child at the Ballet*, and *Classical Child at the Opera*.

Classical Dreams for Kids (Kid Rhino). The Symphony Society Collection includes classical favorites most identified with childhood.

Classical Fantasies for Kids (Kid Rhino). A Symphony Society Collection.

Classical Zoo (Telarc Release). Itzhak Perlman is the narrator. Includes new poems for *Carnival of the Animals* and Respighi's *The Birds*.

Classics for Children (BMG Classics). The Boston Pops with Arthur Fiedler conducting. This wonderful CD has Saint-Saëns' *Carnival of the Animals*, as well as Benjamin Britten's *Young Person's Guide to the Orchestra*, and several other great pieces of children's music and is a *must* for your family collection.

Classics for Kids, Boston Pops (BMG Classics). A wonderful variety of classical music for children on one tape, including Ravel's *Mother Goose Suite*, Bizet's *Childhood Games*, and Schumann's *Dreams*.

Favorite Marches (BMG Classics/RCA Victor).

G'night Wolfgang (Music for Little People).

Heigh-Ho! Mozart (Delos). Favorite tunes in the style of great classical composers.

Jazz-A-Bye Lullabye Classics (proDUCK tunes). Lullaby classics played in the jazz mode.

Jazz-A-Ma-Tazz (Baby Boom). A wonderful jazz album for children.

Kids Classics (EMI release). Subjects include animals, fantasy, lullabies, nature, and toys.

Moving with Mozart (Kimbo). Perfect for children ages three to seven. Combines music and movement to the music of Mozart.

Mozart for Your Mind (Philips Classics). Great music to listen to while studying.

Mozart TV (Delos). Favorite TV tunes in the style of great classical composers.

My Favorite Opera for Children: Pavarotti's Opera Made Easy (London). This is an excellent CD to introduce your child to the exciting world of opera.

Peter and the Wolf (Sony). The Boston Symphony Orchestra with narrator Melissa Joan Hart. This is a delightfully fresh version of not only *Peter and the Wolf,* but also *Carnival of the Animals* and *Young Person's Guide to the Orchestra.*

Peter and the Wolf Play Jazz (Jazzca). By Jon Crosse.

Piano Rags: Scott Joplin/George Gershwin (Quintessence).

Power Classics (Laserlight). A variety of artists and music styles.

Space Classics (BMG Classics). Music of Holst, Grofe, Strauss, and Tchaikovsky.

The Power of Classical Music (Twin Sisters). Classical music perfect for naptime, playtime, or travel time.

This Is My Country (BMG Classics). Wonderful selections of patriotic classical music, including Copland's *Fanfare for the Common Man,* Grofe's *Grand Canyon Suite,* and Gershwin's *Strike Up the Band.*

Thunderous Classics (Vox Cameo Classics). The ultimate in bombastic music.

Classical Music in Movies, Cartoons, and Commercials

There are several CDs available that present music from commercials, cartoons, and the movies. Play a game with your children—write each movie and the music selection on separate strips of paper. Play the music and see if your children can match the correct movie/cartoon/commercial and the music from each. Then rent the movie and see if you can find where, in the movie, the music is played. This is also a great way to introduce classical music to an older child who feels classical music is boring. They'll be surprised at the amount of classical music found in their favorite movies! The recording studios are in parentheses.

Classical Mob Hits (BMG Classics/RCA Victor). Classical music from *The Godfather*, *Casino*, *Prizzi's Honor*, *The Sting*, and other movies.

Greatest Hits Cartoons (Sony Classics). This tape has *Flight of the Bumblebee*, from the cartoon *Melody Time* and *Ride of the Valkyries* from the cartoon *"What's Opera, Doc?"* Both Yo-Yo Ma and Wynton Marsalis are featured artists.

Mad About Cartoons (Deutsche Grammophon).

Mad About Kids' Classics (Deutsche Grammophon). The greatest music from Disney cartoons.

Mad About the Movies (The Sequel) (Deutsche Grammophon). More music from the movies.

Movie Classics (Vox Cameo Classics). Music from *Ace Ventura*, *Four Weddings and a Funeral*, and *Regarding Henry* among other movies.

Opera at the Movies (Vox Cameo Classics). Includes operatic extracts from *Shawshank Redemption*, *Wall Street*, *Apocalypse Now*, *Moonstruck*, and other movies.

TV Classics (Vox Cameo Classics). TV theme tunes from the all-time classical favorites.

TV Classics (BMG Classics/RCA Victor). Arthur Fiedler and the Boston Pops playing classical music from various TV programs.

Music to Study By

The following selections are suggested by Dr. Georgi Lozanov, who has found that music aids in the absorption, retention, and retrieval of information (see Chapter 2).

JOHANN SEBASTIAN BACH

Brandenburg Concertos

Fantasy for Organ in G Major

Fantasy in C Minor

Prelude and Fugue in G Major

Organ Fugue in E Flat Major

LUDWIG VAN BEETHOVEN

Emperor Concerto for Piano, No. 5

Violin Concerto in D

JOHANNES BRAHMS

Concerto for Violin, D Major, Op. 77

ARCANGELO CORELLI

Concerti Grossi, Op. 2, 4, 5, 8, 10, 11, 12

GEORGE FRIDERIC HANDEL

Water Music

Concerto for Organ B-flat Major, Op. 7, 6

JOSEPH HAYDN

Concerto No. 1 for Violin

Concerto No. 2 for Violin

Symphony No. 101, The Clock

Symphony No. 94 in G Major

WOLFGANG AMADEUS MOZART

Mozart for Your Mind. (This CD contains the Piano Concerto in D used in the University of California, Irvine, study to enhance spatial-temporal reasoning.)

Concerto for Piano No. 18 in B-flat Major

Concerto for Piano No. 23 in A Major

Concerto for Violin No. 5 in A Major

Symphony in A Major

Symphony No. 40 in G Minor

Symphony No. 35 in D Major, "Haffner"

Symphony in D Major, Prague

PETER ILYICH TCHAIKOVSKY

Concerto for Violin, Op. 35

Concerto for Piano, No. 1

ANTONIO VIVALDI

The Four Seasons, No. 8

Another good selection to listen to while studying is *Baroque Music for Learning & Relaxation,* Vol. 1, by Optimal Learning. It is available from Success Products, 1725 South Coast Hwy., Oceanside, CA 92054. (Telephone: 619-722-0072)

Reinforcing Your Child's School Experience

Below is a list of twelve different subjects. When your child studies these subjects in school, reinforce their learning at home by playing the classical music and using the books listed. (The books are geared for preschool through elementary.) For instance, if they are studying bees, Rimsky-Korsakov's *Flight of the Bumblebee* is a perfect piece to get their imagination visualizing a bee buzzing.

If they are studying animals, play Saint-Saëns's *Carnival of the Animals.* As you play this music, have your child try to guess which of the thirteen animals is being musically described. If they are studying planets or the universe, Gustav Holst's *The Planets* will get your child's mind soaring through space. When introducing the music, have your child follow these four steps: first, *listen* to the music; second, use rhythm instruments to *beat out* the rhythm; third, *dance* or move to the music; and fourth, *draw* what you hear.

ANIMALS

Music

Carnival of the Animals (Saint-Saëns)

Animal Planet Presents: Sing with the Animals (use Raffi's "Old McDonald Had a Band")

Trout, Quintet (Schubert)

The Birds (Respighi)

Books

Zoo Doings by Jack Prelutsky

Pigericks by Alfred Lobel

Willie Was Different by Norman Rockwell

Brown Bear, Brown Bear and *Polar Bear, Polar Bear* by Bill Martin

The Farm Concert by Joy Cowley

Why Mosquitoes Buzz in People's Ears by Verna Aardema

INSECTS/BEES/ANTS

Music

Flight of the Bumblebee (Rimsky-Korsakov)

Perpetual Motion (Paganini)

Minute Waltz (Chopin)

Moto Perpetuum (Johann Strauss, Jr.)

Books

Buzz, Said the Bee by Wendy C. Lewison

The Tale of the Tsar Sultan by Alexander Pushkin

Insectlopedia by Douglas Florian

TRAINS

Music

"Little Train of the Caipira" with Villa-Lobos, on *Bachiana Brasileira No. 2.*

All Aboard by John Denver. Use this non-classical CD for compare/contrast.

Mostly Railroad Music by Eldon Rathburn. (Crystal Records). Uses the calliope.

Books

Freight Train by Donald Crews

The Little Engine that Could by Watty Piper

Polar Express by Chris Van Allsburg

WEATHER/STORMS

Music

Symphony No. 6 in F, Op. 68
(Pastorale Symphony) (Beethoven)

Thunder and Lightning Polka (Johann Strauss)

Grand Canyon: "Cloudburst" (Grofe)

Appalachian Spring (Aaron Copland)

"Hall of the Mountain King" (Grieg)

"The Thunderer March" (Sousa)

"March to the Scaffold" from *Symphonie Fantastique*, Op. 14
(Berlioz)

Damnation of Faust, Op. 24 ("Rakoczy March") (Berlioz)

Mlada, Cortege (Rimsky-Korsakov)

Books

Cloudy with a Chance of Meatballs by Barrett

Rainbabies by Laura Krauss Melmed

Nimby by Jasper Tomkins

SEASONS

Music

The Four Seasons (Vivaldi)

Spring Song (Mendelssohn)

Sleigh Ride (Mozart)

"Snow Is Dancing" (Debussy)

Books

Weather: A First Discovery Book by Barrons

Snow Lion by David McPhail

NATURE

Music

"Morning Song" from *Peer Gynt* (Edvard Grieg)

Raindrop Prelude (Chopin)

"Snow Is Dancing" (Debussy, from *The Children's Corner Suite*)

Spring Song (Mendelssohn)

Symphony No. 6, in F, Op. 68, (*Pastorale Symphony*) (Beethoven)

Gardens in the Rain (Debussy)

Also Sprach Zarathustra (Strauss) This is great music to conjure images of sunrise.

Books

Rainbabies by Laura Krauss Melmed

If at First You Do Not See, by Ruth Brown

All Falling Down by Gene Zion

SEA/SKY/MOON

Music

La Mer (sea) (Debussy)

Clair de Lune (moon) (Debussy)

Calm Sea (Mendelssohn)

Trout, Quintet (Schubert)

Pachelbel's Canon with Ocean Sounds (Real Music)

Books

Grandfather Twilight by Barbara Berger

Goodnight Moon by Margaret Wise Brown

Ship of Dreams by Dean Morrissey

Moongame by Frank Asch

The Sky is Full of Stars by Franklyn Branley

SOLAR SYSTEM/PLANETS/EARTH/CREATION

Music

The Planets (Gustav Holst). The music from *Star Wars* is very similar to this.

Rite of Spring (Stravinsky). Featured in Disney's *Fantasia*.

Books

The Magic School Bus inside the Earth by Joanna Cole

My First Book About Space by Dinah Mocke

COWBOYS/AMERICA/HORSES/WILD WEST

Music

"Hoedown" from *Rodeo* (Copland)

The Red Pony (Copland)

Appalachian Spring, "Variations on Simple Gifts" (Copland)

Billy the Kid, "Street in a Frontier Town" (Copland)

The Wild Horsemen (Schumann)

William Tell Overture (Rossini)

"The Entertainer" (Joplin)

"Sweet and Low Down" (Gershwin)

Books

Pecos Bill by Steven Kellogg

The Silver Pony by Lynn Ward

Brother Eagle, Sister Sky by Susan Jeffers

MARCHES/FOURTH OF JULY/AMERICA/PATRIOTISM

This music is great to play in the morning while your children are getting ready for school.

Music

"Toreadors" (Bizet)

"Stars and Stripes" (Sousa)

"Grand March" (Verdi)

"Colonel Bogey" (Alford)

"Pomp & Circumstance" (Elgar)

"March of the Toys" (Herbert)

"March of the Soldiers" (Tchaikovsky)

"Funeral March of a Marionette" (Gounod)

March Militaire No. 1 (Schubert)

Book

Where the Wild Things Are by Maurice Sendak. Great to get up and march to.

HOLIDAYS/HALLOWEEN

Music

Danse Macabre (Saint-Saëns). Part of the CD *Bernstein Conducts for Young People*.

"March to the Scaffold" in *Symphonie Fantastique*, Op. 14 (Berlioz)

"*The Hut of Baba Yaga*" (Mussorgsky, *Pictures at an Exhibition* with Ravel)

Toccata and Fugue in D minor (Bach)

Hungarian Dance No. 5 in G Minor (Brahms)

Books

Halloween by Jack Prelutsky

Scary Stories To Tell in the Dark by Alvin Schwartz

The Widow's Broom by Chris Van Allsburg

The Little Old Lady Who Was Not Afraid of Anything by Linda Williams

MUSICAL STORIES/OPERAS/BALLETS

Music

Peter and the Wolf (Prokofiev)

Peter and the Wolf Play Jazz (Crosse)

The Nutcracker (Tchaikovsky)

The Magic Flute (Mozart)

The Sorcerer's Apprentice (Dukas)

Babes in Toyland (Herbert)

Scheherazade (Rimsky-Korsakov)

Peer Gynt Suites (Grieg)

Hansel and Gretel (Humperdinck)

Cinderella (Prokofiev)

Sleeping Beauty (Tchaikovsky)

Swan Lake (Tchaikovsky)

Books

Sing Me a Story by Jane Rosenberg

Dance Me a Story by Jane Rosenberg

The Magic Flute by Anne Gatti

Babes in Toyland by Erin McGonigle Brammer

Swine Lake by James Marshall and Maurice Sendak

Additional Material for Home and Classroom

- *Baby Mozart:* Also included in this series are *Baby Einstein* and *Baby Bach*. These are the most outstanding videos for children ages one month to three years that I have ever seen. They are a playful, imaginative introduction to the music of Mozart and Bach in "video board book" style. Little eyes will light up at the images of brightly colored toys and visually captivating objects while little ears will love the carefully selected and charmingly arranged music of Mozart and Bach. These videos have been featured on CNN, and are a *must* for every baby to experience. I highly recommend them! (Created by Julie Algner-Clark, call 800-793-1454 to order.)

- Bad Wolf Press: This company puts out excellent musical plays for non-music teachers. They are designed to be integrated into kindergarten through eighth grade curricula. Subjects covered include Africa, ancient Greece, ecology, folk tales, literature, Native Americans, oceanography, science, U.S. history, weather, and water. The titles include *The Quest for the Ancient Barometer, Gold Dust or Bust,* and *Theseus and the Minotaur.* This series was created by Ron Fink and John Heath. To order, write to 5391 Spindrift Court, Camarillo, CA, 93012, or call 888-827-8661.

- *Sing a Song of Science:* This CD by Kathleen Carrol includes "Matter Song," "Layers of the Earth," "Tropical Rainforest Story/Rap," "How Animals Move," "Respiratory Rap," and "How the Human Body Works." To order, contact Brain

Friendly Learning, 6801 6th St. NW, Washington, D.C. 20012, or call 202-723-2233.

- *Singin' Smart:* Subjects covered include body systems, history, inventors, explorers, Dewey decimal system, science, aluminum to zinc, and literature. Created by Pamela Peterson. To order, contact Embryo Music, 180 S. 300 West. Suite 450, Salt Lake City, UT 84101, or call 801-532-6114.

- *Rappin' and Rhymin':* This tape is for kindergarten through sixth grades and includes "Parts of Speech," "The Words Spelling Rap," "Vowel Song," "Antonym Song," "Capital Letter Cheer," "Oceans Song," "Continents Song," "Planet Talk," and "Division Rap." Created by Rosella R. Wallace. To order, call Zephyr Press at 520-322-5090.

- *The Alphabet Operetta:* This is an excellent recording to teach the alphabet using alliteration and rhyme. It is done in the operatic style by M. Manley Little and distributed by BMI Release.

Fiction About Music

Abiyoyo. Pete Seeger.

Animal Orchestra. Nick Sharratt.

A Noteworthy Tale. Brenda Mutehnick.

Bat Boy and His Violin. Gavin Curtis.

Ben Franklin's Glass Armonica. Bryna Stevens.

Ben's Trumpet. Rachel Isadora.

Berlioz the Bear. Jan Brett.

Green Horn Blowing. David Birchman.

Hip Cat. Jonathan London.

I Have Another Language: The Language is Dance. Eleanor Schick.

I See A Song. Eric Carle.

Lentil. Robert McCloskey.

Lullabies and Night Songs. William Engvick.

Mandy and Brother Wind. Patricia McKissack.

Max Found Two Sticks. Brian Pinkney.

Moses Goes to a Concert. Isaac Millman.

Mrs. Merriwether's Musical Cat. Carol Purdy.

Musicians of the Sun. Gerald McDermott.

Nana Hannah's Piano. Barbara Bottner.

Onstage & Backstage at the Night Owl Theater. Ann Hayes.

Orchestranimals. Vlasta Van Kampen.

Rondo, Inc. Paul Fleischman.

Second Fiddle. Ronald Kidd.

Sing, Sophie! Dayle Ann Dodds.

Song and Dance Man. Karen Ackerman.

The Banza. Diane Wolkstein.

The Boy Who Loved Music. David Lasker.

The Heart of the Wood. Marguerite W. Davol.

The Little Band. James Sage.

The Maestro Plays. Bill Martin and Vladimir Radunsky.

The Music Box: The Story of Cristofori. Suzanne Guy.

The Old Man and the Fiddle. Michael McCurdy.

The Violin Case Case. Diantha Warfel.

The Violin Close Up. Peter Schaaf.

The Whales' Song. Dyan Sheldon.

Yolonda's Genius. Carol Fenner.

Zin! Zin! Zin! A Violin. Lloyd Moss.

Books About Composers

Amadeus Mozart. Ibi Lepscky.

America, I Hear You. Barbara Mitchell. The story of George Gershwin.

Beethoven Lives Upstairs. Barbara Nichol.

Charlie Parker Played Be Bop. Chris Raschka.

Getting To Know the World's Greatest Composers. Mike Venezia.

Great Men of Music Set. Carol Greene.

Handel and the Famous Sword Swallower of Halle. Bryna Stevens.

Her Piano Sang: A Story About Clara Schumann. Barbara Allman.

Hidden Music: The Life of Fanny Mendelssohn. Gloria Kamen.

If I Only Had A Horn: Young Louis Armstrong. Roxane Orgill.

Introducing the Composers. Roland Vernon.

Isadora Dances. Rachel Isadora.

John Philip Sousa: The March King. Carol Greene.

Lives of the Great Composers, Books 1 and 2. Ian Woodward.

Lives of the Musicians: Good Times, Bad Times (And What the Neighbors Thought). Kathleen Krull.

Magic of Mozart. Ellen Switzer.

Mozart—Scenes from the Childhood of the Great Composer. Catherine Brighton.

Mozart Tonight. Julie Downing.

Raggin': A Story about Scott Joplin. Barbara Mitchell.

Satchmo's Blues. Alan Schroeder.

Young Mozart. Rachel Isadora.

Books About Ballet

A *Midsummer Night's Dream*. William Shakespeare.

Dance Me a Story. Jane Rosenberg.

Illustrated Book of Ballet Stories. Barbara Newman.

Nutcracker. E.T.A. Hoffman. Illustrated by Scott Gustafson.

Petrouchka. Vivian Werner.

Sleeping Beauty. Trina Schart-Hyman.

Swine Lake. James Marshall and Maurice Sendak.

Swan Lake. Margot Fonteyn. Illustrated by Trina Schart-Hyman.

The Firebird. Brad Kessler.

Young Person's Guide to the Ballet. Anita Ganeri.

Books About Opera, Musicals, and Choral Music

A Real Nice Clambake. Oscar Hammerstein and Richard Rodgers.

Aida. Leontyne Price.

Amahl and the Night Visitors. Gian Menotti.

Amazing Grace: The Story of the Hymn. Linda Granfield.

Bantam of the Opera. Mary Jane Auch.

Cumbayah. Floyd Cooper.

Hansel & Gretel: Behind the Curtain. Christian Thee.

I Have a Song to Sing, O! An Introduction to the Songs of Gilbert and Sullivan. Arthur Sullivan.

Messiah: The Wordbook for the Oratorio. George Frideric Handel.

OK! The Story of Oklahoma! Max Wilk.

Opera Stories. Adele Geras.

Opera! What's All the Screaming About? Roger Englander.

Peter and the Wolf. Sergei Prokofiev, retold by Loriot.

Phantom of the Opera. Gaston Leroux.

Sing Me a Story: Metropolitan Opera's Book of Opera Stories for Children. Jane Rosenberg.

The Magic Flute. Anne Gatti.

The Story of Opera. Richard Somerset Ward.

Treemonisha. Angela Medearis. From the opera by Scott Joplin.

Books About the Orchestra and General Music

Alligators and Music. Donald Elliott.

American Indian Music and Musical Instruments. George S. Fichter.

Animal Orchestra. Scott Gustafson.

Brass: An Introduction to Musical Instruments. Dee Lillegard.

Join the Band. Marjorie Pillar.

Long Live Music. Les Chats Peles.

Making Musical Things. Ann Wiseman.

Making Simple Musical Instruments. Bart Hopkin.

Meet the Marching Smithereens. Ann Hayes.

Meet the Orchestra. Ann Hayes.

Music. Carol Greene.

Music. Neil Ardley.

My First Music Book. Helen Drew.

Name the Instrument. Joel Rothman.

A Pianist's Debut: Preparing for the Concert Stage. Barbara Beirne.

Rattles, Bells, and Chiming Bars. Karen Foster.

Rubber-Band Banjos and Java Jive Bass. Alex Sabbeth.

Strings: An Introduction to Musical Instruments. Dee Lillegard.

The Magic of Music. Lisl Weil.

The Marvelous Music Machine: The Story of the Piano. Mary Blocksma.

The Orchestra. Mark Rubin.

The Orchestra: An Introduction to the World Series of Classical Music. Alan Blackwood.

The Philharmonic Gets Dressed. Karla Kuskin.

The Science of Music. Melvin Berger.

This Is an Orchestra. Elsa Posell.

A Very Young Musician. Jill Krementz.

What Instrument Is This? Rosemarie Hausherr.

When Can I Clap, Daddy? Margaret Keith.

A Young Person's Guide to Music. Neil Ardley.

Young Person's Guide to the Orchestra. Anita Ganeri.

Folk Tune Stories

These books, based on folk tunes, are wonderful to use with rhythm instruments. Help your child beat out the sing-song rhythm interwoven in the text.

All God's Critters Got A Place in the Choir. Bill Staines.

America, the Beautiful. Neil Waldman.

Cumbayah. Floyd Cooper.

Dem Bones. Bob Barner.

Earthsong. Sally Rogers (Based on the song *Over in the Endangered Meadow*).

Fiddle-I-Fee. Melissa Sweet.

Five Little Monkeys Sitting in a Tree. Eileen Christelow.

Go Tell Aunt Rhody. Illustrated by Aliki.

Going to the Zoo. Tom Paxton.

How Much Is that Doggie. Bob Merril.

Hush, Little Baby. Shari Halpern.

I'm a Little Teapot. Iza Trapani.

It's Raining, It's Pouring. Rob Gilbert.

John Henry. Brad Kessler.

Little Drummer Boy. Jack Keats.

Mama Don't Allow. Thacher Hurd.

Mary Wore Her Red Dress and Henry Wore His Green Sneakers. Merle Peek.

Miss Mary Mack. Mary Ann Hoberman.

Ms. Macdonald Has a Class. Jan Ormerod.

O Canada. Ted Harrison.

Old Black Fly. Jim Aylesworth.

Over the River and Through the Wood. David Catrow.

Purple Mountain Majesties. Barbara Younger.

Roll Over! Merle Peek.

Silent Night: The Song from Heaven. Linda Granfield.

Simple Gifts. Chris Raschka.

Teddy Bears' Picnic. Jerry Garcia.

The Cat Came Back. Bill Slavin.

The Frog Who Wanted To Be a Singer. Linda Goss.

The Grand Old Duke of York. Maureen Roffey.

The Hokey Pokey. Sheila Hamanaka.

The Itsy Bitsy Spider. Iza Trapani.

The Marvelous Toy. Tom Paxton.

The Star-Spangled Banner. Pete Spier.

There Was an Old Lady. Pam Adams.

There Was an Old Lady Who Swallowed a Pie. Alison Jackson.

There Was an Old Lady Who Swallowed a Trout. Teri Sloat.

This Land is Your Land. Woody Guthrie.

Tingo, Tango, Mango Tree. Marcia Vaughan.

What a Wonderful World. George Weiss.

Who Built the Ark? Pam Paparone.

Yankee Doodle. Steve Kellogg.

You're Adorable. Martha Alexander

Classic Music Videos

Many of these videos can be ordered through the Music in Motion catalog. Call 800 445-0649 to order, or purchase them through your local music stores.

- *Amahl and the Night Visitors* by Menotti. A wonderful opera for children about a crippled boy, Amahl, who is visited by the Three Wise Men en route to Bethlehem.

- *Beethoven Lives Upstairs.* Follows the story from the Classical Kids Series. About Beethoven as seen through the eyes of ten-year-old Christoph. Includes twenty-five excerpts of Beethoven's most famous works.

- *Behind the Scenes with David Hockney!* David Hockney—a world-famous artist in painting, drawing, book illustrations, photo-collage, and set design—shows how modern artists play with perspective, illusion of depth, and the vanishing point.

- *Behind the Scenes with Julie Taymor!* Director of "The Lion King," Taymor creates a visual theater using puppets, masks, and music.

- *Behind the Scenes with Max Roach!* A legendary jazz percussionist and composer, Roach uses layered and funky rhythms to help you feel the beat of the music.

- *Behind the Scenes with Carrie Mae Weems and William Wegman!* These famous photographers show how to use composition and content to create a meaningful photograph.

- *Carnival of the Animals by Saint-Saëns.* The Mormon Youth Symphony with Ogden Nash's delightful verses in an outdoor concert attended by some animal visitors. Live action, live orchestra, live animals.

- *Children's Video Classics.* Includes five ballet and opera productions designed to capture the imaginations of children. They are a wonderful introduction to classical music. The series includes *Cinderella, Hansel and Gretel,* the *Magic Flute* story, *Swan Lake,* and *Alice in Wonderland.*

- Disney's *Peter and the Wolf.* Video includes the famous tale by Prokofiev, a storybook, and two other mini classics, *Music Land* and *Symphony Hour,* where Mickey Mouse conducts the *William Tell Overture.*

- *Hansel and Gretel by Humperdinck.* Metropolitan Opera with Judith Blegen, Frederica von Stade. In English, 100 minutes.

- *Miracle of Mozart.* Babyscapes Video Series teaches children ages eight months to five years about numbers and shapes using computer graphics and Mozart's music.

- *Nutcracker: The Untold Story.* Godfather Drosselmeyer narrates this holiday tale in rhyme. Uses bold 3-D animation of Maurice Sendak's illustrations as well as a live ballet performance. Also takes you behind the scenes to see how this unique version was created.

- *The Orchestra by Mark Rubin*. Narrated by Peter Ustinov, this video introduces the instruments of the orchestra to elementary age children. Music performed by Toronto Philharmonic.

- *Peter and the Wolf: A Prokofiev Fantasy*. Narrated by Sting. Music by Chamber Orchestra of Europe. A hilarious production showing life-sized Spitting Image puppets and the Theatre de Complicite, along with live musicians and characters. Also includes two bonus works for children by Prokofiev, *Overture on Hebrew Themes* and *The Classical Symphony*, where Peter upsets a banquet attended by Bach, Beethoven, Mozart, and others.

- *Reading Rainbow Video Series:* Series includes *Abiyoyo, Barn Dance, Berlioz the Bear, Follow the Drinking Gourd, Hip Cat, Mama Don't Allow, Mufaro's Beautiful Daughters, The Paper Crane, Sophie and Lou, Uncle Jed's Barber Shop,* and *Zin! Zin! Zin!* Suitable for ages pre-kindergarten to three. Introduces children to the many varieties of music through children's literature. This is a two-time Emmy Award-winning series and is hosted by LaVar Burton. Celebrities narrate many of the stories (thirty minutes each).

- *Romeo & Juliet Ballet*. Features the 1976 Bolshoi Ballet performance.

- *Silent Mouse*. This story, featured on PBS, is about the mouse who saves the famous Christmas carol "Silent Night" after the composer Franz Gruber discards it. Narrated by Lynn Redgrave.

- *The Story of Silent Night*. Features the Vienna Boys Choir. Live action retelling the story of how this Christmas carol was written in 1818.

- *Who's Afraid of Opera?* Soprano Joan Sutherland introduces children to opera through her puppet friends and the London Symphony Orchestra.

- *Wynton on Form: Listening for Clues,* by Wynton Marsalis
- *Wynton on Practice: Tackling the* Monster, by Wynton Marsalis
- *Wynton on Rhythm: Why Toes Tap,* by Wynton Marsalis
- *Young People's Concerts: What Does Music Mean?* by Leonard Bernstein
- *Young People's Concerts: What Is Classical Music?* by Leonard Bernstein
- *Young People's Concerts: What Makes Music Symphonic?* by Leonard Bernstein

Internet Sources for Music Information, National Organizations, Curricula, and More

This is not a complete list; there are literally hundreds of Web sites relating to music. But it will get you started on your Internet journey into the fascinating world of music around the globe. Web sites tend to move or be discontinued. These Web sites were available at the time of printing. However, if one does not work, don't be discouraged—just try the next one on the list!

All-in-One Search Page: http://www.albany.net/allinone/

American Music Conference: http://www.amc-music.com/

American Orff-Schulwerk Association: http://www.aosa.org/

ArtsEdge: http://artsedge.kennedy-center.org/

ATMI World Wide Web site: http://www.music.org/atmi/

Band Director's Web sites: http://www.isd77.k12.mn.us/ resources/staffpages/shirk/k12.music.html/newsgroups.html

CAIRSS for Music: http://members.aol.com/Legacy4901/leg.html

Character Classics: http://members.aol.com/Legacy4901/pro.html

Commercial Music Sites:
http://ic.mankato.mn.us/~cshirk/music.html

Children's Music Web Guide:
http://www.cowboy.net/~mharper/Chmusiclist.html

Clarus Music, Ltd.: http://www.clarusmusic.com/

Classical Net: http://www.classical.net/

Composers: http://dir.yahoo.com/Entertainment/Music/
Genres/Classical/Composers/

Family Concert and Educational Orchestra Home Page:
http://www.shore.net/~justin/jlphome.htm

Getty Education Institute for the Arts:
http://www.artsednet.getty.edu

Goals 2000: Arts Education Partnership:
http://www.ccsso.org/

Ideas and Inspirations: http://www.sasked.gov.sk.ca/docs/
.subject.html

Internet Resources for Music Educators: http://www.isd77
.k12.mn.us/resources/staffpages/shirk/music.html

Marsalis on Music: http://www.wnet.org/mom/index.html

Music Education On-line:
http://www.geocities.com/Athens/2405/index.html

Music Education Online Bookstore:
http://www.geocities.com/Athens/2405/bookstore.html

Music Education Launch Site http://www.talentz.com/

Music Educators Lesson Plans and Resources:
http://www.talents.com/

Music Educators National Conference: http://www.menc.org/

Music on the Internet:
http://toltec.lib.utk.edu/~music/net.html

Music Research Information Service: http://imr.utsa.edu/

Music Research Resources: http://www.music.utah.edu/research/

Music Resources on the Internet: http://toltec.lib.utk.edu/~music/resources.html

New Horizons for Learning: http://www.newhorizons.org

Organization of American Kodály Educators: http://www.music.indiana.edu/kodaly/oake.htm

Other WWW Music Resources: http://www.roadkill.com/~burnett/MDB/musicResources.html

Parent and Teacher Links: http://www.staffnet.com/hbogucki/aemes/edulinks.htm

Pepper National Music Network: http://www.jwpepper.com

Teacher Time Savers: http://www.teachertimesavers.com/pub.html

Very Special Arts: http://www.vsarts.org

Worldwide Internet Music Resources: http://www.music.indiana.edu/music_resources/

Yahoo-Music Education List: http://www.yahoo.com/Entertainment/Music/Education/

Arts Resources for Parents and Educators

Music Educators National Conference
1806 Robert Fulton Drive
Reston, VA 22091
703-860-4000

Call and request a list of music education resources. This is a marvelous organization and it's willing to help in any way in making music a reality for every child.

Arts Education Partnership
   (formerly Goals 2000 Arts Education Partnership)
1 Massachusetts Ave., NW, Suite 700
Washington, D.C. 20001
202-326-8693
www.aep-arts.org
   This group is a private, nonprofit coalition of education, arts, business, philanthropic, and government organizations that demonstrates and promotes the essential role of arts education in enabling all students to succeed in school, life, and work. Of particular interest is the information from the report, "Gaining the Arts Advantage: Lessons from School Districts that Value Arts Education." The study was directed by Harriet Mayor Fulbright and Richard J. Deasy on behalf of the President's Committee on the Arts and the Humanities and Arts Education Partnership.

National Education Goals Panel
1255 22nd Street, NW, Suite 502
Washington, D.C. 20037
202-632-0952; Fax: 202-632-0957
   Call for information on Goals 2000 and for a copy of the National Education Goals Report.

National Endowment for the Arts
1100 Pennsylvania Ave., NW
Washington, D.C. 20506
202-682-5400
http://arts.endow.gov
   An informative Web site that provides descriptions of numerous arts programs in the United States and explains the role the NEA plays. Check out their online journal—arts.community—for a variety of interesting arts-related topics.

New Horizons for Learning (Dee Dickinson, CEO)

P.O. Box 15329
Seattle, WA 98115-1329
206-547-7936
www.newhorizons.com

This organization has put together one of the most color-ful, innovative, and informative Web sites ever imagined. It con-tains a wealth of fascinating information on all of the arts disciplines and aspects of life-long learning. Dee, an author of several books, is gracious and willing to help both parents and educators become more informed about the value of arts in edu-cation.

Center for Arts in the Basic Curriculum
   (Eric Oddleifson, chairman)
1319 F Street, NW, Suite 900
Washington, D.C. 20004-1152
202-638-5196

This is a wonderful organization that provides a wealth of information for parents and teachers on the importance of arts education in American schools.

Education Through Music
   (Kathy Damkohler, executive director)
520 Madison Avenue
New York, NY 10022
212-833-1482

This organization promotes the use of an integrated cur-riculum heavily weighted with music and the other arts to in-spire and stimulate elementary and middle school children in their academic studies and general development. Damkohler is more than happy to share her wealth of information with schools across the nation on the effectiveness and success of this program and how to implement the ideas into your school. This program offers comprehensive, sequential learning in the arts.

Arts and Business Council Inc.
  (Business Volunteers for the Arts)
25 West 45th Street, Suite 707
New York, NY 10036
212-819-9287
e-mail: arts&business@internetmci.com
   This organization matches local arts organizations with people who have a passion for the arts and want to share their business expertise in areas such as finance, marketing, strategic planning, and information systems.

Mr. Holland's Opus Foundation
15125 Ventura Blvd., Suite 204
Sherman Oaks, CA 91403
818-784-6787
www.mhopus.org
   The goal of this foundation is to provide and maintain musical instruments for young people whose own school programs cannot afford to do so. Check the web site for guidelines.

Young Musicians Foundation
195 South Beverly Drive, Suite 414
Beverly Hills, CA 90212
310-859-7668; Fax: 310-859-1365
   This nonprofit organization provides encouragement and recognition to gifted young musicians through financial assistance and performance opportunities.

VH1 Save the Music
1515 Broadway, 20th Floor
New York, NY 10036
888-VH1-4-MUSIC
www.vh1.com

This nonprofit organization is dedicated to improving the quality of education in America's public schools by restoring and supporting music programs in cities across the county and by raising public awareness about the importance of music participation for our nation's youth.

Weekend Warriors: National Association of Music Merchants
1806 Robert Fulton Drive, Suite 302
Reston, VA 24010
703-648-9440

The National Association of Music Merchants (NAMM) has a program for people who enjoyed playing a musical instrument when they were younger, but put it aside for family, college, and career responsibilities. Inactive musicians can become active players again when they are hooked up with other musicians in their area. A person is grouped by musical interest and compatibility. In just four short rehearsals, their band, along with others, is ready for a performance at a local venue.

Meet the Composer
c/o New York State Council on the Arts
2112 Broadway, Suite 505
New York, NY 10023
212-787-3601; Fax: 212-787-3745
e-mail: mtc@meetthecomposer.org
www.meetthecomposer.org

Meet the Composer was founded in 1974 by the New York State Council on the Arts. The goal is to bring music to rural communities, small towns, suburban centers, and urban neighborhoods. Meet the Composer-sponsored events put composers into direct personal and professional contact with people of all kinds.

The National PTA

330 North Wabash Ave., Suite 2100

Chicago, IL 60611

Request the "Be Smart, Include Art: A Planning Kit for PTAs" from this organization.

Music Catalogs

MMB Music

3526 Washington Ave.

St. Louis, MO 63103-1019

800-543-3771

Write or call for a catalog on music books, materials, and instruments for home and the classroom.

Music in Motion

P.O. Box 833814

Richardson, TX 75083-3814

800-445-0649

A wonderful music education and gift catalog for all ages.

LMI Music Products for Education

1776 West Armitage Court

Addison, IL 60101

800-456-2334

Offers hundreds of different music products for parents and educators.

Woodwind and Brasswind
19880 State Line Rd.
South Bend, IN 46637
800-348-5003
The catalog contains the world's largest selection of musical instruments and accessories.

NOTES

CHAPTER ONE

1. Ian Crofton and Donald Fraser, *A Dictionary of Musical Quotations*. (New York: Schirmer Bros., 1985).
2. Donald Hodges, "The Influence of Music on Human Behavior," *Handbook of Music Psychology*. (San Antonio: IMR Press, 1996), 497.
3. Hodges, "Influence of Music," 474.
4. Hodges, "Influence of Music," 474, 476, 477.
5. Jon-Roar Bjorkvold, "Canto—ergo sum: Musical Child Cultures in the United States, the Soviet Union, and Norway." In *Music and Child Development* edited by Frank R. Wilson and Franz L. Roehmann, (St. Louis, Missouri: MMB Music Inc., 1990), 118.
6. David Tame, *The Secret Power of Music*. (Rochester, Vermont: Destiny Books, 1984) 237.
7. Tame, *Secret Power*, 236, 239.
8. Cole, K. C. "Scientists Trace Cosmic Blast to Unusual Star." *Los Angeles Times*, September 30, 1998.
9. Richard Huber, scientist, interview with author, August 20, 1998. William F. Allman, "The Musical Brain." *U.S. News & World Report*, June 11, 1990.
10. "Icebreaker Rescues Trapped Whales." *World*, February 1986.
11. Stewart H. Hulse, "Comparative Psychology and Music Perception." In *Music and Child Development* edited by Frank R. Wilson and Franz L. Roehmann, (St. Louis, Missouri: MMB Music Inc., 1990) 139, 153.
12. Glenn Oeland, "Emperors of the Ice." *National Geographic*, vol. 189, no. 3 (March 1996): 64.
13. Alex Sabbeth, *Rubber-Band Banjos and a Java Jive Bass*. (New York: John Wiley & Sons, Inc., 1997) 11, 20.

14. Tony Mickela, "Does Music Have an Impact on the Development of Students?" Prepared for the 1990 state convention of California Music Educators Association. Barbara L. Stein, C. A. Hardy, and Herman Totten, "The Use of Music and Imagery to Enhance and Accelerate Information Retention." *Journal of the Society for Accelerative Learning & Teaching*, vol. 7, no. 4, 341. Laura Saari. "The Sound of Learning." *Orange County Register*. February 6, 1997.
15. Sally J. Rogers, "Theories of Child Development and Musical Ability." In *Music and Child Development* edited by Frank R. Wilson and Franz L. Roehmann, (St. Louis, Missouri: MMB Music Inc., 1990) 3. *Profile of SAT and Achievement Test Takers*. College Entrance Examination Board, Princeton, New Jersey, 1995. Hodges, "Influence of Music," 542. *What Work Requires of Schools: A SCANS Report for America 2000*. (Upland, Pennsylvania: Diane Publishing Co., 1993). Also found in *Visual and Performing Arts Framework*. (Sacramento: California Department of Education, 1996) 13.
16. Hodges, "Influence of Music," 536.
17. Marian Diamond, *Enriching Heredity*. (New York: The Free Press/Simon & Schuster, 1988).
18. Dee Dickinson. "Music and the Mind." (Seattle: New Horizons for Learning, 1993). See also www.newhorizons.org.
19. Robert Lee Hotz, "Study Suggests Music May Someday Help Repair Brain." *Los Angeles Times*, November 9, 1998.
20. Diamond, *Enriching Heredity*.
21. Hotz, "Music May Someday Help."

CHAPTER TWO

1. Alison Motluk, "Can Mozart Make Maths Add Up?" *Science*, March 15, 1997.
2. Frances H. Rauscher, Gordon L. Shaw, and Katherine N. Ky, "Music and Spatial Task Performance." *Nature*, vol. 365, October 14, 1993.

3. Frances H. Rauscher, Gordon L. Shaw, Linda J. Levine, Eric L. Wright, Wendy R. Dennis, and Robert L. Newcomb, "Music Training Causes Long-term Enhancement of Preschool Children's Spatial-Temporal Reasoning." *Neurological Research*, vol. 19, February 1997.

4. Rauscher, et al., "Music and Spatial Task Performance," 1994.

5. Amy B. Graziano, Gordon L. Shaw, and Eric L. Wright, "Music Training Enhances Spatial-Temporal Reasoning in Young Children: Towards Educational Experiments." *Early Childhood Connections*, Summer 1997.

6. Amy B. Graziano, Matthew Peterson, and Gordon L. Shaw, "Enhanced Learning of Proportional Math Through Music Training and Spatial-Temporal Training." *Neurological Research*, vol. 21, no. 2, March 1999.

7. Wendy S. Boettcher, Sabrina S. Hahn, and Gordon L. Shaw, "Mathematics and Music: A Search for Insight into Higher Brain Function." *Leonardo Music Journal*, vol. 4, 1994.

8. G. J. Allman, *Greek Geometry from Thales to Euclid.* (New York: Arno, 1976).

9. A. J. S. Rayl, "Striking a Neural Chord: Musical Links for Scientists and Mathematicians of Tomorrow." *OMNI*, 1995.

10. Marcia Davenport, *Mozart.* (New York: Avon Books, 1979).

11. E. Anderson, *The Letters of Mozart and His Family.* (New York: WW Norton Co., 1985).

12. Martha B. Denckla, "The Paradox of the Gifted/Impaired Child." In *Music and Child Development* edited by Frank R. Wilson and Franz L. Roehmann, (St. Louis, Missouri: MMB Music Inc., 1990) 228.

13. Donald A. Hodges, "Neuromusical Research." *Handbook of Music Psychology.* (San Antonio: IMR Press, 1996) 242.

14. "Neurology: Musical 'Maps' May Grow with Experience." *Washington Post*, April 1998.

15. Laura Saari, "The Sound of Learning." *Orange County Register*, February 6, 1997.

16. Saari, "Sound of Learning."
17. Graziano et al., "Music Training."
18. Boettcher et al., "Mathematics and Music."
19. Ben Carson, *Gifted Hands*. (Grand Rapids, Michigan: Zondervan Publishing House, 1990) 110.
20. Victor Goertzel and Mildred George Goertzel, *Cradles of Eminence: A Provocative Study of the Childhoods of Over 400 Famous 20th Century Men and Women*. (Boston: Little, Brown. 1962) xii.
21. Eric Oddleifson, "The Case for Sequential Music Education in the Core Curriculum of the Public Schools." (East Hampton, New York: Center for the Arts in Basic Curriculum, Spring 1989).
22. Elizabeth Murfee, "Eloquent Evidence: Arts at the Core of Learning." (Washington, D.C.: National Assembly of State Arts Agencies, 1995).
23. Thomas Armstrong, *7 Kinds of Smart*. (New York: Penguin Group, 1993) 59.
24. Oddleifson, "Case for Sequential Music."
25. Anne C. Roark, "How U.S. Failed in Science." *Los Angeles Times*, November 8, 1990.
26. Sara Martin, "Music Lessons Enhance Spatial Reasoning Skills. *Monitor*, 1994.
27. Hodges, "Neuromusical Research," 242.
28. Robert Lee Hotz, "Study Suggests Music May Someday Help Repair Brain." *Los Angeles Times*, November 9, 1998.
29. Tony Mickela, "Does Music Have an Impact on the Development of Students?" Prepared for the 1990 state convention of California Music Educators Association.
30. Mickela, "Does Music Have an Impact?"
31. Howard Gardner, *Art, Mind, and Brain: A Cognitive Approach to Creativity*. (New York: Basic Books, 1982) 329–330.
32. Dee Dickinson, "Music and the Mind." (Seattle: New Horizons for Learning, 1993). Also see www.newhorizons.org.
33. Mickela, "Does Music Have an Impact?"

34. Hotz, "Music May Someday Help."

35. Mickela, "Does Music Have an Impact?"

36. Barbara L. Stein, C. A. Hardy, and Herman Totten, "The Use of Music and Imagery to Enhance and Accelerate Information Retention." *Journal of the Society for Accelerative Learning & Teaching,* vol. 7, no. 4.

37. Sheila Ostrander and Lynn Schroeder, *Superlearning.* (New York: Delacorte Press, 1979).

38. Ostrander, *Superlearning.*

39. Ostrander, *Superlearning.*

40. J. Madeleine Nash, "Fertile Minds." *Time,* February 3, 1997.

41. Nash, "Fertile Minds."

42. Nash, "Fertile Minds."

CHAPTER THREE

1. Thomas Armstrong, *7 Kinds of Smart.* (New York: Penguin Group, 1993) 73.

2. L. Salk. "Mothers' Heartbeat As an Imprinting Stimulus." *Transactions: Journal of the New York Academy of Sciences,* vol. 24, no. 7: 753–763.

3. Donald J. Shetler, "The Inquiry into Prenatal Musical Experience: A Report of the Eastman Project 1980–1987." In *Music and Child Development* edited by Frank R. Wilson and Franz L. Roehmann, (St. Louis, Missouri: MMB Music Inc., 1990) 46.

4. Peter F. Ostwald, "Music in the Organization of Childhood Experience and Emotion." In *Music and Child Development* edited by Frank R. Wilson and Franz L. Roehmann, (St. Louis, Missouri: MMB Music Inc., 1990) 12.

5. Donald A. Hodges, "Neuromusical Research." *Handbook of Music Psychology.* (San Antonio: IMR Press, 1996) 210.

6. S. G. Lopez, "The Effects on Infants of Empathy and Resonance As Reflected in Lullabies and Playsongs: A Musical Developmental Theory." (Ph.D. diss., University of California, San Diego, 1991).

7. Shetler, "Prenatal Musical Experience," 50.

8. Shelter, "Prenatal Musical Experience," 55.

9. Frances H Rauscher, K. D. Robinson, and J. J. Jens, "Improved Maze Learning Through Early Music Exposure in Rats." *Neurological Research* (submitted).

10. Donald Hodges, "Human Musicality." *Handbook of Music Psychology*. (San Antonio: IMR Press, 1996) 47.

11. Peter Ostwald, "Childhood Experience and Emotion."

12. John Baily and Veronica Doubleday, "Patterns of Musical Enculturation in Afghanistan." In *Music and Child Development* edited by Frank R. Wilson and Franz L. Roehmann, (St. Louis, Missouri: MMB Music Inc., 1990) 88.

13. Hodges, "Human Musicality," 47.

14. W. Kessen, J. Levine, and K. A. Wendrich. "The Imitation of Pitch in Infants." *Infant Behavior and Development* 2, 1979, 931–999.

15. Robert Lee Hotz, "The Language of Learning." *Los Angeles Times*, September 18, 1997.

16. Marcel R. Zentner and Jerome Kagan, "Perception of Music by Infants." *Nature*, 383/6595, 1996, 29.

17. Robert Garfias, "Thoughts on the Processes of Language and Music Acquisition." In *Music and Child Development* edited by Frank R. Wilson and Franz L. Roehmann, (St. Louis, Missouri: MMB Music Inc., 1990) 100.

18. Dee Dickinson, "Learning Through the Arts." (Seattle: New Horizons for Learning, 1997) 7. See also www.newhorizons.org.

19. Sally J. Rogers, "Theories of Child Development and Musical Ability." In *Music and Child Development* edited by Frank R. Wilson and Franz L. Roehmann, (St. Louis, Missouri: MMB Music Inc., 1990) 2.

20. Rogers, "Theories of Child Development," 3.

21. Carla Hannaford, *Smart Moves*. (Arlington, Virginia: Great Ocean Publishers, 1995) 107.

22. "Music and Your Child: The Importance of Music to Children's Development." The American Music Conference, 1988.

23. Gordon Shaw, interview with author, April 13, 1999.

24. Jane M. Healy, *Endangered Minds*. (New York: Touchstone Books/Simon & Schuster, 1990) 93.

25. Hannaford, *Smart Moves*, 83.

26. Baily and Doubleday, "Patterns of Musical Enculturation in Afghanistan," 97.

27. *Profile of SAT and Achievement Test Takers for 1995*. College Entrance Examination Board, Princeton, New Jersey, 1995.

CHAPTER FOUR

1. Donald Hodges, "The Influence of Music on Human Behavior." *Handbook of Music Psychology*. (San Antonio: IMR Press, 1996) 498.

2. "What is Orff Schulwerk?" See www.aosa.org/whatis

3. Shinichi Suzuki, *Nurtured by Love*. (New York: Exposition Press, 1964).

4. Sharon Begley, "Your Child's Brain." *Newsweek*, February 19, 1996.

5. John Holt, *Never Too Late: My Musical Life Story*. (New York: Delacorte Press/Seymour Lawrence, 1978) 4.

6. Begley, "Your Child's Brain."

7. "Gallup Poll Reveals Piano and Guitar Still Top the Charts in Popularity." *Music USA*, 1994, NAMM, International Music Products Association.

8. Madeau Stewart, *The Music Lover's Guide to the Instruments of the Orchestra*. (New York: Van Nostrand-Reinhold Co., 1980) 12.

9. Helen Colijn, *Song of Survival: Women Interned*. (Ashland, Oregon: White Cloud Press, 1995).

10. Colijn, *Song of Survival*.

11. Tracy Johnson, "Voices Rising." *Los Angeles Times*, October 2, 1996.

12. Thomas H. Maugh, "Study Finds Piano Lessons Boost Youths' Reasoning." *Los Angeles Times*, February 28, 1997.

13. Roger Von Oech, *A Whack on the Side of the Head*. (New York: Warner Books, 1990).

14. Stewart, *The Music Lover's Guide*.
15. Duane Noriyuki, "Secrets Wonderful and Cruel." *Los Angeles Times Magazine*, August 31, 1997, 8.
16. Ted Libbey, *The NPR Guide to Building a Classical CD Collection*. (New York: Workman Publishing, 1994) 133.
17. Bob Pool, "Singular Act Makes Him a Triple Threat." *Los Angeles Times*, April 15, 1999.
18. Libbey, *The NPR Guide*, 74.
19. Libbey, *The NPR Guide*, 44.
20. Maurice Summerfield, *The Classical Guitar: Its Evolution, Players, and Personalities Since 1800*. (Newcastle-Upon-Tyne, England: Ashley Mark Publishing Company, 1991).
21. Gayla Wise, "A Noteworthy Teacher." *Ensign*, October 1997, 60.
22. Helen Epstein, *Music Talks*. (New York: McGraw-Hill, 1987) 75.
23. Epstein, *Music Talks*, 69.
24. Epstein, *Music Talks*, 87.
25. Epstein, *Music Talks*, 93.

CHAPTER FIVE

1. Eric Oddleifson, "The Case for Sequential Music Education in the Core Curriculum of the Public Schools." (East Hampton, New York: Center for the Arts in the Basic Curriculum, 1989) 29.
2. Melissa Healy, "Fathers at School Give Children an Edge, Study Finds." *Los Angeles Times*, October 3, 1997.
3. Sally J. Rogers, "Theories of Child Development and Musical Ability." In *Music and Child Development* edited by Frank R. Wilson and Franz L. Roehmann, (St. Louis, Missouri: MMB Music Inc., 1990) 3.
4. Patrick Kavanaugh, *Raising Musical Kids*. (Grand Rapids, Michigan: Servant Publications, 1995) 124.
5. Lauren A. Sosniak, "From Tyro to Virtuoso: A Long-term Commitment to Learning." In *Music and Child Development*

edited by Frank R. Wilson and Franz L. Roehmann, (St. Louis, Missouri: MMB Music Inc., 1990) 274-289.

6. Sosniak, "From Tyro to Virtuoso," 281.

7. Helen Epstein, *Music Talks*. (New York: McGraw-Hill, 1987).

8. "Talking with David Frost." Burrelle's Information Services, April 25, 1997.

9. Oddleifson, "Case for Sequential Music Education," 44.

10. Todd Stout, "The Four Utah Varieties of *Papilo indra*." *Utah Lepidopterist*, February 1997, 6.

CHAPTER SIX

1. Thomas Stanley, Ph.D., and William D. Danko, *The Millionaire Next Door: The Surprising Secrets of America's Wealthy*. (Atlanta: Longstreet Press, 1996).

2. Patrick Kavanaugh, *Spiritual Lives of the Great Composers*. (Grand Rapids, Michigan: Zondervan Publishing House, 1992) 31.

3. Anita Bartholomew, "Music Was His Passport." *Reader's Digest*, March 1997.

4. Suzanne Chazin, "She Heard the Music." *Reader's Digest*, February 1997.

5. Stan Miller and Sharon Miller, *Especially for Mormons*. (Provo, Utah: Kellirae Arts, 1973) 69.

6. Alison Murray, "Child Prodigy Scores Big Through Hard Work, Sacrifice." *South Bay Weekly*, Feb. 18, 1999.

7. From "Growing Up Complete: The Imperative for Music Education. Copyright 1991 by Music Educators National Conference. Used with permission.

8. Carol Lynn Pearson, "My Story" from the play *My Turn on Earth*. Lyrics and music by Carol Lynn Pearson.

9. Nona Yates, "Taking Up the Torch." *Los Angeles Times*, October 8, 1996.

10. Tony Mickela, "Does Music Have an Impact on the Development of Students?" Prepared for the 1990 state convention of California Music Educators Association.

11. Mickela, "Does Music Have an Impact?"

12. Lucinda Hahn, "Maestro of Their Dreams." *Readers Digest*, August 1996.

13. Sterling W. Sill, *The Majesty of Books*. (Salt Lake City: Deseret Book Company, 1974) 121.

14. Mickela, 1990.

15. Dan Rather, "Silencing the Sound of Music." *San Diego Union-Tribune*, March 20, 1998.

16. From "Growing Up Complete: The Imperative for Music Education. Copyright 1991 by Music Educators National Conference. Used with permission.

17. Dee Dickinson, "Lifelong Learning for Business: A Global Perspective." Presented at a conference on lifelong learning for European business, Oxford University, October 1992.

18. Daniel Golden, "Building a Better Brain." *Life*, July 1996.

19. Robert Lee Hotz, "Active Mind, Body Linked to Brain Growth." *Los Angeles Times*, February 23, 1999.

20. Don Heckman, "Recalling a Master of Violin Versatility." *Los Angeles Times*, December 2, 1997.

21. Heckman, "Recalling a Master."

22. Marissa Epino, "Eleven Decades of Harmony." *Los Angeles Times, South Bay Weekly*, December 4, 1997.

23. Golden, "Building a Better Brain."

24. Carla Hannaford, *Smart Moves*. (Arlington, Virginia: Great Ocean Publishers, 1995) 83.

25. Elaine Dutka, "88 Keys to Success." *Los Angeles Times*, January 16, 1998.

26. Paul Sullivan, "The Cellist of Sarajevo." *Reader's Digest*, November 1996.

27. Matea Gold, "The Chord of Life." *Los Angeles Times*, April 9, 1997.

28. Gold, "The Chord of Life."

29. Barbara Sande Dimmitt, "Silent Night." *Reader's Digest*. December 1997, 67.

CHAPTER SEVEN

1. Katinka Daniel, interview with author, March 1998.
2. Eric Oddleifson, "The Case for Sequential Music Education in
   the Core Curriculum of the Public School." (East Hampton,
   New York: Center for the Arts in the Basic Curriculum, 1989).
3. Oddleifson, "Case for Sequential Music Education."
4. Oddleifson, "Case for Sequential Music Education."
5. Tom Schultz and Richard Lee Colvin, "U.S. Students Fare
   Poorly in Comparison." *Los Angeles Times*, February 25, 1998.
6. Donald Hodges, *Handbook of Music Psychology*. (San Antonio:
   IMR Press, 1996).
7. Jeanne Akin, "Music Makes a Difference." (Lafayette, California: Lafayette Arts and Science Foundation, 1987). Used
   with permission.
8. Jaye T. Darby and James S. Catterall, "The Fourth R: The
   Arts and Learning," from *Schools, Communities, and the Arts:
   A Research Compendium*, 1994.
9. Eric Oddleifson, "A Fifty School Arts Education Demonstra-
   tion Project." *On the Beam*, vol. XI, no. 1, Fall 1990.
10. Vadim Prokhorov, "Will Piano Lessons Make My Child
    Smarter?" *Parade Magazine*, June 14, 1998.
11. Dee Dickinson, "Learning Through the Arts." (Seattle: New
    Horizons for Learning, 1997). See also www.newhorizons.org.
12. Randy Cohen, "Kellogg Elementary: An Arts in Education
    Program That Works." *Connections Quarterly*, March 1992.
13. Dickinson, "Learning Through the Arts."
14. Hope O'Keeffee, "The Fort Hayes Philosophy." (Washing-
    ton, D.C.: National Endowment for the Arts, 1996).
15. Kathy Damkohler, interview with author, April 1997.
16. Dee Dickinson, "Learning Through Many Kinds of Intelli-
    gence." (Seattle: New Horizons for Learning,) 1997. See
    also www.newhorizons.org.
17. Oddleifson, "Case for Sequential Music Education."

18. Dickinson, "Learning Through the Arts."

19. Dickinson, "Learning Through the Arts."

20. Jocelyn Y. Stewart, "A Renaissance in the Classroom." *Los Angeles Times*, March 5, 1999.

21. Arthur Fisher, "Fragile Future." *Popular Science*, December 1998.

22. Lisa Blake Berke, "Students Sing Opera's Praises." *Los Angeles Times*, January 25, 1999.

23. Danny Feingold, "Schoolhouse Rock." *Los Angeles Times Magazine*, April 11, 1999.

24. LaDawn Jacobs, interview with author, March 24, 1998.

25. From *Growing Up Complete: The Imperative for Music Education*. Copyright 1991 by Music Educators National Conference. Used with permission.

26. Akin, "Music Makes a Difference."

27. James S. Catterall, "Different Ways of Knowing: 1991–94 National Longitudinal Study Final Report." (Tucson: The Morrison Institute of Public Policy, 1995).

28. Murfee, "Eloquent Evidence."

29. Dickinson, "Learning Through the Arts."

30. From *Growing Up Complete: The Imperative for Music Education*. Copyright 1991 by Music Educators National Conference. Used with permission.

31. Bruce O. Boston, "The Changing Workplace Is Changing Our View of Education." *Business Week*, October 28, 1996, 6.

32. Kathy Damkohler, interview with author, April 1997.

33. James S. Catterall, Richard Chapleau, and John Iwanaga. *Involvement in the Arts and Human Development: Extending an Analysis of General Associations and Introducing the Special Cases of Intensive Involvement in Music and in Theater Arts*. Monograph Series No. 11, (Washington, D.C.: Americans for the Arts, Forthcoming Fall 1999).

34. Sharon Begley, "Your Child's Brain." *Newsweek*, February 19, 1996.

35. Begley, "Your Child's Brain."

36. Eric Oddleifson, "To Perceive and to Imagine." (East Hampton, New York: Center for the Arts in the Basic Curriculum, 1996).

37. Roger Kamien, *Music: An Appreciation*. (New York: McGraw Hill, 1988) 142.

38. Richard Dreyfuss, speech to the American Federation of Teachers, August 1996.

39. From *Growing Up Complete: The Imperative for Music Education*. Copyright 1991 by Music Educators National Conference. Used with permission.

CHAPTER EIGHT

1. Brenda Sumberg, interview with author, July 1997.

2. Julie Amparano Lopez, "System Failure." *The Wall Street Journal*, March 31, 1989.

3. Elaine Woo and Richard Lee Colvin, "Lower Standards, Money, Changing Student Body Are the Challenges." *Los Angeles Times*, May 17, 1998.

4. Maura Montellano, "Down but Not Out at Cal State." *Los Angeles Times*, April 11, 1998.

5. Jane M. Healy, *Endangered Minds*. (New York: Simon & Schuster, 1990) 279.

6. Woo and Colvin, "Lower Standards."

7. Richard Lee Colvin, "Too Many Teachers Are Ill-Prepared." *Los Angeles Times*, May 19, 1998.

8. Healy, *Endangered Minds*, 338.

9. Bruce O. Boston, "Educating for the Workplace Through the Arts." *Business Week*, October 28, 1996.

10. Healy, *Endangered Minds*, 338.

11. Boston, "Educating for the Workplace."

12. Eric Oddleifson, "The Case for Sequential Music Education in the Core Curriculum of the Public Schools." (East Hampton, New York: Center for the Arts in the Basic Curriculum, 1989) 31.

13. Boston, "Educating for the Workplace."

14. Todd Oppenheimer, "The Computer Delusion." *Atlantic Monthly*, July 1997.
15. Tom Plate, "One Sacramento Politician with a Pac Rim Vision." *Los Angeles Times*, December 2, 1997.
16. *What Work Requires of Schools: A SCANS Report for America 2000*. (Upland, Pennsylvania: Diane Publishing Co., 1993).
17. Elizabeth Murfee, "Eloquent Evidence: Arts at the Core of Learning." (Washington, D.C.: National Assembly of State Arts Agencies, 1995).
18. Boston, "Educating for the Workplace."
19. Peter F. Drucker, *Innovation and Entrepreneurship: Practice and Principles*. (New York: Harper & Row, 1985) 216.
20. Oddleifson, "Case for Sequential Music."
21. Oppenheimer, "The Computer Delusion."
22. Deborah Belgum, "Redondo Class Gets High-Tech Homework." *Los Angeles Times*, October 19, 1997.
23. Romesh Ratnesar, "Learning by Laptop." *Time*, March 2, 1998.
24. Oppenheimer, "The Computer Delusion."
25. Sharon Begley, "Your Child's Brain." *Newsweek*, February 19, 1996.
26. Oppenheimer, "The Computer Delusion."
27. Ratnesar, "Learning by Laptop." Oppenheimer, "The Computer Delusion."
28. Donald Hodges, "The Influence of Music on Human Behavior." *Handbook of Music Psychology*. (San Antonio: IMR Press, 1996) 478.
29. Tracy Johnson, "Web Writers." *Los Angeles Times*, March 26, 1998.
30. Hodges, "Influence of Music," 480.
31. Dee Dickinson, "Learning Through the Arts." (Seattle: New Horizons for Learning, 1997) 9. See also www.newhorizons.org.
32. Oddleifson, "Case for Sequential Music." 28.
33. Roger Von Oech, *A Whack on the Side of the Head*. (New York: Warner Books, 1990).

34. Robert Wright, "The Man Who Invented the Web." *Time,* May 19 1997.
35. Paul Griffiths, "Don't Blame Modernist for the Empty Seats." *New York Times,* March 22, 1998.
36. Eric Oddleifson, "To Perceive and to Imagine: Unleashing the Talent and Energy of Teachers and Students." (East Hampton, New York: Center for Arts in the Basic Curriculum, 1996) 6.
37. Boston, "Educating for the Workplace."
38. Gretchen C. Van Denthuysen, "Heinz Flavors the Arts with Donation, Contest." *Ashbury Park Press,* June 13, 1996.
39. Miriam Flaherty, interview with author, July 1997.
40. Jana Napoli, interview with author, May 11, 1999.
41. Claudia Barker, *Young Artists and Their Storytelling Chairs.* (Baton Rouge: LSU Press, 1996).
42. "Music Center Education Division, Artists Catalogue." (Los Angeles: Music Center Inc., Education Division, March 1997).
43. Steve Tennen, executive director ArtsConnection, interview with author, November 1997, May 1999.
44. "Young Audiences." *Supplement to the Dallas Business Journal.* June 27–July 3, 1997.
45. "Jobs, the Arts, and the Economy." (Washington, D.C.: National Assembly of Local Arts Agencies, 1994).
46. Elizabeth Murfee, "Eloquent Evidence: Arts at the Core of Learning." (Washington, D.C.: National Assembly of State Arts Agencies, 1995).
47. "The Arts: A Competitive Advantage for California." Washington, D.C.: Policy Economics Group, KPMG Marwick, LLP, October 1994).
48. Joint Legislative Committee on Cultural Affairs. "Economic Impact of the Cultural Industry on South Carolina." (Washington, D.C.: National Endowment for the Arts).
49. From "America's Culture Begins with Education." Copyright 1990 by Music Educators National Conference. Used with permission.

CHAPTER NINE

1. Gary O. Larsen, *American Canvas: An Arts Legacy for Our Community*. (Washington, D.C.: National Endowment for the Arts, 1997).
2. Faye Fiore, "Senators Give Unanimous Nod to New Arts Chairman." *Los Angeles Times*, May 23, 1998.
3. Larsen, *American Canvas*.
4. "National Endowment for the Arts: Did You Know?" (Washington, D.C.: National Endowment for the Arts).
5. *National Endowment for the Arts Annual Report*, 1997. (Washington, D.C.: National Endowment for the Arts).
6. Robert Hughes, "Pulling the Fuse on Culture." *Time*, August 7, 1995, 61.
7. Hughes, "Pulling the Fuse on Culture," 65.
8. Donna Mackay, "Local Music Educators Hope that PVPUSD Program Will Be Extended." *Palos Verdes Peninsula News*, October 29, 1998.
9. Robert Dellinger, "Speaking with Conviction." *Los Angeles Times*, April 15, 1997.
10. Louise Steinman, "Releasing the Artist Within." *Los Angeles Times*, July 8, 1997.
11. Vanora Bennett, "Russia's Artists Try Courting Capitalists." *Los Angeles Times*, February 9, 1998.
12. "Six Myths About the National Endowment for the Arts." (Washington D.C.: National Endowment for the Arts).
13. "Six Myths About the National Endowment for the Arts."
14. "Giving and Volunteering in the Arts."(Washington D.C.: National Endowment for the Arts).
15. "How to Have Fun, Help an Arts Group, and Hone Your Business Skills—All at the Same Time." (Washington D.C.: National Endowment for the Arts).
16. "Life Expectancy and Arts Attendance: Some New Correlations." (Washington D.C.: National Endowment for the Arts).

17. Keith Donohue, editor. *Imagine! Introducing Your Child to the Arts*. (Washington, D.C.: National Endowment for the Arts, 1977), 5–6.

18. Donohue, *Imagine!* 13.

CHAPTER TEN

1. John Naisbitt and Patricia Aburdene, *Megatrends 2000*. (New York: Morrow, 1990).

2. Elaine Dutka, "88 Keys to Success." *Los Angeles Times*, January 16, 1998.

3. Ted Libbey, *The NPR Guide to Building a Classical CD Collection*. (New York: Workman Publishing, 1994) 406.

4. Libbey, *The NPR Guide*, 405.

5. Libbey, *The NPR Guide*.

6. Jim Farber, "Salonen to Take Year Off in 2000." *Daily Breeze*, March 6, 1998.

FINALE

1. Edna Machesny, "Different Strokes." *Good Housekeeping*, February 1988, 206.

2. "A Blind Father Rescues His Daughter from Drowning." *Los Angeles Times* (UPI), June 6, 1973.

3. Mihaly Csikszentmihalyi, *Flow: The Psychology of Optimal Experience*. (New York: Harper & Row, 1990).

4. Eric Oddleifson, "To Perceive and to Imagine." (East Hampton, New York: Center for the Arts in the Basic Curriculum, 1996).

5. Robert A. Jones, "Fast Forward Kids." *Los Angeles Times*, June 22, 1997.

6. *The Lion in Winter*. Part 3 of the documentary *MGM: When the Lion Roars*, Turner Pictures Inc., 1992.

7. Thomas Griffith, "The Waist-High Culture." *Time*, 1959, 188.

8. David O'McKay, *Improvement Era* magazine, June 1964, 445.

9. Michael Ryan, "If You Can't Teach Me, Don't Criticize Me." *Parade*, May 11, 1997.

10. Marian Diamond, *Enriching Heredity*. (New York: The Free Press/Simon & Schuster, 1988).
11. Deborah Fallows, *A Mother's Work*. (Boston: Houghton Mifflin, 1985) 16.
12. Susan Salter Reynolds, "The Family That Plays Together . . . Is the Goal of This Special School Program." *Los Angeles Times*, June 12, 1997.
13. M. Scott Peck, *The Road Less Traveled*. (New York: Touchstone. 1978) 23.

INDEX

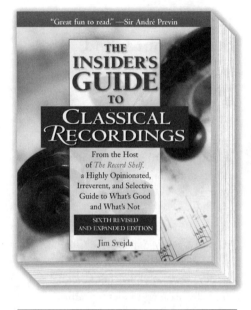

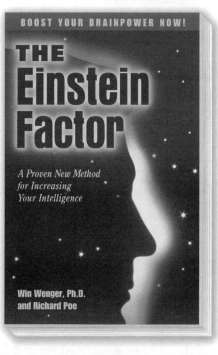

ABOUT THE AUTHOR

Sharlene Habermeyer has lectured for the past sixteen years about the impact music has on children and adults. If you are interested in her giving a lecture in your area, she can be reached by e-mail at shabermeyer@yahoo.com, by phone at 1-800-549-3844, or on the Internet at www.musical-expressions.com.